SHRUB ROSES OF TODAY

SHRUB ROSES
OF TODAY

WRITTEN AND ILLUSTRATED

BY

GRAHAM STUART THOMAS,
OBE, VMH, DHM, VMM

Gardens Consultant to the National Trust

With 8 pages of water-colours,
8 pencil drawings, and 16 photographs

With a Key to the
Major Groups of Cultivated Roses by
GORDON D. ROWLEY, B.SC.

J. M. DENT & SONS LTD

LONDON   MELBOURNE

© Graham Stuart Thomas, 1962, 1974, 1980
Text printed by
Garden City Press Ltd, Letchworth, Herts
Colour plates and drawings printed by
Belmont Press Ltd, Northampton
Photographs printed by
Belmont Press Ltd, Northampton
for
J. M. DENT & SONS LTD
Aldine House, 33 Welbeck St, London W1M 8LX
First published 1962
Second impression 1963
Third impression 1967
Revised edition 1974
Revised edition 1980
Reprinted 1985

ISBN 0 460 04533 4

Contents

Illustrations

Acknowledgments

AFTER completing a book the author has the pleasant task of placing on record the help given to him, and the knowledge freely shared with him by his friends. Therefore I take this opportunity of thanking most warmly my friend Mr Gordon Rowley, formerly Keeper of the National Rose Species collection at the John Innes Institute and at present lecturer in taxonomy at Reading University, who has been good enough not only to make numerous suggestions for the improvement of the book, but has contributed some valuable notes and tables in Chapter 15. I am greatly indebted to him for his painstaking work, and for guiding me so tactfully along the narrow path of taxonomy!

I am equally grateful to the Royal Horticultural Society for the use of their splendid Lindley Library; I have received unstinted attention from the librarian, Mr P. F. M. Stageman, and his staff.

To Mr Wilson Lynes go my thanks for much help with the American roses; and to Mr V. M. Staicov for his valuable contributions to the chapter on fragrance; Miss Alice M. Coats kindly sent me several interesting details. It has been of great assistance to be able to visit the collection of roses at Kew; also those of Mr Harold Hillier and Mr Maurice Mason. And to all other growers and kind enthusiasts, I wish to record my thanks for the numerous details they have provided.

Permission for the inclusion of poems is gratefully acknowledged to the Hon. V. Sackville-West and Michael Joseph Ltd for two quotations from 'The Garden', also to her and to William Heinemann Ltd for a quotation from *The Land*; to the Society of Authors and Dr John Masefield, O.M., for two lines from 'The Rose of the World'; and to the Society of Authors and Miss Ann Wolfe, for a poem and extracts, pages 43, 152, 214; 69; 115 and 165, respectively; and to Messrs Edward Ashdown Ltd for the poem on page 144.

9

Introduction, 1973 & 1980 Editions

Since writing the introduction to the original edition, much, has happened in the shrub rose world. In 1969 Sunningdale Nurseries changed hands, the shrub rose collection was dispersed and I left the firm in 1971. Fortunately in that same year the Royal National Rose Society, propagated and planted practically the whole of my collection of species and old roses at their Display Garden at Bone Hill, St Albans, Herts. In addition the National Trust has planted another all-embracing collection of Old Shrub Roses and Climbers and Ramblers in a charming walled garden complete with box hedges at Mottisfont Abbey, Romsey, Hants. My colleague James Russell is doing the same at Castle Howard, York. Freed from today's limitations connected with commercial enterprises, it is hoped that these three collections, when complete, will preserve our historic roses for the future.

In the preparation for this latest edition I gratefully acknowledge help with various details from Mr J. L. Harkness and Mr D. L. Clarke.

G.S.T.

Introduction to 1962 edition

Who would look dangerously up at Planets that might
safely look down at Plants?

Gerard's Herball, 1597

THE LAST six years have been of particular interest to me. *The Old Shrub Roses* saw the light of day in the autumn of 1955; during 1960 I revised it, and wrote a supplementary chapter for its new edition. In 1956 I severed a long-standing connection with a wholesale nursery firm and re-established my entire rose collection at Sunningdale Nurseries, Windlesham, Surrey, and have been delighted to welcome there many old friends and to be in touch with numerous pen-friends again from that address. I am glad to report that the new collection of Shrub Roses, both old and new, and all the old climbers and ramblers that go with them, have settled down well, after overcoming various difficulties. The collection has been greatly enriched by further old and new varieties received from correspondents around the world, but especially from Herr Wilhelm Kordes in Germany and from my friends and opposite numbers in California, the late Mr Will Tillotson and his helper and successor, Mrs Dorothy Stemler.

At Sunningdale there was already a good collection of the Old Roses, and many established bushes in the nursery borders. The varied terrain, the spacious design of the place, mostly laid out by my friend and colleague James Russell, and a love of beautiful plants and shrubs which we both enjoy, have given zest to this new beginning. From the nursery I issued *The Manual of Shrub Roses* in 1957 which supersedes my older effort *Roses as Flowering Shrubs*, and both the Manual and *The Modern Florilegium* have run to several editions.

In addition to this big upheaval I have spent much of my time in advising the National Trust about their gardens. This has brought me into contact with an entirely new circle of people, all keenly alive to beauty, to jobs well done, and dedicated to maintaining fine buildings, gardens, and county areas for the

enjoyment of the public. Blickling Hall is one of the gardens
where the original Portland Rose is still growing, together with
other historic roses.

The Old Shrub Roses sought to cover all the Old Roses which I
could find, but before I had finished writing it I realized I should
not be able to rest until I had written another book, and I make
no apology for the appearance of this one. Every year or two
brings us a new volume on the more popular roses, until one
wonders how it can all be written differently so many times over.
The Shrub Roses on the other hand suffer from a dearth of the
written word, except as a final chapter in most books, cursorily
dealt with, and very often inaccurately. The present book presents
new light, I think, on Shrub Roses generally. Apart from *The Old
Shrub Roses* no book has been exclusively devoted to Shrub Roses
before; this vigorous type of rose has been neglected by authors
as it has on the show bench. In spite of this the Shrub Roses
continue to grow in popularity. When one considers how the
Shrub Roses and ramblers act as a foil and complement in shape
and form to the brilliant moderns it is the more remarkable that
no London show caters for them. The only show that I have seen
which caters for *all* classes of roses is the comparatively small one
staged annually in Dublin by the Royal Horticultural Society of
Ireland.

In the old days the title of this book might have read 'Shrub
Roses of Today; or, a plea for the greater use of Shrub Roses in
the gardens and pleasure grounds of Ladies and Gentlemen and
of the Nobility'. But such a title could not have been understood;
no 'Shrub Roses' as such were grown. On recourse to the dictionary one will find that a 'shrub' is the same as a 'bush', but
'Shrub Roses' have come to mean something quite different from
'bush roses' since I first started the term just after the Hitler war.
On the Continent they are known as Park Roses.

Today the Shrub Roses command a great public, and this
public is not only the nobility, the ladies and gentlemen, but all
of us hard-working gardeners who know a good plant when we
see it and are thankful for these shrubs which give so much
beauty for so little trouble.

I left off, in *The Old Shrub Roses*, at a point when the revolu-
tionary China Rose had touched up the Old Roses, had created

the Bourbon Roses in their image, but had scarcely been appreciated in its own rights. I went as far as I could, in other words, with the Old Roses and the China Rose hand in hand. The arrival in our gardens of some splendid species roses, mainly from the Far East, brought roses generally into a different light; and, coupled with the trend towards flowering shrubs in gardening, gave them a new significance. William Robinson, Ellen Willmott, Gertrude Jekyll, Walter Easlea, George Beckwith, E. A. Bunyard, A. T. Johnson, Arthur Osborn, and others were writing about them and it is very much in thanks to them that I pen these pages, to those who used and appreciated the species roses, and held them in as great esteem as they did their lilacs and azaleas, mock oranges and forsythias.

To find a concise title for the new volume was not so easy. *The Old Shrub Roses* embraced *Rosa gallica* and its hybrids, and sought to explain, with Dr Hurst's help, how they eventually became the darlings of the nineteenth century; but even these roses are only old in man's esteem. All species were probably growing wild somewhere in the world long before *R. gallica* created its dynasty. But few species were in cultivation during the nineteenth century, so that they may, I feel, be called 'modern' in comparison with the old Gallicas. Then there are all the roses bred or raised since the China Rose came into use; all these are also 'modern' by comparison also, and, even though raised fifty or more years ago, are part of modern rose evolution.

And so here is the book. I have done my best to put into it the sort of information that will be required by gardeners. I have taken up the tale where *The Old Shrub Roses* left off; though some of the Hybrid Perpetuals can scarcely be called 'shrubs' they are included since I saw no real reason to omit their sadly decreased numbers. Almost all Hybrid Teas and Floribundas have been omitted, though I feel they are reaching more and more towards the perpetual-flowering Shrub Rose. In this category we have already gone a long way, with the Hybrid Musks and Rugosas setting a standard of beauty, vigour, and scent which it will be hard to beat; at the other end of the scale are all the species roses, the wild roses of the Northern Hemisphere which have remained mostly untapped by the hybridist, and are available in their unsullied beauty. And there are all those other roses, the first crosses, the experiments, the by-blows, the chance seedlings and foundlings, many of which I should not like to be without. It is a bewildering collection, difficult to group and classify.

The scope of this book, therefore, briefly supplements the earlier volume, and I hope will be accepted by the gardening public with as generous a share of leniency towards its short-comings as that volume received. I hope the notes I have gathered together may help seekers after beauty like myself, and may save those who work after me many hours of searching for original coloured portraits in the journals and books in our libraries.

> The Roses of today exhaust all our powers of admiration, our finite appreciation of the beautiful. The Roses of tomorrow can do no more. The Rosarian may 'raise' hereafter flowers large enough to cradle Cupid—
>
> > Within the petals of a Rose
> > A sleeping love I spied
>
> —but he cannot have a higher delight surveying them than Rivers enjoyed over his George IV one fine morning more than thirty years ago.
>
> Dean Hole: *A Book about Roses*, 1870.

G. S. THOMAS.

Woking, Surrey: January 1962.

The Appeal of the Rose

Ah see the Virgin Rose, how sweetly shee
Doth first peepe forth with bashfull modestee
That fairer seemes, the lesse ye see her may;
Lo see soone after, how more bold and free
Her bared bosome she doth bold display;
Lo see soone after, how she fades, and falles away.

Edmund Spenser (1552–99); The Faerie Queene.

WHAT IS this ROSE that enslaves gardeners? Why should the society concerned solely with the rose be the strongest in members of all our specialist plant societies? Why, in short, does everyone love a rose, and what has it to offer that other flowers lack? These are the questions that must have occurred to many of us in those precious times when our thoughts can muse happily on the subject of our fancy. With me, it is usually when I am weeding. We do not have to *think* when weeding; but the train of thought is sometimes punctured in a decisive way when a thorn is inadvertently grasped. . . . Certainly thorns and prickles do not endear the rose to us—but 'she arayeth her thorn wyth fayr colour and good smell'.

The superficial reason for the present popularity of the rose is undoubtedly because so many dozens of new varieties assail us every year. Our insatiable desire for novelty makes it worth while for the rose breeders of today to spend many hours of their time and large sums of money in order to produce some fresh colour or style to whet our appetites. This craving for novelty has been going on for over a hundred years, and it looks like continuing.

But this is not the whole answer. The rose has been popular for too many centuries for us to rest comfortably in the thought that the numerous varieties of modern roses constitute the whole reason for its popularity. When one reads that it was a religious emblem of the Medes and Persians hundreds of years before Christ, and has been cultivated throughout history, we must think again. For there is ample proof that the rose has been a favourite through the ages, and was grown and loved when mankind had little time for anything but the necessities of life and the battle for survival.

If we look at a wild rose analytically we do not find anything particularly flamboyant: nothing so intriguing as an orchid, so sculptured as an iris, nor so dazzling as a peony or tulip. Its shape, in those far-off days of our western civilization, was mainly single or semi-double, a circular flower, charming but not impressive. In colour it was quiet, white or pink or purplish, with brilliant exceptions in forms of *Rosa foetida* and one or two allied species. Its leaves were small, prettily divided and patterned, but had no great effect upon art, and that it was a shrub rather than a herbaceous plant or bulb can have been no overriding factor in its favour. I have no doubt myself that it owes its perennial popularity to its scent; it was for this priceless quality that it was originally cultivated, not because it was a food. Not only could the dried petals of certain roses, notably those of the Apothecary's Rose, retain their fragrance for years when suitably stored, but 'attar' or 'otto' of roses could be distilled from the freshly picked blooms of the Damask Rose and some others. Throughout history we read of different ways that roses were used to please human beings, and almost always it is the scent that is the principal factor.

Had the rose been a flower of complete insignificance, this inherent yet extractable odour would have ensured its being cultivated; when we add to that odour a flower of pleasing outline and indefinable charm, produced by a plant that grows in beauty yearly, its claim on our senses is wellnigh insuperable.

I have devoted a chapter to fragrance; while it varies greatly in strength and quality, it also varies with hybridization and has become involved in modern roses, infusing the different scents of the parents into a complex strain. Because we have much less appreciation of scent than of colour and shape these two characters have received infinitely more attention by writers over the

I. R. *multibracteata* and its hybrid 'Cerise Bouquet'.

II. Roses with grey-toned leaves: R. *rubrifolia* (R. *glauca*) (top left), R. *fedtschenkoana* (top right) and the Hybrid Perpetual 'Reine des Violettes' (1860).

III. Fruits of roses: 'Nymphenburg' (1954) (top); Hybrid Musk 'Penelope' (1924) (mid-left); R. *moyesii* 'Geranium' (mid-right); R. *rugosa* 'Fru Dagmar Hastrup' (1914) (bottom left); 'Ormiston Roy' (1953), a Burnet hybrid (bottom), and a small spray of R. *filipes* 'Kiftsgate'.

IV. Rugosa roses 'Fru Dagmar Hastrup' (1914) (top) and
'Roseraie de l'Haÿ' (1901); both are scented of cloves.

V   Hybrid Musk roses 'Vanity' (1920) (top) and 'Pax' (1918);
both are very fragrant.

VI. Hybrid Musk 'Buff Beauty', and five stages in the
development of R. *chinensis* ' Mutabilis '.

VII. Two brilliant shrub roses: 'Golden Wings' (1956), a
Burnet hybrid, and 'Erfurt' (1939).

VIII. The deliciously scented 'Nymphenburg' (1954).

years. There is moreover no established vocabulary describing scents.

It seems contradictory that so much sweetness and beauty have to be accompanied by the inhospitable thorny wood. But is it not just another example of how evil accompanies good throughout the walk of life, and does not the evil accentuate the good?

Single Roses

All roses were originally single, composed of five petals, or only four in the species R. *sericea*. Where they grew round early civilizations, perhaps chance seedlings occurred and were treasured and propagated by cuttings or grafting. Thus we can visualize not hundreds of new varieties occurring every year as happens today, but only a few new varieties or forms or hybrids being found and grown in each hundred years. So through its long association with Grecian and Roman civilizations, in China and in Persia and later in Western Europe, more and more colourful and more double roses appeared; some were no doubt lost, others throve and gave of their sports and hybrids over again. The first double rose recorded in literature appears to be in *Urania* by Herodotus (*c.* 470 B.C.), in which he speaks of a rose with sixty 'leaves' in Macedonia. Many of our oldest varieties appeared so long ago that there is no record of them. The first Damask Rose and the first White Rose appeared possibly in the wild, and later perhaps the excellent Autumn Damask, which went on flowering until winter. And so gradually a collection of hybrids and forms was gathered together in different countries and slowly distributed, ready to be depicted and recorded by the first herbalists and botanists. So old are our oldest roses; tough, treasured heirlooms, which shew no signs of the deterioration in vigour that is prophesied by certain writers of today.

I like to think of the excitement in those far-off days when the first fully double rose appeared, perhaps an Alba or a Gallica. How this new form must have set ideas running in design and decoration! And yet what an extraordinary thing it has been that the rose, of all flowers, should be so desirable when doubled. Is it perhaps its shape, a circle in one plane, that allows doubling to take place without destroying its beauty utterly as it does in a

two-dimensional shape such as a daffodil or a lily? It never ceases
to surprise me that a genus whose single flowers are so beautiful
should be the favourite genus selected by our western civilization
for elaboration in doubling. It cannot be denied that the single
rose is more beautiful than the double, but a double has often
more scent, longer lasting powers, and a richness of texture and
shape not found in the singles. Let us examine a little more closely
the various shapes of roses as they have evolved through the
centuries. I feel we must say 'evolved', for though during the last
hundred years or more man has raised millions of seedlings, it is
the rose that has been the prime mover. We cannot bring forth
anything which is not in the rose: all mutations and surprises are
governed by natural laws which we have only recently begun to
grasp through scientific research. As a sport or hybrid occurred,
so was a step forward or back taken by the rose in the eyes of man,
and treasured or discarded by him.

Originally, then, the rose was single, and in its simplicity was
loved and compared with blushing cheeks and the dawn. In fact it
ranked with the lily in being compared in beauty to the human
face by the poets throughout the ages; they had in mind the
'unimproved' beauty of the wild rose, or the rounded sweetness
of R. *centifolia* itself, or the Moss Roses, some of which have
greatest beauty when just opening. Who can deny the beauty of a
wild rose as, for example, our own Dog Rose in its fresh warm
pink, half open at breakfast time? There are many other single
beauties: the great limp-petalled R. *gigantea*, the creamy yellow
prototype of the Tea Roses; the intense colour and matt surface of
R. *moyesii*, with recurved shape; R. *macrophylla* and R. *setipoda*, in
both of which poise is added to perfect shape, and their smooth
beauty is contrasted by a hairy-glandular, purplish receptacle; or
the tiny daintiness of R. *farreri persetosa* and R. *willmottiae*. In fact,
all the wild species have a beauty that is never found in artificial
hybrids. The late E. A. Bunyard, writing in the Royal Horticultural Society's *Journal* in 1916, observed that 'singles are God-
made, doubles are man-made; a perfect flower should have
anthers and pistils'. As a general rule nature cannot be improved
upon, but here and there a hybrid outshines its fellows, and in the
rose there are exceptions as successfully beautiful as two other
examples that come to mind, *Rhododendron* 'Penjerrick' and

Lilium testaceum. These, with the rose 'Mermaid', with 'Früh-lingsmorgen', R. 'Paulii Rosea' and 'Dupontii', have reached the perfection of outline and have the innate charm and poise that one associates with a wild species. These all have a species for one parent, but this is not a prerequisite for perfection in breeding single roses. Every now and again a single arises in the highly evolved modern strains of roses: some years ago we had the Irish group of single Hybrid Teas, including the exquisite 'Irish Fire-flame', 'Isobel', 'Mrs Oakley Fisher' and others, in which the rolled petal of the Hybrid Tea was revealed in a new beauty from the opening of the fluted bud to the starry flower. A particularly good coloured plate of these singles will be found in *Roses of the World in Colour* (McFarland). 'Innocence' and 'Karen Poulsen' came later; Mr Le Grice has been in the forefront of raisers of singles, with his 'Lilac Charm', 'Silver Charm' and others. Those which are not quite single like 'News', 'White Wings', and 'Golden Wings', never reach the same standard. It is good to feel that singles and near singles are still being raised, to act as leavening to the vast numbers of doubles.

Double Roses

The 'doubling' of a flower is simply the replacing of stamens and styles by petals. The first doubles or semi-doubles may have occurred, died out, and occurred again thousands of years before they were first *noticed*, to be lifted from the wayside and put into the first garden. But it was not until about 1820 that any con-siderable number of double roses had been collected together, and not until about the middle of that century that a floral style had been selected. The most nearly perfect doubles among the old roses of the flat or Gallica style were evolved as early as 1825 or thereabouts, witness such varieties as 'd'Aguesseau' (1823), 'Petite Lisette' (1817), 'Félicité Parmentier' (1836), and the incomparable 'Mme Hardy' (1832). 'Mme Hardy' set a floral style that was never surpassed, in spite of many hundreds being raised for the next thirty years in the same style. It was a floral style that reigned until the Tea Rose upset it, with its longer petals resulting in a flower with a higher centre. So long as roses of the old style were raised the flat—'expanded'—floral

style continued, and it was still paramount in many of the early
Hybrid Perpetuals, as is demonstrated by 'Baronne Prévost'
(1842), 'Reine des Violettes' (1860), and 'Souvenir d'Alphonse
Lavallée (1884). Meanwhile the Bourbons had come and gone,
many of them with this old floral style, as found in 'Louise Odier'
(1851) and 'La Reine Victoria' (1872) and its sport.

It was a characteristic of this style, together with the flat fully
expanded flower, that the many petals were short—all the parents
had short petals—and there were so many of them in some
flowers that they were folded into the otherwise empty and futile
receptacle so tightly that they could not open. Often this results in
a 'button eye' which is one of the charms of this old style; the
curved-over petals reveal their lighter undersides in contrast to
the velvety upper surfaces. Good examples are 'Koenigin von
Danemarck' (1826), 'Juno' (1847), and 'Capitaine John Ingram'
(1856). Today this type of flower may be thought peculiar, but it
is nevertheless very appealing when once recognized as a distinct
floral style. There were so many petals that they grew in serried
ranks often imbricated or lying directly on top of one another,
forming the scalloped arrangement that we call 'quartered'. It
was not until the China Rose was used to great effect in breeding,
bringing with it a fewer-petalled, loose flower, and the Tea Rose
had contributed its larger petals, that this floral style gradually
disappeared, and the high-centred Tea-hybrids began, fostered by
the increasing popularity of long buds forced under glass. Con-
currently with the flat old roses there was also another style,
deep-centred—again with short petals—found in R. centifolia, with
its layers of large outer petals creating a great globular bloom.
Gradually, after multitudes of Bourbons and Hybrid Perpetuals
had come, had been appraised and forgotten, after the turn of the
century the shape we know so well in today's Hybrid Teas was
evolved, and the gracious sculptured bud appeared with its high
pointed centre and rolled-back petals.

In the old roses the bud was not of great beauty or importance,
the full beauty not being attained until the flower was full blown,
complete with quartering and button-eye, which were all part of
the fashion. 'Come, and I will show you what is beautiful; it is the
Rose fully blown' (Barbauld, d. 1825).

Today just the opposite obtains. Few Hybrid Teas are very

elegant when full blown, and most varieties are depicted in bud or half open. I always think the real test of a Hybrid Tea is whether it is beautiful when fully open; not many of them have sufficient petals to remain shapely. Quartering or splitting of the petals into different groups is looked at disapprovingly, while a button-eye could not happen with so few petals; the nearest approach to it, the 'balling' of a bloom—when instead of the petals retaining the pointed-bud shape they curve over one another like a spherical cabbage—is always frowned upon. I do not like it myself. 'Mme Caroline Testout' and 'Gipsy Lass' were notable offenders.

It is interesting to look back over the pages of rose history and see how these two totally different styles developed and became perfect. For I believe the best Hybrid Teas with really shapely flowers such as 'Ophelia', 'Eclipse', and 'First Love' *are* perfect in bud and half open. It remains to elongate the petals still more, so that a greater number can be accommodated in a longer bud and thus when full blown they will have a centre that remains beautiful in expansion. 'Gail Borden' and 'Grand'mère Jenny' are two of the most satisfying of Hybrid Teas when fully opened, like well-filled peonies. The rolled-petalled, fully double shape may be recalled in some of the Hybrid Perpetuals such as 'John Hopper' (1862) and 'Eugène Fürst' (1875), and also in 'Paul Ricault' (1845), which I believe is not repeat-flowering, but is a close relative of them; in later times this shape occurred in 'Dame Edith Helen' (1926).

This is perhaps the place to mention roses with fringed petals; they are all double, with the edges of the petals more or less cut, producing the effect of a pink or carnation. 'Fimbriata', 'F. J. Grootendorst', 'Pink Grootendorst', 'Grootendorst Supreme' are all of R. *rugosa* derivation, while 'Serratipetala' and the Green Rose are of fairly pure China descent.

Among the Floribundas something equally interesting is, I believe, developing. So many of the earlier varieties like 'Donald Prior' and 'Frensham' had loose, shapeless blooms but now some varieties are shewing much more form; in some such as 'Nymph', 'Heidelberg', and 'Allotria', we have fairly perfect rosettes, though few-petalled, and in yet some others the old rose style, flat and packed with petals, is reappearing. I refer especially to 'Honeymoon', 'Rosemary Rose', and 'Magenta'.

It may be that among Floribundas, though they may ape the Hybrid Teas in their colour and even approach them in shape and size, the flowers may be preferred when they are on the small side; and personally I should welcome a rather prim rosette shape. I can think of nothing so becoming on a branching stem bearing several flowers all open at one time. But with so much happening among roses today, so many new species being used for hybridizing, and so many 'new' colours appearing, anything may occur, and, compared with the gentle acceleration over a decade or two in the past, we jump from one new character to another in a matter of a few years nowadays. The leisurely progression has ceased: 'progress' has arrived.

Colours in Roses

Having given scent a separate chapter, and having briefly sketched the alterations in shape in the single and double roses, let us now turn to colour, the character of *immediate appeal* to all who see roses, and the character which today seems to outweigh all others. I have written elsewhere how roses were mainly pink in our early western civilization; the Old Roses were predominantly pink in all groups; a few were pure white, and plum-coloured ones appeared among the Gallicas. R. *gallica* brought us the deepest colours, but no really true reds; the Damask Rose was only mid-pink and yellows were practically non-existent. R. *gallica* varied from a deep old-rose-pink to light carmine or crimson, and it was not until R. *chinensis* arrived, and especially 'Slater's Crimson China', that a really true vivid crimson was available for hybridizing.

Throughout the nineteenth century, especially towards its close, garden roses were gradually being selected for their brightness, particular landmarks in bright crimsons being the Portland Rose (prior to 1809), 'Général Jacqueminot', and 'Charles Lefebvre' (1861). After this date bright crimson Hybrid Perpetuals were fairly common, but practically all inherited what has since been considered a failing and what was probably in those days glossed over as inevitable: the flowers developed a bluish tinge as they matured, no doubt inherited from R. *gallica*. We may therefore visualize all the ordinary old garden roses of the nineteenth century being white, pink, deep pink, and crimson, and all or most verging towards the bluish side of the central red of the spectrum. The Tea Rose first produced light yellows among climbers, the Tea Noisettes, and gradually a few pale yellow and salmon-yellow bush Tea Roses were raised. The vivid yellow of R. *foetida* remained locked within itself until 1900 when Pernet-Ducher succeeded in launching 'Soleil d'Or', the ultimate result being the race of Pernetiana roses of vivid colourings, bright yellows, flames, and two-toned varieties which became gradually merged with the Hybrid Teas. And so today we have all these colours within the one hybrid race; many of the reds and flames are almost free of purplish tones when fading.

That is what happened to the popular roses of the busy raisers. Little obvious variety of colour remains to be incorporated; in fact, all species are but variations on the same theme of colour.

Having reached such a pitch of general brilliance it became inevitable that a new colour tone would be welcomed for the sake of variety. A new colour did indeed appear in recognizable quantity in 'Gloria Mundi' (1929) and 'Paul Crampel' (1930), both Poly-poms; this new colour was pelargonidin, a vivid orange tone reminiscent of our greenhouse geraniums or Zonal Pelargoniums. Not only was this colour in the Polypoms, but in descendants from 'Eva', a Hybrid Musk, and it has produced astonishing tones in later roses such as 'Fashion', 'Independence', 'Orangeade', and 'Super Star'. A visit to the Royal National Rose Society's Trial Ground is almost painful to the eye; the blatancy and vividness of the dazzling scarlet, orange, and flame tones predominate to an overwhelming degree. Surely the rose has become bright enough? But in these days of neon lights and fluorescent colours on posters and socks it is, I suppose, comforting to think that the rose can at least hold its own. On the other hand Shakespeare said: 'They are as sick that surfeit with too much, as they that starve with nothing.'

Fortunately there is a comforting thing happening. Some of the colours which have been frowned upon for so long are being given a chance. Mauve and purple, innate in all roses and rightful to them, but suppressed and subordinate for nearly a hundred years, are once again allowed and even encouraged. Some Hybrid Teas and Floribundas such as 'Grey Pearl' (1944), 'Lavender

Pinocchio' (1948), 'Magenta' (1954), 'Twilight' (1955), 'Lilac Time' (1956), 'Sterling Silver' (1957), and 'Maud Cole' (1970) are restoring the balance and perhaps before long we shall have a rose in true *bluish* lilac—although having cried 'wolf' too often, with the latest so-called 'blue' roses, what will the raisers do then? Up to the present I find 'Reine des Violettes' (1860) can hold its own quite comfortably with all these 'latest' colours and it is infinitely more fragrant. Very few genera of plants contain species with red, yellow, and blue flowers. Exceptions are lobelia, gentiana, and delphinium. Blue is not present in any rose except in an adulterated pink, and while selection of these mauve tones may result in our getting *nearer* to blue, I understand that a genetical miracle would have to happen for a true blue rose to appear. Dr Jeffrey Harborne and Mr Gordon Rowley explained this technical point admirably in the *National Rose Society's Annual* for 1959.

To return, 'Masquerade' (1949) and 'Cavalcade' (1950) set a 'new' style also in their chameleon-like changes of colour. It is, however, only the strong influence of the China Rose, which always would turn darker, not lighter, on fading, that has returned. *R. chinensis* ' Mutabilis ', known since before the turn of this century or perhaps eighty or more years previously, has been changing like this regularly every summer. Even 'Peace', 'Grand'mère Jenny', 'Perfecta', and other pale yellow roses with pink edges, and 'Pigalle'—that extraordinary mauve-pink with yellowish reverse—are not new colours. We only have to turn the pages of such a book as the *Journal des Roses* to find that these colours had already been exploited among the Hybrid Perpetuals at the end of the last century. They were of good size too; some of the greatest of these old hybrids with slight Tea admixture must have been monster blooms.

So far my remarks on colour have been mainly concerned with shrub roses and bedding, or bush, roses. Popular progress has begun to make itself felt among ramblers and climbers as well, and I do not think it will be long before 'Chaplin's Pink' and 'American Pillar' will be decked out in flame and orange, and will join hands with climbing sports of the brilliant Hybrid Teas and Floribundas. Fortunately among the ramblers there are already some excellent varieties of purple colouring, 'Violette' (1921),

'Bleu Magenta', and the fragrant 'Veilchenblau' (1909), and some equally good whites.

I can think of nothing so desirable among Hybrid Teas as a rich maroon-purple rose, the colouring of 'Cardinal de Richelieu' with the scent, size, and texture of 'Mme Louise Laperrière', coupled with freedom and vigour. Here would be something worth achieving. And how useful it would be in designing a conventional rose garden with beds in a lawn, and finding one really had an alternative heavy colour to balance the dark crimson varieties. Similarly, when we have an 'Ophelia' or 'Monique' in silvery-lilac it will be a wonderful companion to the yellows and pinks. I should welcome both with open arms. Together with a really reliable white and more soft yellows like the unsurpassed—even unequalled—'Lady Hillingdon', these cool colours would have a vast and sobering effect on the vulgar blatancy that obtains today, while the changes are being run in the tints of the spectrum between yellow and red with frightening and wearying monotony. Of course we need all these softer colours, too, in good hearty Floribundas like 'Frensham' and with a good fragrance.

No doubt in the past many unusual seedling roses were thrown away in disgust by breeders as worthless. Such would have been the fate, I think, if 'Café', 'Blue Moon', or 'Grey Pearl' had appeared in the thirties. But today the craze for novelty and also the delight in quiet and often unusual colouring have given even these strange flowers a place in horticulture. Obviously of less conspicuous value in the garden, these greyish colourings have been appraised by the skilful flower arrangers, among whom none was more grateful for them than the late Mrs Constance Spry, who devoted a chapter to them in her last book, *Favourite Flowers* (Dent, 1959).

Orange and scarlet are splendid and desirable when one is led up to them as a high-light of the border; there they can be enriched with coppery purple and golden foliage, and the whole thing becomes lighted with a Byzantine gorgeousness which can be absolutely thrilling. Miss Jekyll shewed the way, as everyone will agree who saw her borders, and it has been followed by careful gardeners since. But it is done only once, even in big gardens; in small gardens it should never be repeated. Such a furnace of colour is overpowering except in occasional blasts. To have vivid colours distributed round the garden mixed up with the quieter colours is to me like having a stimulant every quarter-hour of the day. It destroys the peace and quiet which is after all what we most desire in a garden and which brings the 'greatest refreshment'.

It is all a question of what one is used to. Those who glory in orange-red flowers of all kinds today find magentas, mauve-pinks, and crimson-purples very difficult to place in the garden. Believe me, it is far easier to cater *for* them than *without* them in a garden of all sorts of plants and shrubs. The 'difficult' colours, when one has a catholic taste in plants, are not the magentas but the hard yellows, the oranges, and yellow-toned reds. These are the colours which look harsh with green—the opposite to red in the spectrum—and as the whole garden must perforce have a background of green, it stands to reason that without the flame-red tints everything blends well with its neighbours, from pale yellow through all greens, blues, mauves, purples, pinks, and crimsons. Plenty of the dark plum colours and crimsons must be included; without these deep bass notes, as it were, the rest are apt to sound a little thin.

Size of Flower

Scent, shape, colour, and now size. Everything today gets bigger and brighter, so I suppose we have not yet seen anything like the limit in size. As the plants are bred for vigour they will develop stronger stalks, and the stronger the stalk the bigger the bloom it can support. While a single flower can nod and still retain its charm and beauty, as in an Iceland poppy, a lily, or a fritillary, a big double flower cannot be allowed this shy charm. We must be prepared for roses that are full to overflowing with colour and petals and, I hope, scent, and bigger and better than ever before. Meanwhile we can fortunately still enjoy some dainty treasures like 'Cécile Brunner', 'Perle d'Or', and 'Alister Stella Gray'; with them we can grow 'Mme Abel Chatenay' and the 'Rose d'Amour', all roses that do not owe everything to size or brilliance. They have a quintessential beauty that can bear long acquaintance and close inspection, and shew the scrolled beauty of bud of the Hybrid Teas in miniature. These little roses have nearly been forgotten: they did not conform to a popular style. 'Cécile Brunner' and 'Perle d'Or' were really the first Polypoms with a leaning towards the China Rose. It so happened that others, raised about the same time, leaned towards R. *multiflora* and became popular. But these had little or no scent and no stylish shape and yet they established a group while no more China-Polypoms—exquisitely shaped, coloured, and scented and only slightly less free-flowering—appeared. This extraordinary fact has a parallel in the two groups of ramblers derived from R. *wichuraiana*. On the one hand are those several intensely fragrant large-flowered roses with glossy leaves like 'Albéric Barbier', which, except for this variety, have not been popular, while various small-flowered, scentless hybrids with poor foliage like 'Excelsa' and 'Dorothy Perkins' are found in every garden.

Roses of the Future

I like to think that this is a fair picture of the rose through the years and today. If I seem to lean towards the older types it is not because I cannot see the beauty and value of modern varieties. I was brought up on Hybrid Teas, and knew and loved them for many years before I came across other types and realized there was more in roses than at first was apparent. It seems to me that, looking at the picture broadly, and once again considering only man-made roses, we had a formalism in late Georgian and Early Victorian times followed by a fulsomeness lacking in refinement, when roses were flowers, not plants. The Tea Rose did not help matters immediately. All of these have succumbed to a dazzling display of colours, scents, and shapes—hard, sharp, clear, fitting to our modern age. The angular buds and petals of some of our modern roses are incredibly far removed from the cosy little round sweeties of a hundred years ago. Colours can usually be sorted and made to look well together with due care; shapes need more attention. I am sure we ought not to let roses get too far removed from a soft outline. Scent is of course paramount, otherwise the rose will lose its pride of place, and charm is an indefinable something without which the rose cannot satisfy as a flower, only as a bedding plant or a giver of colour.

At the moment the rose is on the crest of a wave of popularity. Dare we pause for a while? Nothing stands still: the Hybrid Tea, the choice favourite of today, may be a back number tomorrow, and who knows but that in twenty-five years gardeners will be witnessing a revival of the 'sweet old Hybrid Teas of our forbears'? Judging by the publicity accorded them in shows, trials, catalogues, and magazines, the Floribundas—they may even be Grandifloras, of all ridiculous pretentious names!—may supplant the Hybrid Teas in a few years. The latter do not flower freely enough; they may have charm which at the moment most of the Floribundas have not, but if in a few years these develop charm, will the Hybrid Teas become back numbers? I think they will, in popular esteem, provided that with charm the Floribundas develop scent. When scent, shape, floriferousness, and colour are added to charm then that rose is a paragon. If it can bring with it disease resistance and not be dependent on pruning, then it will sweep the board.

Looking back once again, we must admit that so long as the rose was thrifty and could stand on its own with a modicum of attention all was well; it was not until the Victorian Age brought a surfeit of gardeners that the new roses of the time could be grown successfully; the blooms were not very weatherproof and had to be protected. As labour in the garden dwindled through the years on account of the gradual economic squeeze, roses had to be acceptable and easily grown by amateurs, without professional gardeners, in order to survive. They have amply demonstrated that they are capable of doing this. That is why I think an improved type of Floribunda, with perhaps flowers somewhere between a Hybrid Tea and an old rose in floral style, may be the aim of the present age.

The newer, more vigorous Floribundas of today are every year becoming linked more closely with descendants from the Hybrid Musk group, and 'Heidelberg', 'Gustav Frahm', 'Erfurt', 'Golden Wings', and others are already pointers to the brighter perpetual flowering shrub roses of the future. While tall upright roses like 'Joanna Hill' and 'Queen Elizabeth' are too erect to be classed as flowering shrubs they at least demonstrate how effective a tall modern style of rose can be. It is unfortunate when they are given beds to themselves; their stems are bare 2 feet from the ground, an indication that they should be surrounded by shorter-growing varieties, or should only be grown in the mixed border among shrubs and plants. As yet these big-growing Floribundas have scarcely become shrubs in the sense that the Hybrid Musks are shrubs, but they are a step towards the ideal of perpetual-flowering shrub roses in bright colours. Up to the present no roses can compare with the stature, floriferousness, and far-carrying amazing fragrance of the Hybrid Musks.

The popular roses of today have become more and more givers of colour, and so their demand for use in segregated colours as bedding plants is on the increase. The lower-growing varieties are undoubtedly ideally suited for this form of culture, dull though it may be. With the stronger growers, however, their inclusion in the mixed and shrub borders becomes increasingly popular by discerning gardeners, and it is with this in mind that I turn towards these perpetual-flowering shrub roses which fulfil a long-felt want. The rose has arrived first at what must be man's ultimate goal—the production of new varieties of everything, in all colours, to flower throughout the season. How tiresomely bright the gardens of the future will be!

2

Rose Species in Nature and in the Garden

Would Jove appoint some flower to reign
In matchless beauty on the plain,
The Rose (mankind will all agree),
The Rose the Queen of Flowers should be.

Sappho, Greek poetess, born about 600 B.C. (from *The Book of the Rose*, by A. Foster-Melliar, 1894).

WILD ROSES might be described as prickly deciduous shrubs, with pinnate leaves and usually fragrant flowers borne singly or in clusters, from yellow and white through pink to dark red, normally with five petals; the achenes, or seeds, are contained in a fleshy, usually reddish hep. But how little can be conjured up from those bare phrases; how little they depict the wonderful and varied beauty to be found within the genus!

According to conservative botanists about a hundred and forty species occur in the Northern Hemisphere, from as far north as Alaska and Siberia to Abyssinia and Mexico, but the greatest number come from China and neighbouring countries, and with very few exceptions all are hardy in the southern half of the British Isles. If we take our native Dog Brier, *Rosa canina*, as a yardstick we find about fifty species which are deserving of cultivation in our gardens. The Dog Brier is not usually grown as a garden plant; the reason being, I suppose, that it is too common in our hedgerows and too thorny to be manageable. Nobody will deny its beauty of flower, delicate fragrance, and colourful heps, but even so I would venture to say that all the other species roses that I have included in this book can make a greater appeal to us, either through their flowers or their heps, or both, for inclusion in our gardens. Many are just as thorny and unmanageable as R. *canina,* but their display makes them more valuable.

Some may ask why we trouble to grow wild species of rose when we have so many gay garden hybrids; others may exclaim that the modern bedding roses are so overweening and vulgar that it is a relief to turn to nature's unadulterated beauty. In some districts and on some soils species will grow where Hybrid Teas will not; in some gardens anything but species would be out of place. Fortunately there is such a wide difference between the extremes of taste in gardening that there is enough demand even for the more obscure roses to warrant nurserymen growing them, although it is probably equally true that for every species that is sold, a hundred or more modern bedding roses find sales.

Some of us are brought up on Gilbert and Sullivan and develop later in life a taste for Bach. Whether the obvious is thrust on us or not there comes a time in most people's lives when the discerning mind needs more than the obvious for its refreshment, and I know many gardeners who have graduated from dahlias and nasturtiums to species of flowering shrubs and lilies. But I should not like it to be thought that I have no use for the obvious, nor that I want all gardeners to grow species roses. When we are confronted by such variety as we find in the genus *Rosa,* only then can we say that there is a rose for every taste and every garden; and there is abundant latitude for all tastes.

Their Place in the Garden

As we study and seek to appreciate all kinds of roses so does our appreciation become deeper, finding more and more delight in colour, form, shape, scent, and all other characters that are spread before us, and gradually roses fall into fairly clearly marked groups in our minds—groups which are not botanical, nor of colour, nor of size, but which bring together certain styles of roses. These styles become associated with styles of gardening and the gardens with styles of houses, and of course with types of people. Then there are the different areas of each type of garden to be considered. Thus, putting forth a few generalizations— however dangerous they may be—a small modern house in a new estate may suit Floribundas very well; but if the garden is large, the farther away from the house one goes the less prim one's ideas can become, and at the end of the plot wild species might not come amiss. Species can easily predominate in a country garden of large size, but I feel they are not happily placed near the house; that is where the Hybrid Teas can go, or China Roses; and to link one group with another there are the roses of sophisticated colouring, modern in tone, but gay and perpetual-flowering, such as the Hybrid Musks, which can link the moderns with the species. And of course there is the period house around which only the Old Roses look well, with species appearing more and more frequently as one recedes farther into the depths of the shrub borders. I hope this does not sound fanciful. In my opinion in this country today we are far too fond of collecting plants and not nearly careful enough over their placing. Our gardens are frequently like a junk shop where a bit of Old Chelsea lies cheek by jowl with a Japanese fan, an elephant's tusk, a piece of modern pottery, or a Roman coin. We are far too prone to go round the garden looking for a site for a new acquisition than to sit quietly and think out the best plant to give effect in a certain place. In the first instance the gardener is a *collector* and in the second he is a *selector*, and may well be an artist. Occasionally these two qualities are found in an individual.

Putting it simply, I like a slight sense of orderliness and prefer my Hybrid Teas, my Floribundas, or my Old Roses fairly near the house; they are man-made and assort well with seats and paths, vegetable plots, formal lawns, and flower beds. At the other end of the scale are the species roses, breathing of fresh air and freedom and the wild countryside; appealing but not perhaps showy; of a beauty which needs other natural things around it in herbaceous or woody plants. Between the two extremes we are lucky in having today an ever-growing new category of roses, those which have perhaps modern colours but are big shrubs.

Having indicated the place in the garden generally that the wild species roses might occupy, let us now examine these roses and see what they have to offer us for our garden furnishing. No sweeping statements can be made. There is as much variety among them as is found in the majority of garden genera—in fact *more*. For they vary from little bushes of a couple of feet to climbers achieving a height of over 50 feet. They may grow into stalwart shrubs of 12 feet or may lie prone on the ground, exceeding that figure in length. They may make shrubs with a single woody stump giving off branches, or may colonize the ground with a thicket of ever-increasing suckering stems, and roots that travel as fast as couch grass. Some will do best climbing up into bushes and trees, others seem more at home sprawling downwards. Some are impossibly prickly; a very few are devoid of all thorns. Their lovely colours we have already sounded, and theirs is also the beauty of fruit; the heps may be tiny and round or long, bottle-shaped, and bristly. Given reasonably well-drained soil and freedom from dense overhead shade, there is not a position in any garden where a species rose would not thrive. Certainly they like full sunshine, but they will be beautiful in light shade, often taking on in such conditions a grace and delicacy not otherwise shewn.

In this book I have felt it best to group the species botanically, following Mr B. O. Mulligan's key to the species in the Royal Horticultural Society's *Dictionary of Gardening*, incorporating recent changes in nomenclature from the eighth edition of Bean's *Trees & Shrubs Hardy in the British Isles* (1980). Every now and again one receives a jolt and finds that two species which one had always considered were alike belong in fact to widely separated botanical groups! However, this once again demonstrates that gardeners and botanists do not think alike; it also demonstrates that the botanists' presupposed idea that all wild species should fall conveniently into botanical compartments is a hope without foundation. After all, why should they? They have been evolved through hundreds of thousands of years, and were successfully established denizens on this planet before mankind had invented anything, let alone a botanical 'key' to the species. Various groups of species, shall we call them, had established themselves over the earth; as an example we may cite the Musk Roses which extend from Madeira through the Himalayas to Japan, and, when introduced by seed from their native habitats, usually breed true to type. Geographical segregation is one of the factors which break up such an array of related plants into local species. When these 'species', separated in nature by a varying terrain, are brought into cultivation and propagated by seeds over a generation or two, they may lose their identity; they may become one, or become totally different roses by hybridization with an unrelated species or garden hybrid.

This is what makes the study of species so difficult. Few of us can afford the time to refer to a pressed specimen in the British Museum, for instance, collected by a plant-hunter in western China, and have to be content with knowing the plant as grown in cultivation. Fortunately variation of this kind can seldom be blamed upon the nurseryman. His long-practised method of reproduction has been by budding; he may be maligned when—on a wayward Dog Rose seedling that prefers a suckering life, or when his budding has been effected too high upon the 'neck' of the stock and thus allows the latter to start life on its own—a rose comes up which is nothing like the plant that was sold; but he can at least claim that all his propagation has been to maintain the *status quo*. Much confusion has been caused in many genera of plants by the distribution of open-pollinated seeds of plants that inter-hybridize freely. One can sympathize with the keen amateur gardener who, having received seeds of some species from a noted botanical source, finds out after years of proud distribution of resulting plants to his friends that he has given away hosts of hybrid individuals none of which is the true species which he tried to acquire. Roses interbreed so freely that seed-raising is not recommended; yet, let us remember the numerous seedlings that have been raised deliberately or under nature's care; I need only cite R. ' Highdownensis ' as an example.

To return, as in succeeding chapters I have devoted some trouble to the grouping of the species botanically, I think this is the place to examine them horticulturally, so that when the artist goes into a brown study to find the right growth for his given spot he may perhaps be helped by the following notes, always remembering, however, that two seekers for quality in plants seldom see eye to eye. The beauty of plants is so infinite in its variety when nature has alone been the artist that we each discern different beauty on contemplation.

Ground-covering Species

It may be as well to start our review with a few completely

prostrate roses, among which none is so flat and flowing as R. *wichuraiana*, and it has an added advantage among species: it is late-flowering. In the south of England the month of August usually arrives before the first flowers open. The dappling of creamy white small flowers over the close carpet of tiny, glossy leaves is a sight well worth waiting for, to say nothing of the fragrance. This is a rose which thrives well in sandy soil; it grows well at Wisley and at Talbot Manor and is a dense carpeter for any sunny slope or flat ground. Slightly higher off the ground is a hybrid between it and R. *rugosa*, 'Max Graf', which is a splendid colonizer, rooting as it goes. The next most important low ground-coverer is the vigorous and prickly R. ' Paulii '; this will cover 12 feet square in a few years, and not exceed 2½ feet in height. Various of the true Wichuraiana Ramblers such as 'Albéric Barbier' and 'François Juranville' are also excellent when allowed to grow flat. The former is particularly effective near the Japanese temple at Nymans. But lovely as they are when grown in this way, they are not sufficiently dense to smother weeds, and it is not an easy or pleasant job hand-weeding among their prickly trails. So long as a rose can make a dense mass to exclude weeds I class it as a ground-cover plant; less dense roses are best used as ramblers and trained on supports, and do not lie within the scope of this book.

There are several more rather higher growing sprawling roses which make a dense covering; among the best are R. ' Macrantha ' and its form ' Daisy Hill ', ' Raubritter ', and R. × *polliniana*. They all make wonderful hummocks of blossom, the first two being considerably stronger than the last two. One of the loveliest annual sights that I know is the flowering of a huge planting of 'Daisy Hill' at the back of a flower border. Practically no pruning is required. In the foreground of shrub borders, and on the fringe of woodland or grassy slopes and to cover low walls, these sprawling roses are invaluable. Many of them root as they go, and thus when suited will cover large areas of ground.

Colonizing Species

In some gardens one sees an area given to heathers, which

finish abruptly and give way to shrubs or other plants. As heathers are essentially plants of the wild, their surroundings should be made as harmonious as possible, and this is best done by planting dwarf rhododendrons, of which there are many that enjoy full sunshine, prostrate junipers, and dwarf brooms. Where the heathers are winter-flowering varieties or hybrids of *Erica carnea*, the ground may be limy and the rhododendrons must be excluded, but dwarf shrubby potentillas and some of the dwarf roses then come into their own, although they will of course do equally well, perhaps better, where there is no lime. The two really dwarf roses that are ideal for the heather garden and the outskirts of the rock garden are R. *nitida* and R. *pendulina* ' Pyrenaica '. They grow to only about 18 inches in height and are free colonizers, with single pink flowers and red heps, and with autumn colour from the first named. Slightly taller and of similar uses are three little species, the first two with aromatic foliage: R. *glutinosa*, R. *serafinii*, and R. *nanothamnus*.

Rather taller and suitable for use where the heathers merge into shrubs proper, some of the bigger colonizing roses, so thrifty on sandy soils, may be used; these are notably R. *spinosissima* in its many forms and colours, R. *virginiana*, R. *reversa*, R. *foliolosa*, and R. *rugosa*. One or other of them would be flowering from the end of May till the end of September. I must repeat here a warning I have given under R. *spinosissima*: that if you plant these roses you must be prepared for the nuisance of running roots. R. *rugosa* is considerably bigger than the others, but both thrive on light soils which are not usually given to roses, and even when the soil is really sandy—dunes or heathland—all these species will thrive amazingly. And in their likes as well as in their size and habit they are very suitable for the heather garden area. Many other species increase steadily at the root.

For Screens and Hedges

Many rose species will withstand the salt of the sea, but none makes so excellent a windbreak even on the dunes as R. *rugosa*. This hardy species in its typical forms is one of the best hedging roses we have. Its naturally bushy habit can be enhanced by clipping it every spring, and the clipping will result in a longer display of flower, for the best flowers are produced on the strong young shoots of the current year. Others which are dense and bushy and make good windbreaks are R. 'Coryana', R.× *micrugosa*, and 'Frühlingsanfang'. R. *virginiana* is lower and also excellent. Equally bushy is 'Felicia', a Hybrid Musk, and the great 'Nevada' is as good and dense as any. To create a really dense screen the first three and 'Nevada' should be planted at 4 feet apart, and the others at 3 feet, and they will all attain 5 to 7 feet in height. If greater sturdy height is needed from roses, I should interplant them at every 8 feet with one of the much taller types such as R. 'Highdownensis'. The riot of colour from such a mixture—and thorny tangle!—would be superb.

While on the subject of hedges I may perhaps call attention to some of the upright Gallica roses—'Officinalis' and 'Rosa Mundi', 'Charles de Mills' and 'Tuscany Superb'—all will stand annual February clipping and will reach to about 3–4 feet. 'Great Maiden's Blush' comes to mind for an informal hedge and many of the Hybrid Musks; in fact any bushy rose is admirable for hedging. But let us return to the species.

Good Foliage

It is not generally realized what a big part roses can play in the colour schemes of the garden from the foliage point of view. RR.× *alba*, *murielae*, *fedtschenkoana*, *soulieana*, and *beggerana* have grey-green leaves and white flowers. When they are in flower they give a nearly all-white effect. By grouping them with silvery foliage of other plants, santolinas, artemisias, *Elaeagnus argentea*, and the Cardoon, interspersed with white lilies, galtonias, and perhaps white phloxes and the rose 'Gruss an Aachen', a spread of cool colours can be achieved with very little trouble. To come upon such a planting round a bend in a path after a rich Byzantine mixture as visualized on page 89 would startle the most phlegmatic mortal. The two colour schemes could be linked together by another rose, R. *rubrifolia*, whose leaves are greyish-green, overlaid with coppery-mauve. This is an invaluable species in the garden, being quite dusky and purplish in full sun, but pale and greyish in the shade. Other species have leaves which are variations in greens, though with considerable variety in shape, size, and texture, from the tiny foliage of R. *farreri* and R. *spinosossima* to great limp leaves of R. *centifolia* ' Bullata ' and R. *brunonii*. But they all conform to a fairly regular pattern except R. *sinowilsonii*, which grows well on a wall at Kew and in the open at Wakehurst. It has wonderful lustrous, dark green leaves which are shining red brown beneath, and if I had a sunny wall available, it would have an honoured place. There is one variegated-leaved rose, R. *wichuraiana* ' Variegata ', not very vigorous but producing dainty sprays of tiny leaves of shrimp pink turning to creamy white, with a few green flecks which become more prominent as the leaves age.

The genus is not noted for its autumn foliage colour but there are a few species and varieties which make a decided contribution. Best known perhaps is the clear yellow of R. *rugosa*. The American species RR. *virginiana, foliolosa,* and *nitida* can be brilliant in their red and orange, especially the first named. For more subtle and long-lasting tones ' Morletii ' should be planted; its coppery pinks and soft orange will sometimes last in mild autumns until December.

Large Shrubs for Flower and Hep

Having combed out the dwarfs, the trailers, the dense low-growers, and foliage roses, we now have left all the usual big bushes from 6 to 10 feet high and wide. The group headed by R. *moyesii*—R. *moyesii* ' Fargesii ' and the forms ' Geranium ', ' Sealing Wax ', and others; R. *setipoda*, R. *davidii*, R. *sweginzowii*, and R. *macrophylla*—are all noted for their rather gaunt growth and magnificent flagon-shaped heps, which are at their best from August to October. Rather more bushy are three hybrids, R. ' Highdownensis ', R. ' Hillieri ', and ' Autumn Fire '. All of these must be expected to exceed 10 feet in height and it is useless trying to keep them bushy by pruning. The more they are pruned the stronger they grow, and the less flower will be produced. It is best to encourage them to grow upright, and to make a wide ferny canopy over one's head, through which will appear the glowing flowers. The weight of the fruits will cause the branches to arch gracefully and at that time nothing can surpass them for beauty in the garden. Small clematis species like C. *macropetala* and C.

alpina can be planted to grace their gaunt stems, and to add colour and interest in the spring.

This great group does not exhaust the fruiting roses. One of the most glittering and brilliant is R. *webbiana*, a very pretty, bushy, wiry shrub. And R. *canina* ' Andersonii ', R. *rubiginosa*, R. *rubrifolia*, R. × *alba* ' Semi-Plena ', and some of the Hybrid Sweet Briers also are very good, but this group has the usual oval heps, not the striking flagon-shaped kind of R. *moyesii*. The main difference in the shape is that while both groups have oval heps, those of R. *moyesii* and its relatives have a persistent calyx which adds the flange, as it were, to the flagon. R. *rugosa* also has a persistent calyx, but its heps are rounded like tomatoes; R. *soulieana* has small orange heps. And apart from the species several other roses are noted for their autumn fruits. 'Wilhelm' and 'Will Scarlet', two Hybrid Musks, hold their colour through the winter; 'St Nicholas', a Damask, and 'Cupid', 'Düsterlohe', 'Scarlet Fire', and many others come to mind.

From their size alone the big species would not be suitably placed in conventional beds. The fringe of woodland is an excellent place for them, or the back of wide shrub borders. They assort well with other shrubs and bring to a collection good late colour, just at a time when shrubs are looking most dull. I remember seeing a particularly happy grouping of R. ' Highdownensis ' used behind *Senecio* 'Sunshine', the arching sprays of red heps weeping over the grey-leaved hummocks of *Senecio*; I have used R. *sweginzowii* behind the silvery grey of *Atriplex halimus*; the dark red of ' Europeana ' Floribunda coupled with *Clematis* ' Royal Velour ' is wonderful when lightened by the orange-red sprays of heps of R. *moyesii* ' Geranium '. Their period of beauty is so much longer when in fruit than when in flower that it comes to me more naturally to arrange schemes for that period. In May and June one welcomes every flower that comes to fill that glorious time, and all flowers contribute to the gaiety of the garden. But a display of certain colour in August and September is worth catering for: the weeks in the garden stand still, the flowers of the period are lasting, and all is poised in a quiet maturing way for the final autumn pageant. Even in July and August certain late-flowering species with only the one normal flowering period are at their best, notably RR. *multibracteata*, *foliolosa, virginiana, davidii, setigera,* and the prostrate R. *wichuraiana* mentioned earlier in this chapter.

I have made no attempt in the following pages, devoted to species roses and their more immediate relatives, to describe the roses botanically. Full descriptions can be found in the standard works on the subject of woody plants. Rather have I done my best to give a brief description of the garden merits, disadvantages, or peculiarities which may be of service to gardeners.

Notes in regard to the descriptions

Names in large capitals denote species.

Names in small capitals denote sub-species, recognized botanical varieties and hybrids; the latter are prefixed by ×.

Names in bold type and quotes denote garden forms, varieties, and hybrids, called 'cultivars'.

Wherever possible the name of the introducer or raiser, together with the date of introduction, has been given, together with synonyms and parentage.

All the references are to coloured illustrations, and they are not in any particular order.

For details of books consulted, see bibliography, page 221.

Where two sets of figures are given, the first refers to the height and the second to the width that the bushes may attain. All such measurements are approximate and vary with local conditions.

A 'sport' is a shoot which is different in growth from the parent plant; these shoots usually remain constant when vegetatively propagated.

A 'clone' is the vegetatively produced progeny of a single individual.

A 'perpetual' rose flowers more or less continuously during the growing season; 'remontant' or 'recurrent' roses usually have two crops, but are not necessarily 'perpetual'.

Descriptions of Shrub Roses

PART 1

Species, Varieties,
and
Hybrids
not having Affinity to
the China Rose

3

The Dog Rose and its Relatives

We know the dog-rose, flinging free
Whip-lashes in the hedgerow, starred with pale
Shell blossom as a Canterbury Tale,
The candid English genius, fresh and pink
As Chaucer made us think,
Singing of adolescent meads in May.

V. Sackville-West, The Garden, 1946.

OUR BELOVED native wild rose, *Rosa canina*, the Dog Brier, a fine tough shrub of great sweetness and beauty, is well enrolled among the most important ancestral species, for it will be recalled how it became united with the Damask Rose and produced a race we now call the Alba Roses. These I described at some length in *The Old Shrub Roses*. Of all the old races of roses, the Albas alone had large, widely spaced prickles, hard greyish leaves, excessive vigour, delicious fragrance, and clarity of colour, all of which characters can be traced back to R. *canina*. Although later varieties of Alba Roses became mixed up with all sorts of others, including no doubt the China Rose, no obvious influence of R. *canina* has transmitted itself to our newer groups. Its influence may be said to have died out, but we must always bless it for its part in producing a few roses of such great beauty and charm that they were and still are in many ways peerless.

All roses in our present group are natives of the Old World, and are mainly vigorous shrubs with scattered hooked prickles, and bear their flowers singly or in clusters; in nearly all species the heps become bald, that is, they lose their calyces on maturity. Many of the remaining species are not worthy of garden cultivation, in fact if we take R. *canina* as our criterion very many wild roses are ruled out, for this species sets quite a high standard of beauty. I have included two small species, R. *glutinosa* and R. *serafinii*, which are connoisseurs' plants and which add a leaf fragrance to their obvious charms. The most noted of all fragrant-leaved roses, the Sweet Brier, or R. *rubiginosa*, is similar in many outward appearances to R. *canina*, but with its brighter pink flowers, greater freedom of flower, and equal brilliance of hep, coupled with its delicious scent of flower and leaf, it would stand in my opinion very high in the ranks of flowering shrubs—if only it were not so frightfully prickly. It may well be that a thornless form will appear one day; thornless forms of R. *canina* have appeared from time to time—in fact it is usually considered that a thornless (or nearly so) form was the parent of R. *alba*—and today there are less thorny forms being developed as understocks for budding. If the Sweet Brier ever gives us this priceless boon, a new and very favoured flowering shrub will have arrived. Few shrubs have greater beauty at two seasons of the year.

R. *villosa* flowers early in the season, and I know of few more satisfying sights than the cool combination of clear light pink flowers scattered all over the pale jade-green leaves. Great bushes at Mottisfont and at Bone Hill flower wonderfully every year. But perhaps the most valuable rose in the group from a gardening point of view is R. *rubrifolia*, on account of the colour—a soft greyish-green tinted with coppery-mauve. It is indispensable for colour schemes in the garden or home, but has been surprisingly little used for hybridizing. This species is widely separated botanically from R. *murielae*, R. *fedtschenkoana*, and R. *beggerana*, all of which have pale grey-green leaves and white flowers, but will hybridize readily with them, and herein may lie the germ of a series of grey-leaved roses of the future.

CANINA. Europe. The Dog Rose. Few wish to grow this species in their gardens; it is scarcely showy enough, and is such a common hedgerow wilding that it may well be left to grace the countryside. The Sweet Brier, R. *rubiginosa*, has all its qualities coupled with fragrant foliage.

This species is raised by the million every year for the production of understocks for budding. It is not generally realized that when a 'maiden' rose is bought—that is a plant of one summer's growth—no less than four autumns have passed since the seed was picked to produce the understock. The seed needs stratifying for a year, and another year to grow; another summer passes when the rose is budded, and yet another year's growth for the scion. Looked at in this way maiden roses are really four years old from the picking of the seed, and the price paid for the finished article has to cover these long years of patient and careful preparation by skilled workmen. First there is the harvesting, cleaning, and stratifying of the seeds, sowing and cultivating; next year lifting, grading, planting, cultivating, staking or tying, labelling, lifting, grading, and packing—and so to the customer's door. I wonder how many purchasers have any idea of all this work?

Roessig, Plate 21. 'Le Rosier canin.'

Andrews, Plate 4. R. *canina*, the 'Dog' Rose: 'a title but ill adapted to designate wild nature's blushing maids'.

Lawrance, Plate 81. 'Dog' Rose or 'Hip Tree'.

Duhamel, vol. vii, Plate 11. Bois and Trechslin, Plate 1.

Schlechtendal, t.2629. Hoffman, Plate 1.

I grow three seedlings of R. *canina*:

'Abbotswood'. 1954. A seedling rose which cropped up in a hedgerow in the kitchen garden at Abbotswood, Stow-on-the-Wold, Gloucestershire, the home of Mr and Mrs Harry Ferguson. Mr F. Tustin, then their head gardener, pointed it out to me and I subsequently named and distributed it. It is a vigorous plant, but more manageable than R. *canina* itself, and carries normal armature and light green foliage. The flowers are of true Dog Brier pink, fairly double, borne along the arching branches. Heps oval, orange-red, showy. Sweetly scented like R. *canina*, and a spray cut with half-open blooms can be very charming. Should reach 6 feet by 6 feet. (Photograph, Plate 2.)

From the following illustrations it is obvious that chance hybrids or forms of this type must have occurred before:

Andrews, Plate 6, R. *canina var. flore pleno*. Very similar to 'Abbotswood'.

Lawrance, Plate 60, Double 'Dog Rose'. Ditto.

'Andersonii'. Known before 1912, when it was first recorded by Hillier, but of unknown origin. It is believed to be a hybrid of

R. *canina* with one of the other diploid roses. Be this as it may, from the garden point of view it can be considered as a very worthwhile variant of the Dog Rose, for its flowers are not only considerably larger than those of that species, but of a rich and brilliant rose pink. Leaves dark, leaden green, long, pointed. Unlike R. *canina*, its leaves are hairy beneath, while the heps are equal in brilliance and size to those of that species. It make a wide arching bush, some 6 feet by 8 feet. Rich fragrance of raspberry-drops.
Willmott, Plate 379.

'**Kiese**'. Kiese, 1910. 'Général Jacqueminot' × R. *canina*. A big, vigorous bush or semi-climber with dark green glossy leaves, and heads of semi-double or nearly single flowers, of bright cherry-red. 6 feet by 6 feet.

× HIBERNICA. 1802. R. *canina* × R. *spinosissima*. Mrs Gore, in *The Rose Fancier's Manual*, 1838, mentions that 'the environs of Belfast produce an insignificant shrub, known as the *Rose Hibernica*, for the discovery of which Mr Templeton received a premium of fifty guineas from the Botanical Society of Dublin, as being a new indigenous plant'. I have been amused by and not a little jealous of Mr Templeton's prowess; such a reward from such a quarter would be inconceivable today. It is a very pretty little shrub, now known to be a hybrid between R. *canina* and R. *spinosissima*, thanks to Mr Rowley's patient work. Mrs Gore refers to the difference in growth on poor or rich soil in her absurd remarks; with her it apparently varied considerably in vigour, but my plant, received from Lady Moore some years ago, has never departed from its normal appearance, which is in effect a large bush with greyish leaves and cream-pink single flowers, leaning considerably towards R. *canina*. About 6 feet by 10 feet.
Willmott, Plate 289.

GLUTINOSA. S.E. Europe, W. Asia. R. *pulverulenta*, R. *dalmatica*. This rose is seldom seen, but should be in collections when possible on account of its aromatic foliage, which smells like a pine forest on a hot day. The odour comes from innumerable sticky glands on both sides of the small leaves, which cluster the dense growth thickly. The twiggy shoots branch freely, bearing prickles of all sizes, and make a bushy plant up to 2 or 3 feet and as much wide. The flowers are small, of clear pink, and resemble those of the sweet brier, but the heps are large, of rich dark red, and covered with bristly hairs; the display of heps creates a more telling effect than that of the flowers. By some authorities it is considered a relative of R. *rubiginosa*. Tall forms are native to some localities.

Willmott, Plate 467.

Sibthorp, vol. v, Plate 482.

Botanical Magazine, t.8826. R. *glutinosa dalmatica*, a closely related geographical form with larger fruits.

RUBIGINOSA. Europe. The Sweet Brier, or Eglantine. R. *eglanteria*. One of the most treasured of English wild plants, and rightly so, for its flowers are clear pink, beautifully fashioned, and deliciously fragrant; a fragrance that has its richer counterpart in the aromatic foliage. It forms an arching shrub 8 feet or more high and as much through, and is very heavily armed with hooked prickles, so that it will make an impenetrable and beautiful hedge. In autumn the masses of glittering oval heps transform it into a vivid spectacle lasting well into the winter. It will make a dense hedge if pruned annually in spring, although thereby all the best flowering shoots will be removed; for this purpose it should be planted about 3 feet apart, and be allowed to make a mass some 6 feet wide. It is best to plant it to the south and west of the garden if possible, since its leaves release their fragrance most in warm moist wind. 'Not even among the roses shall we find a more delicious perfume' (Dean Hole).

An interesting and beautiful hybrid is 'Eos'. See page 61.

Schlechtendal, t.2630.

Duhamel, vol. vii, Plate 7. A small spray.

Andrews, Plate 109.

Lawrance, Plate 56.

Jacquin, *Florae Austriacae*, vol. i, Plate 50.

Around 1800 several forms of Sweet Brier were growing, as recorded in old books, but very few of them have come down to us. I have found only two. And yet the Sweet Brier must have been a great favourite in old times if only on account of its aromatic leaves. No form or hybrid that I have so far examined is as aromatic as the type species, and I have not yet seen a double pink form closely resembling the species, with anything like the beauty of 'Abbotswood', a double R. *canina*. R. *rubiginosa* seems to convey to its progeny a rather coarse appearance which is much at variance with its natural form.

'Janet's Pride'. Introduced in 1892 by W. Paul and Sons, but Mr Shepherd tells us it was known prior to that date under the name of 'Clementine'. On the other hand Miss Willmott records a statement by the Rev. C. Wolley-Dod that this 'Janet's Pride' was found growing wild in a Cheshire lane, far from garden influence. It is thought to be a hybrid, perhaps with R. *damascena*, is less vigorous and prickly than R. *rubiginosa*, and bears faintly aromatic foliage. The flowers are of fair size, with an extra two or three petals, bright cherry pink with nearly white centre, the pale colour running out into the pink in veins and occasional flashes, giving a charming effect. 6 feet by 5 feet.
Willmott, Plate 449.

'La Belle Distinguée'. The 'Double Scarlet Sweet Brier'. I have been unable to trace its origin, but it is no doubt a hybrid, for it is not very thorny, of dense rather upright growth to about 4 feet by 3 feet; leaves very dark green, tough, scarcely fragrant. Flowers flat, very double, deep cherry red, not very fragrant. It is a showy little bush. A few small dull red heps are produced.
Andrews, Plate 118. R. *eglanteria rubra*, 'Red-flowered Eglantine Rose'. A similar, larger-flowered form, not identical to the above.

'Manning's Blush Sweet Brier'. The excellent plate of this little double rose in Miss Lawrance's volume proves that it was in cultivation prior to 1797. Fortunately, although we do not know its origin or parentage, it inherits the fragrant foliage of R. *rubiginosa*, but it is very much more compact in growth, about 5 feet high and wide. It is really a miniature both in stature and in the size of the flowers, which about cover a florin, and are fully double, blush-white, with a flush of pink in the bud and half-open flower. Foliage small, rich green, on an arching fairly dense bush. Somewhat mossy calyx.

Andrews, Plate 115. The paler of the two depicted. Rather highly coloured.

Lawrance, Plate 41.

Lawrance, Plate 72. Depicts a double, mossy, Sweet Brier of dark colouring.

It is thought that the charming bright colouring of 'Janet's Pride' prompted Lord Penzance to start breeding with R. *rubiginosa*, which he did about 1890, creating a fairly uniform group of vigorous shrubs by using pollen principally from Hybrid Perpetuals and Bourbons, and two others from R. *foetida* or its progeny. No less than fifteen hybrids were put on the market between 1894 and 1895, many of them being rather similar. The two descended from R. *foetida*, 'Lord Penzance' and 'Lady Penzance', are not so vigorous as the others, which may frequently attain 10 feet in height, and as much through; these are strong growers therefore, suitable only for the largest plantings, where they will make a magnificent show at midsummer and not be without colour later from the heps, which most of them carry; those which I have examined have foliage somewhat aromatic but of less potency than their parent.

Although, since these are hybrids, they rightly belong to Chapter 14, I prefer to list them here on account of their affinity to the Sweet Brier.

'Amy Robsart'. 1894. Deep rose pink, large, semi-double. Scarlet heps.

'Anne of Geierstein'. 1894. Dark crimson, single. Scarlet heps.

'Brenda'. 1894. Peach-blossom pink, single. I have not grown this variety.

'Catherine Seyton'. 1894. Soft pink, single. Aromatic foliage. I have not grown this variety.

'Edith Bellenden'. 1895. Pale pink, single. Aromatic foliage. Not in my collection.

'Flora McIvor'. White, flushed with pink, single. Aromatic. Mansfield, Plate 52.

'**Greenmantle**'. 1895. Rosy crimson, with white eye, single. Aromatic foliage.

'**Jeannie Deans**'. 1895. Brilliant crimson-scarlet, semi-double. Aromatic foliage.
Kingsley, p. 44.

'**Julia Mannering**'. 1895. Bright, clear, delicate pink, with darker veins; nearly single.

'**Lady Penzance**'. 1894. R. *rubiginosa* × R. *foetida bicolor*. Single, bright yellow centre, with coppery-salmon flush over most of the petal area. Pretty arching growth, foliage somewhat aromatic. Scent of flowers reminiscent of R. *foetida*.
Mansfield, Plate 52 (poor).

'**Lord Penzance**'. 1894. R. *rubiginosa* × 'Harison's Yellow'. Single; rosy-fawn-yellow, lemon centre. Sweet scent; fragrant foliage.

'**Lucy Ashton**'. 1894. A distinct pink edge adds colour to the pure white, single flowers. Aromatic foliage.

'**Lucy Bertram**'. 1895. Dark, vivid crimson with white centre; single; aromatic leaves. Scarlet heps.

'**Meg Merrilies**'. 1894. Rosy crimson, nearly single. Aromatic foliage. Scarlet heps.

'**Minna**'. 1895. Clear salmon-rose with white centre. Sweet scent. Very aromatic foliage.

'**Rose Bradwardine**'. 1894. Rose pink, single. Aromatic foliage.

In 1916 Hesse, the German nurseryman, put on the market 'Magnifica', which was the result of 'selfing' a seedling from 'Lucy Ashton'. It is a vigorous plant, with large, semi-double, deep pink, cupped blooms, deliciously scented, and has been used extensively by Herr Wilhelm Kordes for the production of widely differing hybrids. Miss Ann Wylie gave a very clear family tree in the Royal Horticultural Society's *Journal* for February 1955, shewing all the derivatives, including Floribundas. We need only concern ourselves, however, with certain of the shrubby seedlings, one of which is of superlative beauty for general use, 'Fritz

Nobis'. Herr Kordes's aim is the production of gay Floribundas and others which will have greater hardiness and resistance to disease owing to the influx of new blood from R. *rubiginosa*, and he has successfully launched several varieties and used the progeny for further experimentation. These newer shrubby types will be found included with others in Chapter 14.

RUBRIFOLIA. Mountains of Central and Southern Europe. *R. glauca*, *R. ferruginea*. There are very few shrubs with such distinctive garden value as this open-growing species, with no great pretensions apart from the colouring of its leaves. It is practically thornless, apart from the bases of the strong violet-coloured young shoots, and in winter imparts a warm red-brown effect, reaching up to 6 or 8 feet in height and as much through. The growth and leaves resemble somewhat the Dog Brier, but all the leaves, from spring till autumn, have a unique glaucous colouring; in shady cool places they are usually broad and luxuriant and grey-green, with a hint of mauve, while in sunshine they are smaller and suffused with a rich coppery-mauve tint. The flowers are borne in bunches, the long calyx-lobes creating a hairy effect around each bunch, and they open flat; they are of clear pink, enhanced by the white centre area which in turn is crowned by light yellow stamens. The buds and young wood are dark purplish-copper. Later the heps, of an unusual brownish-red, crop in bunches and give further colouring to the bush, as they are usually very free. Little scent. (Plate II).

Redouté, vol. i, Plate 31. 'Le Rosier à feuilles rougeâtres.'
Willmott, Plate 399. Beautiful and true to nature in every way.
Duhamel, vol. vii, Plate 10.
Schlechtendal, t.2627. Does not shew the usual white centre.
Botanical Register, vol. v, t.430. A poor little spray.
Andrews, Plate 92. *R. lurida*. A somewhat pithy comment on this fine portrait showing an amazing number of flowers occurs in the *Botanical Register*: 'Andrews has a figure of it in a most luxuriant state under the name of *lurida*, by which it is known in the nurseries.' One might understand that nurserymen's flair for exaggeration was not unknown in those days.

'**Carmenetta**'. (R. × *rubrosa*.) R. *rubrifolia* × R. *rugosa*. 1930.

Raised at Ottawa. This plant is very near to R. *rubrifolia*, but from R. *rugosa* it inherits coarseness and thorns. On the whole I think it inferior to R. *rubrifolia*; it has a stronger growth, equally good leaves, larger flowers in larger bunches, and the fruits are very similar. In some soils where for any reason R. *rubrifolia* might not thrive—possibly those which are light and sandy—'Carmenetta' should be tried. The leaves are glaucous blue-grey with violet tints above, grey-green beneath.

SERAFINII. Mediterranean. R. *apennina*. An exceedingly dense twiggy plant, growing to about 3 feet in height, and copiously armed with small hooked thorns. The thin, wiry, short-jointed twigs interlace freely and bear numerous small rounded leaves with five or seven small rounded leaflets, densely glandular on the margin and stalk, and thus gummy and fragrant. Pretty little pale pink single blooms appear at midsummer, followed by a good show of small, bright red, rounded fruits. A gay little shrub suitable for planting in heath gardens and such places where a breath of the wild without unmannerliness is needed. Willmott, Plate 475. A good portrait.

SHERARDII. Northern and Central Europe. R. *omissa*. Comparatively new to me, this rose grows well at Talbot Manor, Norfolk, making a well-filled shrub, covered with bluish-green leaves, up to about 5 feet high and wide. The shapely single pink flowers are of a particularly clear fresh pink and contrast well with the foliage. This rose might be a good substitute in small gardens for the similarly coloured large-growing R. *villosa*. Bright oval heps.

VILLOSA. R. *pomifera*. 'The Apple Rose.' Europe, West Asia. This most beautiful species makes a large shrub, fairly compact, up to 7 feet high and rather wider. The large grey-green leaves are downy on both surfaces and give exactly the right contrast to the single pink flowers, which are of a particularly clear and lovely pink, and prettily crinkled. At flowering time it is not eclipsed in beauty by any other species. Through the summer the foliage remains greyish although it loses its first cool fresh-ness, and later makes another lovely foil for the huge heps, which turn from orange-red to rich plum-crimson, densely set with bristly hairs. Slightly fragrant.

It has been used as an understock for budding from time to time, and Dean Hole recalls in his *A Book About Roses* a hedge of R. *villosa* twenty years old at Kilkenny in 1834, belonging to a Mr Robertson, which was 'about 8 or 10 feet high, which is a sheet of bloom every May, and throughout the rest of the season flowers with the Boursault, Noisette, Hybrid China, and other Roses which are budded on it'. Andrews refers to a similar hedge 13 feet high with sixteen varieties of roses budded on it. All this might be a pointer towards bigger and better roses for the future.

Willmott, Plate 435. A rather poor flower. R. *pomifera*.

Andrews, Plate 34.

Lawrance, Plate 33. 'The single apple-bearing rose.' Very highly coloured.

Botanical Magazine, t.7241. An admirable portrait of the flowers and remarkable fruits.

Schlechtendal, t.2632. A good portrait.

Roessig, Plate 30. 'Le rosier vélu ou à fruits épineux.' R. *pomifera*, R. *villosa*. An excellent plate.

Duhamel, vol. vii, Plate 15. R. *villosa*.

Redouté, vol. i, Plate 67. 'Le Rosier vélu.'

'Wolley-Dod'. R. *villosa* 'Duplex', R. *pomifera* 'Duplex'. A semi-double hybrid of the 'Apple Rose' and of equal vigour, 'Wolley-Dod's Rose' is undoubtedly a hybrid between R. *villosa* and a tetraploid garden rose, according to the chromosome count. The figure in Willmott's *Genus Rosa* was from the Rev. Wolley-Dod's garden and is therefore authentic. That this plant was an original seedling is not recorded by her, but semi-double forms were known earlier, witness two other plates cited. It has little scent; its chief merits are the exquisite blend of the flowers and later the heavy dark red heps with the leaves. It is not quite so free of fruits as the species.

Willmott, Plate 436. R. *pomifera* variety.

Andrews, Plate 34.

Lawrance, Plate 29. 'The double apple-bearing rose.'

4

The Cinnamon Rose and its Old World Relatives

The Canell or Cinnamon Rose, or the rose smelling like
Cinnamon, hath leaves like unto those of Eglantine, but
smaller and greener, of the savour or smell of Cinnamon,
whereof it tooke his name, and not of the smell of his
floures which have little or no savour at all.

Gerard's *Herball*, 1597.

THE MAJORITY of our garden rose species belong to what the
botanists call the Cinnamomeae group, exemplified by *Rosa
cinnamomea*, a singular honour for a not very important small
European species in a group comprising some forty species,
including such horticultural giants as R. *rugosa* and R. *moyesii*.
In botanical works, without which we should have difficulty in
finding our way through the morass of species at all, mere size
and colour of flower or hep are not so important as such obscure
points as the shape of the style in the flower, the placing of the
seeds in the hep, or the fusion of the stipules to the leaf-stalk.

I find it impossible to give a group of characters by which all
species in this section can be distinguished. There are exceptions
to every rule, but the section resolves itself fairly easily into several
recognizable groups. There are R. *rugosa*, R. *kamtschatica*, and R.
acicularis at one end, we might say, covered with prickles and
bristles, whereas R. *pendulina* is thornless. Almost all species have
persistent sepals, projecting erectly above the hep except in R.
willmottiae. The great group of species allied to R. *moyesii* have
long flagon-shaped heps, and do in fact constitute the bulk of the

species included in this chapter, which is devoted to the Old World representatives of the Cinnamomeae Group, apart from R. *rugosa*, which has a chapter to itself. The New World species will be found in Chapter 5.

BEGGERANA. Temperate Asia. The first alphabetically of a trio of roses with grey leaves and white flowers. From R. *fedtschenkoana* and R. *murielae* it is separated by minor botanical differences, and they all provide an exceptional pale grey-green effect in the garden, and are thus valuable for colour schemes. This species is perhaps the least grey and the least ornamental of the three. Its hooked prickles distinguish it from the other two, and also from R. *soulieana*, another valuable grey-leaved rose which belongs to a separate group. The fragrant leaves are of medium size with 5 to 9 leaflets, and the flowers are borne in small clusters. They have a peculiar scent—reminiscent of R. *foetida*—and appear over a long period, the later ones having as companions dark-red heps from earlier flowers; these heps eventually turn to maroon colour, and lose their sepals—an exception to the rule. It is of tall, spreading habit, up to 8 feet high and wide.
Willmott, Plate 171.

CINNAMOMEA. Europe, N. and W. Asia. Reaching 6 feet or so in height, this is a small-leaved shrub of no great merit for the garden. The flowers are of dark pink, up to $2\frac{1}{2}$ inches across, borne in small clusters or singly. Stipules very wide. I have been unable to detect any cinnamon scent though Gerard & Parkinson ascribe it to the foliage and the flowers respectively. Possibly ' cinnamon ' refers to the colour of the stems.
Willmott, Plate 141.
Andrews, Plate 96.
Schlechtendal, t.2626.
Redouté, vol. i, Plate 133. *Rosa cinnamomea flore simplici*, 'Le Rosier de Mai à fleurs simples'.

CINNAMOMEA ' Plena '. ' Rose de Mai ', *Rosa majalis*; ' Rose du Saint-Sacrement', 'Rose des Pâques'. Miss Willmott claims that the original R. *cinnamomea* ' Plena ' was of a much deeper colouring than her figure to which she gives the above synonym. Probably doubling has occurred several times and slightly different colour forms have been the subject of separate records, but all that I have seen have had a dark lilac-pink tone, and I have not considered them of much value. It is true that it is one of the oldest recorded double roses and as such is worthy of a place in a collector's garden. Mrs Gore, 1838, states 'this sub variety is a favourite in all gardens'. It is extremely early flowering, as its popular names suggest, and this may have been one of the causes of its popularity. About 4 feet by 3 feet.

Lindley, Plate 5. A good portrait of the flowers in bud.

Willmott, Plate 143. Possibly not authentic.

Lawrance, Plate 34. 'The Double Cinnamon rose.'

Andrews, Plate 97. R. *cinnamomea multiplex*, the 'Double Cinnamon Rose', said to have been introduced from Southern Europe in 1569.

Roessig, Plate 3. ' Le Rosier de Mai ', *Rosa majalis*. Excellent.

Redouté, vol. i, Plate 105. *Rosa cinnamomea majalis*. 'Le Rosier de Mai.' A rather elongated drawing.

DAVIDII. E. Tibet, W. China. A tall, open shrub reaching 9 to 10 feet in height, with erect but arching light green shoots and a few reddish prickles. The leaves are deeply veined, giving a corrugated yet matt effect, elegantly poised. The flowers do not appear until most species are over, and are borne in big bunches all the way up the stems, smelling of peonies, loosely nodding, with sticky, hairy stalks and long calyx lobes; their soft mallow-pink is a welcome change at that time from the vivid Floribundas. The resulting bunches of small, flagon-shaped heps are most attractive. A useful species on account of its late-flowering habit and slender grace.

Botanical Magazine, t.8679.

DAVIDII ELONGATA. A form with rather longer fruits in smaller clusters, and longer leaflets.

FARRERI. N.W. China. The wild species is not in cultivation. Today's correct name is R. *elegantula*.

FARRERI ' Persetosa '. The ' Threepenny Bit Rose ', so called because of the size of its flowers. This variety was noted by

E. A. Bowles among a batch of seedlings of R. *farreri* (Farrer No. 774), and was named specially because of its excessive crop of hair-like thorns which occur all the way up the stems, and its richer colouring. The species makes a charming plant about 6 feet high and sometimes twice as wide, as in Lady Moore's garden near Dublin or at Spetchley Park, with graceful shoots set with the tiniest of leaves with 7 to 9 leaflets. It has quite an airy effect, like a veil, and when the clear salmon-pink flowers from coral buds appear it is a plant of great distinction. Small, orange heps follow.

It is the flimsiest of roses, like R. *willmottiae* but with leaves and flowers of half the size, and with the grace of R. *webbiana*. In the garden it appears to flourish best in cooler places, even in partial shade, when its ferny grace is the more apparent. In hot positions the foliage is frequently burnished or purple-tinted. *Botanical Magazine*, t.8877.

FEDTSCHENKOANA. Turkestan. Shrubs with pale grey-green leaves are not many and for this reason alone this species has considerable garden value. It is similar to R. *beggerana* and R. *murielae* and also R. *soulieana* in this greyness but noticeable characters separating it from all these are the hispid calyx tube and persistent sepals. Apart from these small botanical points it has another great attribute, for it produces its flowers continuously through the summer, one or a few together at the ends of short side-shoots; they are white, 2 inches across, with yellow stamens, and the later crop coincides with the earliest of the orange-red bristly heps. The scent of the flowers reminds me of that of R. *foetida*. It forms an erect bush up to 9 feet and about 6 feet wide, well filled with small branches, and spreads freely by underground shoots. The strong, young, grey shoots, covered all over with pinkish bristly thorns, are of great beauty. It is altogether a valuable rose, interesting and charming throughout the growing season. Leaflets 5 to 9. (Plate II). Willmott, Plate 155. A good portrait.
Botanical Magazine, t.7770. A good portrait.

FORRESTIANA. Western China. A vigorous bush, with strong arching branches and straight thorns; fresh green copious foliage with 5 to 7 leaflets; very free flowering and a splendid sight both then and when in fruit. The flowers are deep carmine pink, single, like R. *moyesii* in shape, with creamy-yellow stamens, very fragrant. They are borne on short side-shoots, but their stalks are almost absent, the flowers being clustered four or five together in a very tight bunch. The heps are large and hairy, bottle-shaped, bright red, and are framed in the persistent green bracts. 7 feet by 6 feet.

MACROPHYLLA. Himalaya. One of the largest of shrubby roses, reaching 15 feet in height and as much or more in width. An old plant in Cambridge Botanic Garden once achieved '18 feet in height by 25 feet—10 feet in excess of given height' (R. Irwin Lynch in the Royal Horticultural Society's *Journal*, 1915). It creates ferny shade, and often with the flowers above one it can be passed unnoticed, but the flowers when seen are not likely to be forgotten. They have much of the poise of those of R. *setipoda*, and are of warm clear pink, followed by bristly, long, flagon-shaped fruits. It is often without prickles, and the leaflets, from 7 to 9 in number, are hairy beneath. The whole plant is elegant and owes not a little to the beauty of the pruinose young shoots, and the maroon setae on the receptacle. Few roses have such an elegant poise of bloom.

Two subsequent collections by Forrest (14958 and 15309) have been named by Mr Hillier 'Glaucescens' and 'Rubricaulis'. In the former the leaves are particularly glaucous and in the latter the plum-like bloom on the dark reddish stems is a distinguishing feature. 'Rubricaulis' has not proved so hardy as the other forms in cultivation, but is of exceptional beauty and richly coloured.

An interesting hybrid is 'Auguste Roussel' (page 169).
Willmott, Plate 157.
Wallich, vol. ii, Plate 117.

'Doncasteri'. A form of R. *macrophylla* put on the market between the wars by Mr Doncaster of Messrs. J. Burrell and Co. of Cambridge, but probably one of Dr Hurst's seedlings. It has narrower, darker green leaves than the type, with smaller, darker flowers, and a less free and graceful habit. Its chief glory is the sumptuous display of large, red, flagon-shaped heps in early autumn.

Other species related to these and allied to R. *moyesii* are R. *caudata*, R. *hemsleyana* (*Botanical Magazine*, t.8569), R. *banksiopsis*; all have some merit but I would not choose any of them in preference to the species I have described.

MOYESII. Western China. This is not only a very fine species of unique qualities and colouring, but is also a landmark in rose history. It was introduced into cultivation in 1908, and its intense red flowers and magnificent heps at once gave the growing of wild roses a fillip; R. *hugonis* had recently appeared in cultivation and the two of them placed rose species well to the fore among flowering shrubs—a position to which the many rather insignificant pink species would never have brought them. It is undoubtedly one of the finest of all flowering shrubs and one of E. H. Wilson's greatest treasures from the Far East.

Unfortunately it is of gaunt, tall habit which at first might make it appear unsuitable for all but the largest of gardens, attaining as it often does 12 feet in height, the branches above supported by relatively few, extremely stout, thorny stems. But where it thrives it forms a lofty canopy of small leaves with 7 to 13 leaflets of dark, rather bluish green, and the resulting broken shade provides the ideal condition for plants that cannot stand full sunshine. The flowers are borne in small clusters, and are of intense blood-red colouring, with dark-coloured stamens. When seen against the blue sky their colouring is enhanced. This blood-red type is not the most common in its native habitat, but takes priority in naming. The pink form, to which seedlings often revert, is more common and is known as R. *m.* ' Fargesii '.

Although the flowers are of such wonderful colour I would go so far as to say that the heps were probably of more value in getting it the recognition it deserved. For apart from its allied species, all introduced about the same time (except R. *macrophylla*), no other rose or shrub had such striking large fruits of so unusual a shape. They are bulbous at the base, narrowing above before widening again below the persistent calyx lobes, and thus shaped like a flask or flagon, with which they are often compared. The heps are at their best in August, and this applies to the allied species as well. Berried shrubs were not of much

account in the nineteenth century, so that here again its introduction was most opportune, when the numerous new flowering shrubs were awakening the public to fresh beauty for their
gardens.

The Garden, October 1916, p. 514. Flowers and fruits; very fine.
Revue Horticole, 1926-7, p. 334.
Botanical Magazine, t.8338. Poor.
Willmott, Plate 229. A splendid portrait.

MOYESII ' Fargesii '. This is so near to R. *moyesii* as not to be
distinguished from a garden point of view, except in floral
colour. It has rose-red flowers and the usual heps. On the other
hand the chromosome count—it is a tetraploid—makes it a
possible parent for 'Nevada' and other similar crosses rather
than R. *moyesii* itself, which is a hexaploid.

MOYESII ROSEA. R. *holodonta*. These two names are sometimes
used for pink-flowered forms of R. *moyesii*. R. *holodonta* in
reality relates to R. *davidii elongata*.
Botanical Magazine, t.9248. This is R. *sweginzowii*.

GARDEN FORMS AND HYBRIDS OF R. *moyesii*

'Fred Streeter'. Jackman, 1951. A seedling R. *moyesii* which
originated at Petworth, Sussex, and was originally distributed
as R. *moyesii* 'Petworth'. Considerably more bushy, with fine,
dense, arching habit and fresh green leaves. The flowers are of
bright cerise pink. Large flagon-shaped crimson-red heps. This
is no doubt a form of R. *moyesii* ' Fargesii ' and resembles
'Sealing Wax' and R. *wintoniensis*.

'Geranium'. 1938. This excellent form, raised at Wisley and
selected by Mr B. O. Mulligan, is of more compact growth than
the type, with more copious, larger, fresh-green leaves. The
flowers are a magnificent blazing red, and the heps are larger
and smoother than those of the average R. *moyesii*, and of
equally good colour. Undoubtedly the best type for the average
garden, or at least for those gardeners who prefer a reasonably
compact erect bush up to 10 feet by about 7 feet, rather than a
gawky tree-like shrub creating overhead shade. It has few
thorns. (Plate III, heps.)

'**Sealing Wax** '. 1938. A form or hybrid of R. *moyesii* ' Fargesii ' of the same origin as ' Geranium ', selected for its splendid scarlet heps. Vivid pink flowers in the R. *moyesii* style. Possibly a hybrid with R. *sweginzowii*.

The following are known or presumed to be hybrids of R. *moyesii* but are sufficiently like a species rose to be included here.

'**Eos**'. Ruys, 1950. R. *moyesii* × 'Magnifica'. With two such vigorous parents a vigorous offspring would be expected, and this plant can achieve 12 feet in a few seasons after planting, sending up stiff yet arching shoots daintily set with small *moyesii* foliage in dark leaden green; the next spring they become wands of coral red, from the clusters of nearly single flat flowers borne along their entire length. Stamens yellow. It is a most arresting sight; worthily named after the Goddess of the Dawn, for just those flaming tints appear at sunrise. No heps. For late May and early June display few roses can compete with its brilliance. It is best planted well behind other shrubs to cover its gaunt lower stems. Spiky red thorns.

' **Highdownensis** '. 1928. A seedling from R. *moyesii* raised by Sir Frederick Stern at Highdown, Goring-by-Sea, Sussex. The original plant is still a fine sight on a chalky slope. Although it is less of a vivid red colour than a selected R. *moyesii* it is in many ways a much more satisfactory and spectacular plant, being more bushy, and bearing elegant deeply tinted leaves. The single flowers are borne in conspicuous clusters, of vivid cerise crimson, and are followed by large flagon-shaped orange-scarlet heps. At both flowering and fruiting time it can hold its own with anything in the garden. Its general good behaviour and vigour recommend it for all large plantings of shrub roses; it makes a fine shrub of some 10 feet by 10 feet. The strongest shoots are very beautiful with colourful prickles and bristles and coppery leaves. Little fragrance.
Gardeners' Chronicle, 6 January 1934.

' **Hillieri** '. R. *hillieri*; Hillier, *c.* 1920. The darkest-flowered single rose, resembling R. *moyesii* in shape and type of flower, but the growth is more graceful, the branches forking and interlacing, making a large mass sparsely covered with small pretty leaves. A few fine heps are produced, flagon-shaped, orange-red. It is best placed so that the sun shines through the maroon crimson of the flowers, greatly enhancing their colour. Young wood glaucous green with few large thorns. 10 feet by 12 feet. Usually considered to be a hybrid between R. *moyesii* and R. *willmottiae*, but Mr Rowley tells me that the chromosome count of R. *willmottiae* would preclude this cross. Sometimes classed under R. × *pruhoniciana*.

WINTONIENSIS. Hillier. R. *moyesii* × *setipoda*. A big bushy fresh green leafy plant, whose foliage is scented, like that of R. *setipoda*. Single vivid cerise- to rose-pink flowers with paler centres, and the general appearance of R. *moyesii* ' Fargesii '. Has purplish setae on the young heps. 12 feet by 12 feet.

MULTIBRACTEATA. Western China. A vigorous shrub up to 7 feet and often more in width, sending up prickly stout shoots, green while young, with mahogany-coloured prickles which turn later to grey, on red-brown wood. These stout shoots branch freely in subsequent years producing numerous fine zigzag twigs heavily set with tiny leaves of 7 to 9 greyish leaflets, rounded and grey-green, giving an effect of dots of green at a distance. The flowers are small but numerous, en-shrouded with multitudes of grey-green bracts, the same size as the leaves, in long arching branching sprays; cool lilac-pink with creamy stamens, they are borne late in the season—often into August—and are thus doubly welcome. When growing vigorously it is luxuriant in its beauty, creating a curtain of flower and leaf. The scent is unusual, and related to that of R. *foetida*. Small bright red cerise-tinted rounded heps. 'Cerise Bouquet' is a beautiful hybrid (see Chapter 14). Both are depicted on Plate 1.

MURIELAE. Western China. The third of our trio of grey-leaved roses and larger than the others, making an arching shrub up to 6 or 8 feet and as wide, producing underground stems. The smaller shoots are drooping and make a dense curtain of foliage, pale grey-green, among which the small white flowers are disposed in clusters of 3 or 7. Leaflets 9 to 15, borne on downy, prickly stalks. The sepals have leafy tips and stay on the elliptical red heps, which are glabrous. In common with R. *fedtschenkoana* its strong young shoots are heavily armed with pinkish bristles, and a few prickles which are straight. Before the collection of rose species at Kew was reorganized, a plant had grown to large proportions, arching and weeping to the ground and creating a beautiful effect, some 7 feet high by 12 feet wide.

NANOTHAMNUS. China, Central Asia. R. *webbiana microphylla* or R. *w. pustulata*. An extremely pretty small species near to R. *webbiana*, but only about 18 inches or 2 feet high, composed of small, freely branching twiggy shoots, straight thorns, and tiny leaves with serrations only on the upper third of the leaflets. The flowers, borne on very short flower stalks, are pink, single, small and dainty, but not unusual in any way; in fruit, however, the bush is really brilliant, with shining oval scarlet heps.

PENDULINA. Central and Southern Europe, R. *alpina*. This mountain shrub figures in all the illustrated Alpine floras, and it is surprising that it is found so seldom in gardens, being practically thornless. The reddish, sometimes purplish stems make an open, arching shrub up to 4 or 5 feet high and wide. As many as 11 leaflets sometimes occur but usually these are between 5 and 9, creating an airy effect. The flowers are about 2 inches across, of rich, light crimson with a purplish suffusion; stamens light yellow. The long fruit, more or less narrowed to a flask shape at the end, is bright red and decorative, but by no means as large as that of R. *moyesii*. It flowers very early in the season. Among its progeny are ' Mrs Colville ' and R. × *reversa*. For years it has been claimed to be the ancestor of the old Boursault Roses (R. *lheritierana* or R. × *reclinata*); from chromosome counts taken at Bayfordbury Mr Rowley tells me that this is highly suspect and that some other species, perhaps R. *blanda*, is probably concerned in the parentage of this old group of roses.

Botanical Register, vol. v, t.424. Poor colour.
Lawrance, Plate 9. Good portrait, vivid colour.

Willmott, Plate 293.

Schlechtendal, t.2625. Light pink.

Andrews, Plate 88. *R. inermis.*

Jacquin, *Florae Austriacae,* vol. iii, Plate 279.

Redouté, vol. i, Plate 57.

PENDULINA FLORE PLENO, see ' Morletii ', Chapter 14.

PENDULINA ' Pyrenaica '. This charming dwarf Pyrenean form
was recorded in cultivation in 1815, and has enjoyed a certain
amount of popularity among rock garden enthusiasts. It runs
freely at the root and its plum-coloured stems ascend to about
1 foot. It is more prickly than the type species, but not heavily
armed, and the scattering of single crimson flowers can give a
lovely effect among other plants. It has a densely glandular
receptacle and calyx, giving a pine-like hint to a lemony
fragrance, and later bears slender scarlet heps. Like all shrubs
that are invasive it can become a nuisance. It is easily grown in
any well-drained soil in sun. *R. pendulina* ' Nana '.

Jacquin, *Horti Schoenbrunnensis,* Plate 416. Probably not a
portrait of the dwarf clone described above.

Botanical Magazine, t.6724.

OXYODON. *R. haematodes.* A native of the Caucasus and sometimes
considered a variety of *R. pendulina,* and, like that species,
practically thornless, with reddish-purple stems. The leaves,
composed of 7 to 9 leaflets, are of greyish-green with reddish
stipules. It is not particularly striking when producing its
clusters of single, deep pink flowers with yellow stamens and
long sepals, but the bulky, flagon-shaped heps in dark red turn
it into a thing of splendour in late summer. 4 to 5 feet.

'Mount Everest'. Prior to 1938. Probably *R. pendulina* crossed
with a nearer relative of *R. moyesii.* Elegant foliage on strong
stems, purplish below, and plentiful, single, carmine-pink
flowers in the early season. The brilliant, shining fruit, of the
colour and almost of the glossiness of a ripe red currant, are of
the usual bottle shape but with very little neck. They are at their
best colour in late August or early September, and my plants
usually have purplish-tinted foliage at that season, creating an
attractive display. Probably 10 feet.

PRATTII. Western China. A shrub with small leaves and small deep pink flowers in clusters, followed by small, long-shaped, red fruits.

SERTATA. Central and Western China. A species up to about 7 feet with slender prickles and thin leaves, coppery-tinted while young. Clean pink flowers with white centres and creamy yellow stamens, above a glandular-hairy receptacle. The bottle-shaped heps are bright red and glandular-hairy. Nearly related to R. *macrophylla* and R. *willmottiae*.
Botanical Magazine, t.8473.

SETIPODA. Western China. R. *macrophylla crasse-aculeata*. The individual bloom in shape, colouring, and poise can be supreme among wild roses. A few large, handsome, flat prickles beset the stout stems, which reach 9 feet in height and width, forming an open, arching shrub. Leaflets 7 to 9, rather long for this group, grey beneath; large stipules. The flowers are borne on hairy purple stalks with hairy purple calyx-tubes; the calyx lobes are long, with leafy tips enshrining a large, wide bloom of exquisite beauty. Perhaps the flower is nothing very great on its own, but I always feel its deeply notched petals, clear pink colouring fading to white in the centre around the creamy-yellow stamens, and the contrast of the purplish stalks and long calyces are of special merit; and they are poised so beautifully. Very large flagon-shaped heps follow in the R. *moyesii* tradition, freely set with sticky hairs. The glandular-hairy flower stalks and calyx-tubes are redolent of pine, and the flowers of green-apple scent; in addition the leaves have a fragrance of Sweet Brier, but not so strong. (Fig. 1, heps.)
Botanical Magazine, t.8569.

SOULIEANA. Western China. Although this species was introduced as long ago as 1896 it is still a rare plant in cultivation. It belongs to the entirely separate botanical group of Synstylae, all the others of which are great climbers, like R. *moschata*; as R. *soulieana* is a grey-leaved shrub it fits best here horticulturally, and has considerable value in the artistry of the garden, in common with RR. *fedtschenkoana*, *murielae*, and *beggerana*. It is a large-growing rose of arching, sprawling habit, and possibly its scarcity in gardens is due to its size, for it can grow to 10 feet or so eventually, mounding itself up, and has an equal spread. I could take more interest in the beauty of the young grey stems set with yellowish prickles if the latter were not so numerous. Be this as it may, nobody can deny that the general effect is charming; the leaves are of cool, greyish green, usually with 7 leaflets, and the inch-wide white flowers are carried in bunches of several, emerging from ivory-yellow buds. When the crop of flowers is half open the plants are of extraordinary beauty, only equalled a few days later when the whole thing disappears under a snowy covering of petals, giving a rich, fruity fragrance. In the white garden at Kiftsgate, Gloucestershire, it is of outstanding merit.

It has a further unusual attraction, for the heps, which are small and round, are orange, not red, a tint which combines well with the deeper grey-green of late summer and early autumn.

It is not absolutely hardy; I have had strong growths of the summer killed to the ground by autumn frost, but it soon recovers and I think it becomes hardier when its excessive early vigour has somewhat spent itself.

Willmott, Plate 57.

Botanical Magazine, t.8158. Rather too yellow.

SWEGINZOWII. N.W. China, Kansu. A great shrub up to 12 feet and sometimes as wide, more bushy than R. *moyesii*, but armed with large, flattened prickles and many bristly thorns; the bases of the strong basal shoots are repellent. Leaflets 7 to 11, pubescent beneath, borne on prickly reddish stalks, and with prickly stipules; the prickles are glandular. The flowers are bright pink, carried singly or a few together, with glandular-hairy stalks and calyces. The hep is smaller and with less neck than that of R. *moyesii*, more or less hispid, but bright red and shining. As a garden plant it is more vigorous than R. *moyesii* 'Fargesii', and apart from its prickliness, more desirable. In common with all similar species the heps are usually tarnished by mid September.

Botanical Magazine, t.9248 (as R. *holodonta*).

SWEGINZOWII MACROCARPA. Sangerhausen, intro. Kordes; a similar shrub to the type species, darker pink, with larger and more handsome heps. Fruits mature early. Superlative.

WARDII. S.E. Tibet. The species is represented in cultivation by:

WARDII CULTA (Kingdon Ward 6101). Although this form has been in cultivation since 1924, it has never become widely known. Probably a rose that acquired the nickname 'white *moyesii*' would not be likely to become popular, but the beauty and refinement of the solid, creamy-white blooms with their rich mahogany red central disc and yellow stamens leave little to be desired. A. T. Johnson grew it well; it is of pretty, arching growth with light green leaves of *moyesii* persuasion, reaching perhaps 6 feet by 6 feet. Almost thornless.

WEBBIANA. W. Himalaya. One of the prettiest of rose species, making dense bushes filled with arching, interlacing twigs, up to 6 feet high and wide. The wiry stems are of rich plum-brown with a purplish bloom when young, with scattered long straight pale-yellowish thorns mostly at the base. Leaflets tiny, 7 to 9. The pale lilac-pink flowers, up to 2 inches across and with yellow stamens, make a most charming, airy picture early in the season. As the twigs interlace so much many flowers are borne inside the bush but the smallness of the leaves allows them to be seen. In late summer the bushes are once more alive with colour, for the narrow bottle-shaped heps are of brilliant sealing-wax scarlet and highly polished, with persistent sepals; it is one of the showiest of roses in fruit. In cold districts this species should be given a sheltered position. The flowers have a faint fresh scent.
Willmott, Plate 233.

WILLMOTTIAE. Western China. I look upon R. *farreri* ' Persetosa ', R. *webbiana*, R. *willmottiae*, and R. *multibracteata* as four most exquisite and elegant species. R. *webbiana* is the smoothest and most wiry, R. *willmottiae* and R. *farreri* ' Persetosa' have multitudes of tiny bristles and thorns, while R. *multibracteata* is covered, as its name suggests, with many bracts below the flowers. All have pretty, tiny leaflets and comparatively small flowers, but make up for this in their plenteous crop.

R. *willmottiae* forms a dense bush up to about 6 feet and

considerably wider, every twig arching gracefully over the one below it. The young shoots have a pinkish effect from the tinted thorns and bear greyish, tiny leaves with 7 to 9 leaflets. The flowers, rich lilac pink with cream stamens, approach the size of R. *farreri* ' Persetosa '. Later the small, pear-shaped heps of orange-scarlet decorate the bushes; they are very distinct from those of R. *webbiana*, since the sepals are deciduous. *Botanical Magazine*, t.8186.

Postscript 1973 Edition

'Autumn Fire'. Kordes, 1961. 'Herbstfeuer'. Having tested this for many years I think it is a worthy addition to autumn-fruiting roses, to say nothing of its midsummer display (with a few later) of dark blood-red blooms touched with scarlet and maroon. They are semi-double, borne along arching branches. In late autumn the heps take on red colouring; they are bottle-shaped and the longest and largest in the genus. 6 feet by 8 feet.

MACROPHYLLA 'Master Hugh'. 1966. Raised by Mr L. Maurice Mason from seed collected in China by Messrs Stainton, Sykes and W'lliams, No. 7822. Not only is it beautiful in its typical R. *macrophylla* flowers but also in its splendid bottle-shaped frcits; both are of great size and quality. Probably 8 feet by 10 feet.

5

Some American Wild Roses

. . . on the wild-rose spray the blackbirds sing
'O Rose of all the world, O lovely thing.'

John Masefield.

IN THIS chapter we have five species, RR. *carolina, foliolosa, palustris, nitida,* and *virginiana,* which are often classed in a group called Carolinae, but I feel it simpler to group them together, with the remaining species of the Cinnamomeae. All are native only to the Western Hemisphere, and many of them have an obvious resemblance to one another, even to a non-botanist. It will be understood therefore that the remaining species, i.e. RR. *blanda, californica, nutkana,* and *woodsii,* have been extracted from Chapter 4—which was quite full enough—and included here. Fairly constant botanical minutiae which would have in the past supported the separation of the Carolinae from the Cinnamomeae are that the sepals remain on the hep and curve over it—instead of remaining erect or dropping off—and that the seeds are usually attached only to the base of the receptacle, instead of to the bottom and sides.

RR. *californica, carolina, palustris,* and *foliolosa* are rather open-growing shrubs; R. *virginiana* is a dense-growing, wide bushy plant, while R. *nitida* more nearly approaches the growth of R. *spinosissima,* and is a dwarf. They all sucker freely. R. *nutkana* and R. *woodsii* are the most spectacular in fruit. RR. *nitida, foliolosa,* and *virginiana* are noted for their autumn leaf-colour, in fact the last is unsurpassed among roses for its brilliant display, and takes a high place among shrubs in general which are noted for this asset. They do not stand high in garden value, apart from this autumnal brilliance, but some of them have charming double-flowered forms. The portraits of the Carolinae are much confused in old books but I have done my best to sort them out.

BLANDA. Eastern and Central North America. A nearly thornless species with limp, smooth, pale green leaves and clusters of single pink flowers. Its smooth hep, persistent sepals, and freedom from prickles place it near to R. *pendulina*. The hep is almost globose. Its most noticeable character is the very wide stipules, as much as an inch across. 5 feet. It has no great garden merit. Willmott, Plate 307.

'**Amurensis**'. Probably a hybrid of R. *blanda*. A name which has been used apparently without foundation; I believe it is traceable to the collection of Messrs Späth of Berlin, who listed it and distributed it before 1939. It forms a leafy bush of loose appearance owing to its light grey-green, limp, smooth leaves and very broad pale grey-green stipules and bracts. The calyx tube is pale green and both this and the pedicel are slightly hairy. The flowers are semi-double, soft rose pink, loosely petalled, with yellow stamens, eventually fading to blush and reflexing. Sweet cucumber scent. Pear-shaped heps. A pretty bush of cool fresh appearance growing to about 6 feet by 6 feet.

CALIFORNICA. California. The single-flowered species has no particular garden merit, and makes a shrub up to 6 feet in height.

CALIFORNICA 'Plena'. One of the most free-flowering of the species-like roses, this makes a pleasing, leafy, dense yet graceful bush, freely set with fresh green somewhat hairy and folded leaves. The flowers are borne in arching sprays with conspicuous leafy bracts. They are rich dark pink with good yellow stamens. It is a splendid garden shrub. My stock of this rose was a gift from Mrs Fleischmann, and her plant came from Messrs Bobbink and Atkins, of Rutherford, New Jersey. Wood and thorns greenish when young; later the thorns are grey and the wood becomes a red-brown. 6 feet by 6 feet. (Photograph, Plate 1.) 'Theano' (1894) was a similar rose. Willmott, Plate 223. A doubtful portrait.

CAROLINA. Eastern United States. R. *humilis*, R. *parviflora*. A shrub very variable in nature, often only 3 feet in height, bearing pairs of short, straight thorns at the junction of stem and leaf-stalk. The leaves are somewhat lustrous, composed of usually seven leaflets with fine serrations. The long calyx-lobes are characteristic, projecting well beyond the bud, and even shewing well beyond the flower when it is wide open; flowers single, pink; receptacle usually glandular hispid.

Redouté, vol. i, Plate 81. R. *carolina corymbosa*; shows a particularly large corymb of flowers.

Lawrance, Plate 24. R. *carolina*.

Andrews, Plate 100. R. *pennsylvanica*.

Andrews, Plate 103. R. *carolina pimpinellifolia*.

Willmott, Plate 201. R. *humilis*.

Jennings, vol. ii, Plate 88.

Meehan, Thomas, vol. ii, Plate 9. As R. *lucida*. Colour too flame in tone.

CAROLINA ' Plena '. A few years ago Mr and Mrs Wilson Lynes of Taberg, New York State, rediscovered this exquisite little rose and kindly sent me plants. It is a double form of perhaps the smallest variant of this species and will reach probably no more than 2 feet in height; growth twiggy, dense, and bushy. My plants, four years old, are at last growing well after a very slow start and are increasing by suckers. The leaves are smooth and dark green above, small, narrow, and pointed, freely serrated for three-quarters of their length, and the stipules are guarded by a pair of short, straight thorns. Flower-stalk, receptacle, and calyx are glandular-hairy, and the calyx lobes project well beyond the bud. The blooms are fully double, opening from pretty little shapely buds; they are of clear almost salmon pink, deeply coloured in the folded centre—often with a slight button eye—but rapidly fade on the wide outer petals, which become nearly white. It is exceedingly attractive; a half-open bloom surrounded by its five long wisps of calyx is very neat and strange. Unfortunately many buds do not open, but I think this was due to the extremes of summer weather that we experienced during 1959–61. (Fig. 2.)

The name given above is a new combination devised by Mr

Lynes, and the names in the following list of illustrations are synonymous with it. I am much indebted to Mr Lynes for so promptly sharing the results of his investigations with me.

Andrews, Plate 102. *R. pennsylvanica var. flore pleno.* 'The Pennsylvanian Rose, double-flowered variety.' He states: 'This delicate little rose is a most desirable variety . . . of dwarf growth . . . in dry weather the sun frequently extracts so much of the colour from the outer petals as to leave them almost bleached.' A charming picture, true to nature.

Redouté, vol. ii, Plate 73. *Rosa parviflora var. flore multiplici.* 'Le Rosier à petites fleurs'; 'Rosier de Caroline'; 'Rosier Caroline du Roi'; 'Rosier de Virginie'; 'Rosier Pennsylvanie à fleurs doubles', etc. Thory gives a long careful description finishing with the statement that the flowers have many rows of petals, paler in the centre than in the circumference of the flower, but the plate does not shew this.

Lawrance, Plate 66. *Rose carolina, A*; Double Pennsylvanian Rose.

FOLIOLOSA, S.E. United States. Another species which suckers freely and thrives in light soil; but it does not usually make a dense thicket; the few rather weak stems are greenish brown, and bear narrow leaves with 7 to 9 leaflets, light in colour and fairly glossy above. The very long sepals project beyond the open flowers, which are of vivid cerise pink; they do not appear until well past midsummer, continuing into September, and have peculiarly short pedicels, thus distinguishing them from the others of this group. Small sub-globose red heps. Excellent autumn colour. 4 feet.

Botanical Magazine, t.8513. Very vivid colouring.

Willmott, Plate 219.

Mrs Léonie P. Bell of Pennsylvania writes that she has acquired the white form once again.

NITIDA. Eastern North America. In many ways this little shrub resembles the Burnet roses—in its dwarf, twiggy habit, seldom exceeding 2 feet in height, its masses of slender prickles and bristles all the way up the freely suckering reddish stems, and in its 7 to 9 leaflets; but here the similarity stops, for the leaflets are narrow and pointed, shining green above, and turning to vivid scarlet in the autumn. In addition the flowers are of bright deep pink with yellow stamens, and the heps red and bristly, without the persistent sepals of the Burnets. The young basal shoots are of great beauty, for the masses of thorns are of rich reddish colouring.

In the wild it grows in low-lying, often marshy, places, but in the garden seems happy in ordinary soils including sand and heavy loam, although it has usually taken some time to settle down under my care. I should feel this to be an attractive rose for a dwarf bushy hedge were it not for its questing roots. It is, however, one of the very best of dwarf shrubs for autumn colour and is therefore valuable for the foreground of shrub beds and borders, for heath and wild garden areas.

Unfortunately the true plant is very scarce; more vigorous, erect, poor hybrids do duty for it.

Willmott, Plate 215.

Lawrance, Plate 36. 'Upright Carolina Rose.' From its thorns this may be intended for R. *nitida*.

NUTKANA. Western North America. A species closely related to R. *blanda*, growing to 5 feet. The fairly wide single pink flowers are pleasing but the main horticultural value of this open-growing shrub is found in the heps, which are rounded and persist on the bush until the severe frosts of winter cause them to decay.

'Cantab'. 1927. This hybrid, R. *nutkana* × 'Red Letter Day', was raised by Dr C. C. Hurst while working on the genetics of the rose at Cambridge University Botanic Garden. It is in effect a vigorous, species-like rose with normal prickly stems and has 7 to 9 small, lead-green leaflets. The flowers are big and single, of deep pink, lilac-tinted, with creamy stamens, and create a good display at midsummer. Fragrant. The large, oval heps last through the winter, in bright orange-red, with persistent calyces. 7 to 8 feet by 6 to 7 feet. On good soil can make an impressive and colourful bush at two seasons of the year.

PALUSTRIS. Eastern North America. In spite of its name this rose will grow and flower well in poor, sandy, dry soil. It has few garden merits apart from the production of its bright yet deep pink flowers in July, when most species are over. It forms an erect sparse shrub up to 6 feet high.

Redouté, vol. i, Plate 95. *R. hudsoniana.*

Willmott, Plate 211. *R. carolina,* but I think applies to *R. palustris.*

Addisonia, 1923, p. 275. 'The Swamp Rose.' A good example of flowers and heps.

Jennings, vol. ii, Plate 87.

SETIGERA. Prairie Rose. Eastern United States. A species with procumbent stems, arching and capable of climbing into shrubs and small trees. The branches may reach 12 feet or so, bearing along their length clusters of single mallow-pink flowers with broad petals, which are very fragrant in spite of numerous statements to the contrary. In nature I am told this varies from white to crimson in colour but over here I have never seen anything but pink forms. From its habitat one would think this rose would thrive particularly in sandy soils. It has been a parent of several climbing roses. It is not spectacular, but is useful as it does not flower until after most species are over, together with RR. *davidii, multibracteata,* and *wichuraiana.* There are thornless forms. This species belongs to the Synstylae group, which are mainly climbers, but as this is a sprawling shrub rather than a climber it fits best horticulturally here.

Willmott, Plate 71.

Meehan, Thomas, vol. viii, Plate 5.

VIRGINIANA. Eastern North America. The synonym, *R. lucida,* calls attention to the shining leaves, a very lovely attribute of this plant. Frequently the young foliage is richly tinted, soon covering up the thicket of suckering stems, which are fairly free of thorns except at the base; in the autumn the leaves become beetroot-coloured with the approach of cold weather, and later turn to vivid orange-red, those in the centre of the bush frequently turning to yellow only, thus adding to the very brilliant display. Usually 9 leaflets.

In July appear the pointed vivid buds opening to cerise-pink flowers, with paler centres crowned with yellow stamens; together with others of this group, *R. setigera, R. wichuraiana,* and the Noisette known as 'Autumnalis', it is one of the latest roses to flower and continues well into August. Bristly receptacle. By October the clusters of blooms have given rise to bunches of glittering rounded heps, which last long after the leaves have fallen. In winter these and the red-brown twigs give a warm glow. There are few shrubs in any genera which have such manifold attractions, and it therefore must be reckoned with the very best, being suitable for almost any soil, but particularly those of a light nature, where it will colonize the ground freely, making an ever-spreading thicket up to 5 feet high. Although sometimes recommended for hedges its suckering habit makes it rather too wide for this purpose except where ample space is available.

Redouté, vol. i, Plate 45. R. *lucida*. 'Le Rosier luisant.'

Duhamel, vol. vii, Plate 7.

Andrews. The portrait of R. *lucida* (vol. ii, Plate 78) refers to a totally different species, R. *bracteata*, also with very glossy leaves.

Willmott, Plate 197. Unfortunately Miss Willmott's paragraphs are confusing. Thus on page 198 she mentions the double form in the second paragraph; the last paragraph on the same page also refers to this double form, but the intervening two paragraphs obviously refer to the single-flowered species, except for the line in the fourth paragraph where she mentions the fading of the outer petals; this reference I take to refer to the double form.

Lawrance, Plates 54 and 68. No thorns. These plates are not very definite.

VIRGINIANA 'Alba'. A beautiful white-flowered rose, having less shiny leaves than R. *virginiana*. The whole bush reveals its albinoid derivation, even carried as far as the stems, which are green instead of brown; the foliage is also light green. So far it has remained compact with me, but that is no doubt because I have it only as a budded plant on a rootstock of R. *canina*. The heps, in common with those of the species, lose their calyces, but are surmounted by a tiny tuft of grey-white hairs. The foliage does not colour much in autumn. Its various characters suggest that it may be a hybrid with R. *carolina*.

Willmott, Plate 198.

'Rose d'Amour'. I have distributed this double-flowered rose wrongly for years under the name of R. *virginiana plena*; it is also known as 'St Mark's Rose'. The last name refers to its flowering in Venice on St Mark's Day, 25 April, a statement of Miss Willmott's which I find hard to believe, since it is so late in the summer season with us. I have never been able to find authentic portraits of it in the old books, but recently Mr Wilson Lynes has done a lot of research and has kindly sent me his findings. It is probably a hybrid as, while it bears much resemblance to R. *virginiana*, it has thin terete prickles and less lustrous leaves; perhaps R. *carolina* was the other parent. On account of the broad hep a similar hybrid was known as R. *rapa*, or 'Le Rosier de Turneps', and this may be found figured in Redouté, vol. ii, Plate 7. With the usual allowance one has to make with Redouté's portraits, the magnificent rose depicted can perhaps be our little ' Rose d'Amour '.

Though it has small flowers, the ' Rose d'Amour ' is not a small shrub. At Wisley in sandy soil it has achieved 10 feet in height on a wall, and great bushes may also be seen at Kiftsgate, at Mellerstain, Berwickshire, and elsewhere. It is practically thornless; the leaves are composed of 5 to 7 leaflets, neat and serrated, with very wide stipules. It does not start flowering in Surrey until mid July, and in cool seasons and districts may still be in flower in early September. The exquisite buds, with long calyces, are slender, neatly rolled, and remain in half-open form for a few days in cool weather, eventually opening with wide outer petals and revealing a fairly well-filled centre. They are of deep pink in bud, the outer petals fading to pale pink, those in the centre retaining their colour well. In the fullness of midsummer the flowers are packed with petals, often causing a button-eye.

I know of few roses that can compare in daintiness with this flower; 'Céleste' has perhaps an even more beautiful bud, but is less good on opening; the only others which approach it in beauty of bud are the 'Cécile Brunner' group; and R. *carolina* ' Plena ', which is neater when fully open. It cannot be called a spectacular plant, but its freedom of flower over a long period and its vigour should ensure its continual popularity. A well-flowered bush can create a good pink effect for some weeks.

This 'Rose d'Amour' must not be confused with the single-flowered Gallica rose depicted by Redouté: vol. ii, Plate 63. There is a good photograph in Jekyll, between pages 74 and 75.

WOODSII. Central and Western North America. Inferior to R. *w. fendleri*. Reaches 6 feet or so, flowers pink, sometimes white, small rounded heps. Not of great garden value.
Willmott, Plate 235.
Willmott, Plate 236. White form.
Botanical Register, vol. xii, t.976.

WOODSII FENDLERI. Of rather more southerly distribution than R. *woodsii* itself, extending from British Columbia to Mexico. A most pleasing, graceful variety, with greyish leaves and clear, soft, lilac-pink flowers with cream stamens, borne very early in the season. Few thorns, reddish, on smooth green wood. The brilliant, rounded, red heps, the size of marbles, last into late autumn or winter; their weight causes the slender branches to hang vertically, and the result is like a series of strings of large red currants. 6 feet by 5 feet.
Willmott, Plate 175.

NOTE:
A useful survey of these species by E. W. Erlanson occurred in the *American Rose Annual* for 1932.

Postscript 1980 Edition

' D'Orsay '. For many years I considered this rose, named at Hidcote by Miss Nancy Lindsay, to be synonymous with ' Rose d'Amour '. In earlier editions of this book the pencil drawing facing page 49 was wrongly captioned ' Rose d'Amour '. It is more vigorous and a richer colour than ' D'Orsay '. This rose is reported to have been a favourite for a buttonhole by the Comte d'Orsay. For further notes see my article in the Rose Annual, R.N.R.S., for 1977, page 27. 4–5 ft.

6

The Wild Burnet Roses
and their Garden Forms

The Pimpinell Rose ... groweth ... in a pasture as you goe
from a village hard by London called Knights bridge unto
Fulham, a village thereby.

Gerard's *Herball*, 1597.

FROM THE above early reference no doubt Linnaeus's name of R.
pimpinellifolia sprang. Botanists have differed over the desirability
of using one or two names for these roses. Miss Willmott decided
to call them R. *spinosissima* and R. *s. pimpinellifolia*, using the latter
for those forms without glandular hairs on the peduncles.*
Nowadays they are usually grouped under one or the other
species, and for our purpose I will adopt R. *spinosissima*, being the
better known of the two. The species has the widest distribution
of any, and it will be readily understood therefore that a great
variation occurs in nature, since it grows from Iceland to
Eastern Siberia, and as far south as the Caucasus and Armenia.
Around the coasts of Britain it grows in sandy dunes, often only
reaching 9 inches in height, while tallest variants may achieve 6
feet. This species is included in the botanical group *Pimpinellifoliae*, together with the roses in the next chapter.
The species spreads freely by underground stolons, or suckers,
and bears an excessive number of straight prickles accompanied
by multitudes of fine bristles, and has small leaves divided into 7 to
9 leaflets. The flowers are also small, and are borne singly on short
stalks from the leaf axils; they appear in spring, usually in May or

* The name *pimpinellifolia* is accepted today for all types. (Footnote 1980.)

very early June, and are followed in late summer by maroon-black heps, round and shining like huge black currants, with the characteristic of retaining the old calyx lobes. Towards autumn these dark fruits often add to a remarkable display of sombre leaf colour; grey-brown and plum colour vie with maroon and dark red in intensity, with an orange or yellow leaf here and there. The wide hummocky bushes thus contribute something unique to the autumn pageant, and I know gardens where this contribution is greatly valued.

It is of course their floral display that has been the main attraction to gardeners through the centuries. They are nearly as prolific of their flowers as they are of their leaves and thorns. A bush in full flower is a wonderful sight, the wiry shoots bending under the weight of the blossoms, and the whole creating a brilliant effect. Mere plenitude would not be enough however; they fortunately have a sweet charm all of their own, an exhilarating fresh scent—like lily of the valley in its revivifying purity—and they flower in early summer just when we are ready to welcome roses, before the hot days of midsummer bring forth the greater garden varieties. There is no doubt too that their extreme hardiness and thriftiness have made them favourites, for they will grow and luxuriate in the poorest of sandy soils and do not suffer from any extremes of cold that we experience in this country.

Looking back through the history of gardening we find that these roses reached a high popularity for a brief period rather before the middle of the nineteenth century, over two hundred forms, supposedly distinct, being listed by Scottish nurserymen. They did not meet with such favour in England; in 1848 William Paul listed only seventy-six, all with fancy names and descriptions of two or three words only. They found even less favour in France. They are easy to raise from their abundant seed and this no doubt contributed to the multitudes of named varieties, but unfortunately very few of the plants growing today can be authentically connected with the names published in the lists over one hundred years ago. No careful descriptions appear to be available. Today it is more usual to be given a root which the owner calls 'double red' or 'single pink', or knows by some proprietary name recording its finding in a district or garden, than to find a plant bearing an authentic name such as 'William III'. The laxity in this matter is so great that varieties are known by different names in different counties and countries today, and nomenclature could not be more vague or unfathomable.

Their flowers run to no striking floral style, being just single, or with extra rows of petals, and almost always shewing the bright yellow stamens; fully double forms usually remain fairly globular. Their colours range in strange mixtures from white to pink and dark plum crimson, and from pale to dark yellow, with a few biscuit tones thrown in. Some are mottled or two-toned, and frequently there is a marked difference between the colour on the front of the petals and that of the reverse. I suspect that all yellow forms are really hybrids with R. *foetida*; in some the scent proves this without doubt. I have not found yellow variants growing wild.

SPINOSISSIMA. Europe, Asia. R. *spinosissima* has been given much attention by artists:
Botanical Register, vol. v, t.431.
Roessig, Plate 9. 'Le Rosier blanc à fleurs de pimprenelle', single, white, smooth peduncle.
Andrews, Plate 121. R. *spinosissima*, single white; excellent portrait.
Schlechtendal, t.2623.
Lawrance, Plate 48. R. *spinosissima*, 'the Common Scotch Rose'. Good.
Lawrance, Plate 19. A tall form of R. *spinosissima*.

SPINOSISSIMA ' Altaica ' or R. ' Grandiflora ' of gardens (not R. *s. altaica* botanically). This beautiful rose is well represented in gardens, even where roses are not usually grown, for it is a very thrifty plant, freely increasing underground and of vigorous upright habit, with comparatively few, large prickles. The leaves also are larger than those of the species. In the full glory of its short flowering season few shrubs are more attractive, the branches drooping beneath the numerous wide, creamy-ivory flowers, suffused on opening with primrose yellow. The heps are conspicuous, of dark shining maroon-black. 6 feet. 'Dunwichensis', a form found growing at Dunwich, Suffolk, does not differ from a horticultural point of view from R. *s.* ' Altaica ', but only in a slight difference in chromosomes. ' Altaica ' has produced many good hybrids, including some of the 'Frühlings' group, also 'Karl Foerster' (see Chapter 14).

Willmott, Plate 257.

Lawrance, Plate 19. R. *spinosissima*, 'The tall Scotch rose'.

The Garden, 1898, vol. liii. An artist's impression.

Botanical Register, vol. xi, t.888. R. *spinosissima grandiflora*.

SPINOSISSIMA 'Hispida'. Siberia. Noted for its bristles, rather than prickles, which densely cover the branches and twigs. This was a great favourite of A. T. Johnson's, and indeed it is as beautiful as R. *spinosissima* 'Altaica', which is giving high praise. It is not so bushy nor so free of its suckers, however, which possibly accounts for its scarcity, but the almost furry branches with few hurtful prickles, and opaque, soft creamy yellow flowers are very appealing. 5 feet.

Botanical Magazine, t.1570.

Willmott, Plate 259. Incorrect, probably R. *spinosissima luteola*, since it lacks the numerous hair-like thorns.

The Garden, 1899, vol. lvi, p. 398. An artist's impression, shewing no thorns. The accompanying article, by W. J. Bean, states that it breeds true from seeds and was cultivated as far back as 1781 at Islington.

SPINOSISSIMA 'Lutea Maxima' (R. *spinosissima* 'Lutea'). On account of its scent, and apart from any other characters, it is probably a hybrid with R. *foetida*. This is also a well-known rose and, if we except R. *ecae* and R. *foetida*, is the brightest of the early yellow single roses. The dark wood and few thorns, twigs somewhat tortuous and weak, leaves downy beneath, and vivid canary-yellow of the flowers are all characteristic of it. It is a most satisfactory garden plant, the copious bright green foliage giving a lush appearance with the flowers. Fruits black. 4 feet. Spreads fairly freely.

Redouté, vol. iii, Plate 19.

SPINOSISSIMA LUTEOLA. Russia. R. *pimpinellifolia ochroleuca*. Of more open habit and taller than the last two, this has pale flowers which often remain in a half-open state. It is hardly worth cultivating, for it cannot compare with R. *hugonis*, R. 'Cantabrigiensis', and others. 6 to 9 feet.

Willmott, Plate 255.

SPINOSISSIMA MYRIACANTHA. Spain and France to Armenia.
R. *myriacantha*. An interesting and constant variant which even
in this prickly group is noted for its dense mass of long, sharp,
straight prickles. It makes a twiggy shrub not more than 3 feet
in height, and its flowers and fruits are much like those of the
type species, in creamy white. The dark prickles add to its
attraction. A noticeable feature is the glandular under-surface
of the leaves. A slow spreader.
Willmott, Plate 261.
Lindley, Plate 10. A very good portrait.
Redouté, vol. iii, Plate 11. 'Le Rosier à mille Épines.' Thory
states that it has been in cultivation a long time. An excellent
portrait.

GARDEN FORMS OF THE BURNET ROSES

Sabine records how Robert Brown and his brother transplanted
some wild plants of the Burnet rose from the Hill of Kinnoul into
their neighbouring nursery garden near Perth. One bore flowers
tinged with red, and subsequent seedlings from this started the
fashion in selecting colour variants of this rose in Scotland and
England.

The most extraordinary thing about these garden variants is that
in the largest list of them, in an old catalogue of Messrs Austin and
McAslan of Glasgow—kindly lent to me by Mr H. Stewart-Paton
—there is no mention of any of the names which are found today.
The list of two hundred and eight varieties, with colour descriptions reduced to one or a combination of two adjectives, of which
there were only eleven used, is surely the best example of economy
ever produced in a nurseryman's catalogue! There is an account of
these roses in the Royal Horticultural Society's *Journal* for 1822 by
Sabine, but here again there are no useful descriptions. All of them
spread freely.

'**Andrewsii**'. Miss Willmott records that this is the most commonly
found in French gardens. In England it is less common, there
being several double pink varieties extant, but no others have I
encountered with the clarity of colour found in this variety. It
grows particularly well in Sir Cedric Morris's garden in Suffolk,

and also in my sandy soil in Surrey. The semi-double or double, somewhat cupped, flowers are as large as any, of clear rose-pink without a trace of blue. Being of dense, bushy growth it makes an excellent hedge. 3 to 4 feet. Willmott, Plate 263.

'Bicolor'. There were many bicolor and 'tinged' varieties; mine is of rosy-lilac, reverse paler, fading to lilac-white at the edges. Yellow stamens. Semi-double. 3 to 4 feet.

'Double Blush'. Rich blush centre, fading outwards, and with nearly white reverse. A charming pale pink variety, probably reaching to 4 feet.

'Double White'. This is perhaps 'William IV' (recorded by Rivers) or 'Duchess of Montrose' (listed by Austin and McAslan) and is a well-known garden plant, very free in growth, reaching 4 to 6 feet. The double flowers have much longer petals than most of these little roses, and do not open so widely, and thus are more cup-shaped or even goblet-shaped. Pure white with the most wonderful penetrating, delicious scent, as fresh as lily of the valley. A splendid, vigorous plant, exceedingly free in flower. Andrews's portrait of a double white (Plate 122) shews a very dwarf plant.

'Falkland'. I regard this as one of the most beautiful. It has greyish leaves, making a charming soft background to the semi-double, shapely flowers which are of the softest, palest, 'Céleste pink' imaginable, with a hint of palest lilac. It fades nearly to white in hot sunshine. 4 feet.

'Glory of Edzell'. An unrecorded name which denotes an early-flowering, tall-growing form, perhaps a hybrid, with clear, light pink, single flowers. 6 to 7 feet.

'Irish Rich Marbled'. Rounded, soft pink buds opening deep cherry pink with lilac-pink reverse; the colour fades towards the edges. Semi-double, three rows of broad petals, the outer ones reflexing conspicuously. Yellow centre around the stamens. Probably 4 feet.

'Loch Leven'. This name indicates a form found growing in the castle garden at Loch Leven, where Mary Queen of Scots was imprisoned. It is very free-growing and flowering, with semi-double, creamy-blush flowers, heavily mottled and delicately pencilled with rose pink. Probably 4–5 feet.

'Mary Queen of Scots'. A most beautiful form grown by Lady Moore in Dublin, and the story goes that it was brought from France by the queen and eventually reached Northern Ireland, where it is found in many gardens. Lady Moore found it in 1921 in Antrim. The grey-lilac buds open to fairly double blooms, the surface of the petals being nearly as richly plum-tinted as in 'William III'. The grey-lilac and the plum make a fascinating contrast, a souvenir of a sad life. Probably 4 feet.

'Purpurea Plena'. Soft mallow-purple or deep old rose with mauve tint, fading to lilac pink, reverse pale pink. Double. Creamy yellow stamens. 3 to 4 feet.

'Single Cherry'. Bluish-green foliage. The bright rose-pink buds open to vivid single flowers of intense cherry red; the colour is splashed and flushed so thickly on a blush ground that it appears uniform. Probably 3 to 4 feet.

'Townsend'. A tall-growing, very prolific plant. Almost double, blush-pink fading to ivory, base of petals yellow. It is not of clear colouring, and creates rather a dirty effect. Small black heps. 5 to 6 feet.

'William III'. Very dwarf, but vigorous. Grey-green leaves densely covering the dense thicket of tiny twigs. Semi-double flowers shewing a few golden stamens, magenta crimson changing to rich plum colour and fading to dark lilac-pink. Reverse paler. Black heps. 1 to 2 feet.

I have come across a few portraits of coloured garden forms of the Burnet roses, and although I do not feel anything very definite can be achieved in nomenclature it may be worth recording them here.

Roses et Rosiers, Plate 30. A double pink.

Botanical Cabinet, vol. vii, Plate 687. R. *spinosissima picta*. Single, maroon-splashed.

Andrews, Plate 121. White, also touched pink.

Andrews, Plates 122–8. Various colour forms, dwarf and tall.

Lawrance, Plate 78. 'Marbled Scotch.' Single, dark, maroon-veined.

Lawrance, Plate 15. 'Striped Scotch.'

Lawrance, Plate 62. A good plate of single red variety.

Nestel's Rosengarten shews two plates of rather highly coloured and enlarged forms.

HYBRIDS OF THE BURNET ROSES

These being mostly old and not generally related to the China Rose, I consider they should be included in this chapter.

'Allard'. R. *xanthina allardii.* Originated in the Botanic Garden at Lyons, France; listed by Messrs Hesse in 1927. I suspect it to be a seedling of R. × *harisonii,* or of similar parentage, and it probably has no affinity with R. *xanthina.* It has similar leaves to R. × *harisonii* and thorny dark wood; a bristly squat receptacle, glandular calyx, and small down-curved thorns on the pedicel. The flowers are nearly double, with petaloid centre and yellow stigmata; true bright yellow and a fresh scent. Probably 4 feet.

× HARISONII. 'Harison's Yellow'. R. *spinosissima harisonii.* Rehder adds further synonymy: R. *lutea hoggii,* ' Hogg's Double Yellow Briar ': *Horticulture,* vol. v is cited, but in this I have found no coloured plate as stated, only a short note in regard to a seedling of ' Harison's Yellow '. Bunyard states that this rose was raised by George Harison of New York in 1830. ' Hogg's Double Yellow' was obtained, according to Sweet's *The British Flower Garden,* 1838, Series II, vol. iv, p. 410, from Mr Thomas Hogg, a nurseryman of New York, and it had been raised from seed of the 'single yellow rose'. I have been unable to trace the origins further, but it is quite possible that Harison's and Hogg's plants were the same. In those days the only yellow rose which could have been used was R. *foetida,* the Austrian Brier, and it is probably a hybrid of this species and R. *spinosissima.* It is quite distinct from 'Williams' Double Yellow' (R. *spino-sissima lutea plena, q.v.*) in that it has yellow stamens, whereas 'Williams'' has green carpels, in the centre of the flowers.

'Harison's' is free-growing and free-flowering in brilliant sulphur-yellow, loosely double and somewhat cupped, and has a gaunt upright habit reaching 6 feet. It does not sucker freely. It bears the scent of R. *foetida*. A useful erect rose for planting among other more bushy shrubs, creating a brilliant effect in early summer. Has been used freely in hybridizing: 'Rustica', 'Sonnenlicht', 'Wildenfels Gelb', and others: see Chapter 14. Sweet, 1838, Series II, vol. iv, Plate 410. 'Hogg's Double Yellow.'

×INVOLUTA. R. *tomentosa*×*spinosissima*. A spontaneous hybrid recorded first in 1800 from the Hebrides. Has much of the appearance of R. *spinosissima* and is a rapid runner underground. Single, usually white, flowers, richly tinted with pink in the bud. Long reddish heps. 3 to 4 feet.

'Mrs Colville'. No doubt a hybrid with R. *pendulina*, indicated by its rather smooth red-brown wood, and long, plum-red heps. Nearly single, of intense crimson-purple with a white zone round the yellow stamens. Suckers freely. 3 to 4 feet.

'Ormiston Roy'. Doorenbos, 1938. 'Allard' × R. *spinosissima*. Mr Doorenbos tells me that this rose of his often produces blooms late in the summer as well as at the normal time. It appeared in the F2 generation and was named after a friend in Montreal. The well-formed, clear yellow, single flowers are beautifully veined. Large black-maroon heps and pedicels. Compact habit, about 4 feet. It is a parent of 'Golden Wings', see Chapter 14. (Plate III, heps.)

×REVERSA. Prior to 1820. R. *spinosissima*×R. *pendulina*. R. *rubella*. A neat little bush with obvious leanings towards R. *spinosissima* in its suckering thicket of thorny stems and profuse, fresh green, small leaves. The form I grow is a very gay plant and has rich carmine-pink blooms, single, followed by dark red heps, oval and nodding as in R. *pendulina*; they are produced in late summer. R. *malyi* is of similar parentage. 4 feet. Schlechtendal, t.2624.

'Stanwell Perpetual'. A most treasured possession, and is likely to remain in cultivation as long as roses are grown, for it is perpetual-flowering and has a very sweet scent. It was a chance seedling in a garden at Stanwell, Mddx., and was put on the market by the nurseryman Lee, of Hammersmith, in 1838. That is all that is known about it; but presumably it owes its perpetual habit and floral style to one of the Gallica group, probably an Autumn Damask. In good soil it makes a lax, thorny, twiggy bush up to 5 feet or so, with greyish small leaves resembling those of R. *spinosissima*, which is no doubt its other parent. The flowers are of pale blush-pink, opening flat, with quilled and quartered petals. The main display is at midsummer, but it is never without flowers. Favoured by Miss Jekyll.

Kingsley, Plate 45. Exquisite portrait.

Willmott, Plate 253. Rather fewer petals than usual.

Trechslin & Coggiatti. Very good.

'Williams' Double Yellow'. R. *spinosissima lutea plena*. This was raised about 1828 by Mr John Williams of Pitmaston near Worcester from seeds obtained from the single yellow rose (R. *foetida*). It is thus of the same parentage as R. × *harisonii*, but the present 'Old Double Yellow Scots Rose', as it is often called, is very distinct. It would seem to be much nearer to the Burnet Roses than R. *harisonii*, making a freely suckering, branching, thorny bush about 4 feet high, with neat leaves and loosely double, bright yellow flowers. These have a bunch of green carpels in the centre; 'Harison's Yellow' has yellow stamens, and this at once distinguishes them, apart from other characters. The heavy scent of R. *foetida* pervades them both. In shape the flowers are inclined to reflex, and the petals stay on the bush for a long time after turning brown, a sad disadvantage. It is used effectively with the clear lavender of *Nepeta faasenii* (*N. mussinii*) against the yellow-brown stone of Upton House near Banbury, a property of the National Trust. It is often encountered in gardens in the Western Highlands, where it is known as 'Prince Charlie's Rose'.

Sweet, 1838, Series II, vol. iv, Plate 353. R. *spinosissima lutea plena*; 'Williams' Double Yellow'.

7

The Wild Yellow Roses
and Related Species

The Yellow Rose (as divers do report) was by Art so
coloured, and altered from his first estate, by grafting a
wilde Rose upon a Broome-stalke; whereby (say they)
it doth not only change his colour but his smell and force.

Gerard's *Herball*, 1597.

IT SO HAPPENS that most of the few yellow-flowered wild roses fit
botanically into a convenient group, the Pimpinellifoliae, including two white-flowered species, and these few species are
distributed only through the Old World from Eastern Europe to
China. So far only two of them—R. *foetida*, the Austrian Brier,
and R. *spinosissima*, the Burnet Rose—have been used to any
extent by hybridizers, and possibly untold advances in yellow
roses are at hand through some of the other species.

These roses form a rather diverse group from a garden point of
view, but botanically they are governed by a few characters
common to them all. They are erect-growing shrubs, with
straight or almost straight prickles; leaves small, with anything
from 5 to 19 leaflets; stipules narrow and joined to the petiole for
about half their length; bracts absent; the sepals are vertical and
stay on the heps, which are rounded and orange, red, or maroon.

It will be seen, therefore, that we have ordinary shrubs with
small leaves to deal with; no great attraction in the heps, but only
in the colour of the flowers, and there is no doubt that the species
in this group do add something very valuable not only to roses in

general but to the whole of horticulture. For where would our early summer shrub display be without the dainty grace of R. *hugonis* or R. ' Cantabrigiensis ', or without the glory of ' Frühlingsgold '?—to say nothing of our modern roses, which owe almost their entire yellow and flame colouring to R. *foetida* and its latent characters.

In the garden all these roses except R. *ecae*, and also R. *foetida* and its varieties, blend happily with everything else, their tones being cool and refreshing; the soft mauves of rhododendrons or the flaming colours of azaleas are all the better for a few pale yellow or white roses; likewise irises and peonies are enhanced by big bushes of pale yellow behind them.

A very different approach is needed for R. *foetida* and its more startling varieties; I do not feel happy with them in any combination of roses apart from their own derivatives. Their yellow is so harsh and insistent that it needs the rich background of a copper beech hedge to add tone. The gorgeous warmth of the 'Austrian Copper' Brier is equally difficult to place with other roses, but it is such a glorious personage itself that I prefer it on its own. Against varied greenery or copper leaves it can be the focal point for the whole garden for its few brief weeks of flowering, then sink into insignificance for the rest of the season. Even so I prefer to lead up to such brilliance as this with other brilliant plants, such as potentillas and geums, which diffuse the dazzling colour in a kaleidoscopic mixture, and through their varied warmth and overlapping flowering periods prolong the display so that the given spot can retain a barbaric splendour through the summer. I referred briefly to this colouring in Chapter 1, and at risk of repeating myself would like to enlarge upon it here, as among species roses R. *foetida* and R. *f.* ' Bicolor ' do need such careful placing in the garden, and need to be approached in colours of gathering strength. This method is indeed practised in several famous gardens today and excellent examples may be seen in the purple-and-orange garden at Crathes Castle, Kincardineshire, in the red-and-purple borders at Hidcote, Gloucestershire, in the red-and-yellow borders at Tintinhull, Somerset, and beds of gorgeous colour assortments at Sissinghurst Castle, Kent, Newby Hall, Yorkshire, and Blickling Hall, Norfolk. Let it not be thought, however, that roses provide necessarily the bulk of colour in these blends. Probably the reverse would be true. But there is no doubt that the 'Austrian Copper' and some of its near relatives can add very greatly to such displays. I need only call attention to 'Réveil Dijonnais' and some of the flame-and-yellow Hybrid Teas and vivid Floribundas to conjure up some wonderful 'hot' colour schemes.

This type of colour work cannot depend upon normal greenery for its ultimate success. As I mentioned earlier, the copper foliage of a beech, prunus or berberis hedge is to my mind almost essential to give the grouping warmth and richness, and provides of course the inestimable asset of permanent colour through the various flowering seasons.

ECAE. Afghanistan. The strange name commemorates Mrs Aitchison—E. C. A.—the wife of the botanist who named it. This rose is unique; slender, upright growth with long reddish twigs set with reddish thorns and small, smooth, dark green leaves. It is quite startling when in flower, for the blooms are of intense, deep buttercup-yellow. 5 feet by 4 feet, or considerably more on good soil. Needs full sunshine and well-drained soil, and contrasts well with blue spring-flowering ceanothuses. Willmott, Plate 277. Wrongly captioned R. *xanthina*. *Botanical Magazine*, t.7666. Ditto.

FOETIDA. Western Asia. The Austrian Brier. Although marked by an intensity of yellow bordering on the colour of sulphur, a scent that one could hardly call attractive, and possessing a name which calls attention to its heavy odour, this rose had a profound influence on our modern garden roses mainly through its famous variety R. *f*. ' Persiana '. In the old books the species was called R. *lutea* and was known and grown before 1600. The shining, rich brown stems are set with straight grey prickles, and bear small leaves of intense parsley green. The wide-open flowers create a very startling effect. In my experience, despite the fact that it is a native of hot, arid districts, it appears to thrive best in the cooler counties of Britain; this is also true of other roses from the Middle East. Pruning seldom improves the results. 5 feet by 4 feet. The quotation at the head of this chapter applies to this rose. Lawrance, Plate 12. Excellent portrait. *Botanical Magazine*, t.363.

Roessig, Plate 2. 'Le Rosier jaune, à fleurs simples couleur de cire.'

Revue Horticole, 1865, p. 191. Not very exact.

Andrews, Plate 120. *R. lutea.*

Willmott, Plate 267. Good colour.

Schlechtendal, t.2622. Poor.

Redouté, vol. i, Plate 69. 'Le Rosier Eglantier.'

The Garden, January 1898, p. 22. Artist's impression shewing *R. foetida* and *R. f.* ' Persiana '.

FOETIDA ' Bicolor '. *R. lutea punicea.* The famous ' Austrian Copper Brier' has been known since before 1590. The reverse of the petals is much the same colour as that of *R. foetida*, but shews through the thin texture some of the intense nasturtium-red of the face of the flower. Occasionally this dazzling rose reverts on an odd branch or two to the vivid yellow of the species. In the garden it grows best in the same conditions as *R. foetida*, and both of them, on account of their colour, should be kept well away from the many roses which flower with them early in the season, and which have those soft tones of mauve pink which are so prevalent in the genus. Miss Willmott tells us it is known in France by the name of 'Rose Capucine' and used to be known as 'Rose Comtesse'. I wish we could find the double form, which was apparently recorded in 1815 or there-abouts—although it could scarcely be an improvement on the single. In most of the portraits cited the artists have obviously been carried away with the unusual colouring of the flowers; we can imagine what a relief it must be to have a rose to paint of such brilliance when so many are mauve-pink.

Paul, 9th edition, Plate 8. Rather exaggerated.

Roses et Rosiers, Plate 5. 'R. Eglantier variété couleur ponceau.'
    The name of 'Eglantine' was given to this rose erroneously by Linnaeus. 'Poppy-coloured' is one of its best descriptions. Good portrait.

Roessig, Plate 5. 'Le Rosier à fleurs couleur d'orange ou de feu.'
    R. punicea.

Journal des Roses, Février 1890. 'Rose capucine jaune bicolore.'
    A colourful impression.

Step, vol. ii, Plate 81. Very good.

Trechslin & Coggiatti. Superb.
Revue Horticole, 1865, p. 191. Not very exact.
Andrews, Plate 120. *R. lutea bicolor.*
Lawrance, Plate 6. *R. lutea bicolor.* Very good, but colour too
  brown.
Botanical Magazine, t.1077, *R. foetida bicolor.*
Willmott, Plate 269. Excellent portrait.
Redouté, vol. i, Plate 71. 'Le Rosier Eglantier var. couleur
  Ponceau.'
Duhamel, vol. vii, Plate 14. 'Rose Eglantine.'
Harvey, Plate 1.

FOETIDA PERSIANA. The Persian Yellow Rose was introduced
  to this country by Sir Henry Willock in 1838, and was welcomed by growers as the most brilliant and satisfactory of the
  double yellow roses for the garden. To us, with so many fine
  yellow roses around us, it is difficult to imagine a time when the
  only double roses of this colour were the little Burnets and R.
  hemisphaerica. The latter seldom produced flowers worth
  looking at except in good weather, so we can appreciate with
  what enthusiasm 'Persian Yellow' must have been greeted. In
  the *Gardeners' Chronicle* for 1843 plants were advertised at 15s.
  each, a fabulous sum in those days for a new rose, and the
  equivalent of over 3 guineas today. Eventually its pollen was
  made to produce fine yellow modern roses, such as had never
  been seen before. 5 feet by 4 feet.
     The famous nurseryman of Lyon, Pernet-Ducher, made a
  determined effort in 1883 and subsequent years, pollinating
  thousands of Hybrid Perpetuals with the 'Persian Yellow', and
  eventually succeeded in raising two seedlings, one of which subsequently gave rise to 'Soleil d'Or', the first of the 'Pernet' race
  of roses. They have since been merged into the Hybrid Teas and,
  with the brilliant colouring of R. *foetida* 'Bicolor', have also
  given us the two-tone effect which occurs in the 'Austrian
  Copper'.
Jamain and Forney, Plate 55. Not very representative.
Journal des Roses, Mars 1882. Exaggerated flower.
Komlosy. Yellow too dark, but a good drawing.

Paul, 8th edition, 1881, Plate 4.
Choix des Plus Belles Roses, Plate 36.
Flore des Serres, vol. iv. Plate 374.
Trechslin & Coggiatti. Superb.

HEMISPHAERICA. Western Asia. R. *sulphurea*, R. *glauco-phylla*. The 'Sulphur Rose'. Known and grown before 1625. A famous rose which is not really suited to the British climate, but, prior to the introduction of the 'Persian Yellow', it was the only large double yellow rose in cultivation. On account of its size of bloom it was often called the 'Yellow Provence Rose' although in growth and general appearance it bears no resemblance to the true 'Provence Rose', R. *centifolia*.

Its synonym, R. *glaucophylla*, gives us the key to its foliage, which is of a distinctly greyish hue, and it has hooked prickles, distinguishing it again from R. *foetida*, even without the flowers. It is of rather loose habit, and the twigs droop with the weight of the large globular blooms, filled with petals, of a brilliant sulphur yellow, and sweetly scented. Unfortunately, except in particularly warm, dry weather, and in the right conditions, it seldom gives perfect blooms. They tend to 'ball' and decay without opening. It grows and flowers at Highdown, Sussex, the famous chalky garden created by Sir Frederick Stern. Mr Gordon Rowley suggests that this rose was derived as a sport from a single-flowered species, R. *rapinii*. As, however, the double-flowered rose was named first, the name of this single-flowered species would be R. *hemisphaerica rapinii*. This species is a native of Asiatic Turkey to N.W. Persia. About 4 feet.

There is a very full account of these roses and an excellent plate in Miss Willmott's book *The Genus Rosa*. The double variety was depicted by Van Huysum and others in some of the great Dutch flower pictures of the seventeenth century, and its vivid colour and occasionally superb blooms made it greatly prized.
Willmott, Plate 273. Very good.
Andrews, Plate 91. *Rosa sulphurea*. A splendid spray, shewing the buds well.
Lawrance, Plate 77. The 'Double Yellow Rose'.
Komlosy. *Rosa sulphurea;* the colouring is too dark, but an excellent portrait.

Roessig, Plate 43. *Rosa glaucophylla.* Poor flower.
Botanical Register, vol. i, t.46.
Redouté, vol. i, Plate 29. R. *sulphurea.* 'Le Rosier jaune de
Soufre.'

HUGONIS. Central China. With R. *moyesii* this is one of the
two most famous roses which, being brought from the Far
East at the turn of the century, revolutionized the horticultural
appraisal of the wild roses. An established plant is nearly thornless, but the bases of the young shoots are often crimson, with
bristly hairs and prickles. This exquisite species has tiny,
smooth leaves, creating a fern-like effect on a shrub some 7 feet
high and wide. The flowers are charmingly disposed along the
arching wiry twigs, and are of cool butter yellow, with a hint of
primrose; they seldom open fully, remaining in a cupped shape,
crinkled and silky. Surpassed by some of its offspring. It is at
its best on its own roots, when it will thrive even on chalky
soils. The small maroon-coloured heps are not conspicuous but
the foliage often turns to purplish brown in the autumn.
Willmott, Plate 279. Bois and Trechslin, plate 4.
Botanical Magazine, t.8004. Scarcely recognizable.

OMEIENSIS. See R. *sericea.*

PRIMULA. Turkestan to Northern China. The 'Incense Rose' is
so called because of the rich aroma which emanates from the
young foliage, which is dark green, smooth, narrow, and of a
somewhat glaucous tint. Some leaves have as many as 15
leaflets. The plants are upright and a pretty sight when in
flower, the tone of yellow being very pale and transparent like
that of a primrose. It can make a fine effect when loaded with
flowers; at Highdown it has reached some 6 feet by 10 feet.
Heps reddish, not conspicuous, but the young growth is
reddish brown with red thorns.

SERICEA and OMEIENSIS. Separated as they are only
by minor botanical differences, it is best to class these two
species together for our present purpose. They are the only
roses which have four petals instead of the usual five. They
make tall, rather open, shrubs up to some 9 feet high and wide;

the stout young shoots are often densely bristly, giving way to almost smooth wood, which is irregularly set with wide, flattened, triangular prickles, most evident in the variety R. s. pteracantha. Numerous rich green leaflets give the plant the ferny appearance peculiar to several of these roses. In August and September in a good season the bushes are brilliant with small pear-shaped glossy heps in bright scarlet; in R. s. omeiensis they have a thickened yellow stalk. In addition R. s. omeiensis has nearly glaucous leaflets up to 17, whereas those of R. s. sericea are silky-pubescent beneath, and not more than 11. In spite of all this Mr Gordon Rowley considers, from Hurst's hybridizations and from recent observations on living material under his care at Bayfordbury, Hertfordshire, that these roses should be united under R. sericea.

They are attractive shrubs for the garden, giving the unsophisticated effect that is the prerogative of dainty wild species, and are really exquisite in flower. The petals are beautifully shaped and slightly veined, remaining in a wide cup formation for most of their short life. Their flowers are normally white.

SERICEA. Himalaya, introduced 1822.
Willmott, Plate 163.
Botanical Magazine, t.5200.

OMEIENSIS. Szechwan, Western China, introduced 1901.

SERICEA CHRYSOCARPA. A form with beautiful yellow heps.

SERICEA DENUDATA. A thornless form.

SERICEA 'Heather Muir'. A superb form, named after the creator of the Kiftsgate garden, who purchased it many years previously as a seedling from E. A. Bunyard. A most beautiful large shrub with extra large white flowers produced over a long period, followed by orange-red heps on orange-red stalks. In flower May to July. 9 feet by 9 feet.

SERICEA POLYPHYLLA. *R. sericea inermis glandulosa*, *R. sericea omeiensis*. A form with numerous leaflets, and not many prickles.

SERICEA PTERACANTHA. *R. omeiensis pteracantha*. A rose well known for its large flattened prickles. These are borne on stiff, straight stems, being sometimes so numerous and wide that they make a vertical line of red among the small ferny leaves. Some prickles are an inch or more wide at the base. The flowers are white, and the plant is much like the species but less graceful. In the garden this variety should be placed so that the sun can shine through the prickles, giving a rich colour effect. In their second season the prickles become grey; thus pruning to encourage constant new shoots is desirable. Introduced from Western China in 1890. 8 feet by 6 feet.

Botanical Magazine, t.8218. Shows the thickened red stalk to the fruit.

The Garden, 2 June 1906, vol. lxix, p. 300. Shewing thorns and foliage only. Excellent picture.

XANTHINA. This, the double-flowered form, has been cultivated for over a hundred years in Northern China and Korea, and has been known in Britain as R. *slingeri*. The growth is less free than that of its single parent and the flowers, though a good colour and fairly double, are less beautiful and effective. 6 feet by 6 feet. Unlike 'Canary Bird', which is sometimes called R. *xanthina spontanea*, it has prickles.

McFarland, *Roses of the World*, p. 285.

XANTHINA SPONTANEA. N. China and Korea. Although this was introduced in 1907 it has never become widely known, having been overshadowed by 'Canary Bird' (q.v.). It is vigorous, reaching in Mr Hillier's garden 8 to 9 feet, with the usual light green, ferny foliage of the group, and large light-yellow single flowers.

HYBRIDS OF THE YELLOW ROSES

'Canary Bird'. At one time distributed as R. *xanthina spontanea*, under the impression that it was the wild type of R. *xanthina*, it has since been considered a hybrid, perhaps R. *hugonis* × *xanthina* or *spinosissima*. I have found no record of its origin. The richly coloured brown stems have a few prickles towards the base, and are noticeably warty, i.e. covered with tiny excrescences. The leaves are of bright, fresh green, luxuriant but small and fern-like; they are hairy beneath, and also in the folds above. The flowers open wide, and are of clear, bright yellow, creating a really splendid effect on the arching young branches and small twigs. Unfortunately it is subject to 'die back' like R. *hugonis*, but appears to be most at home in the drier parts of the country on well-drained soils. Heps maroon or blackish, not conspicuous. 7 feet by 7 feet. Reputedly raised at Osterley Park.

'Cantabrigiensis'. 1931. A chance seedling which occurred at Cambridge Botanic Garden. I regard this and R. *headleyensis* as the most satisfactory of the species-like yellow roses. R. 'Cantabrigiensis' makes an erect bush 7 feet by 6 feet or more, densely covered in tiny hairy bristles on strong young growth, but without winglike prickles; with the same ferny leaf effect of its parents, but a shapely well-filled habit. The five-petalled flowers are very slightly paler than those of R. *hugonis*, but still a good clear yellow, and are far more shapely and open wider than those of that species. Extremely free-flowering and a wonderful sight in full bloom; small orange-red heps in late summer. Fragrant. Not subject to ' die-back ' in my experience, where it scores over R. *hugonis* and ' Canary Bird '.

'Earldomensis'. R. *pteragonis pteragonis*. R. *hugonis* × *sericea pteracantha*. Raised in Mr Courtenay Page's garden, Earldom, Haywards Heath, where the National Rose Society's trials were held for many years. Forms a bushy, thorny shrub with some of the reddish flattened prickles of the second parent. Small pretty foliage and bright yellow single flowers early in the season. 6 to 7 feet high and wide.

'Headleyensis'. This was raised at Boidier, then the home of Sir Oscar Warburg, at Headley near Epsom about 1920. The seed parent was R. *hugonis*, presumably pollinated by R. *spinosissima altaica*. Dr Bertram Smith at Pewsey, Wiltshire, has the best plant I know, which is about 9 feet high by 12 feet wide. This vigorous and healthy plant has the general ferny appearance of the parents, as one would expect, with particularly handsome creamy yellow single flowers. Very fragrant. I consider this is the most ornamental of all the hybrids of R. *hugonis* that I have seen so far; its wide flowers, graceful growth, and clear soft colouring make it an important garden plant, and it is amazing that it has remained so long in obscurity. (Photograph, Plate 4.) A rose of similar parentage is 'Albert Edwards'; Hillier, 1938.

'**Helen Knight**'. F. P. Knight collected seeds from R. *ecae* at Wisley, which had presumably been crossed with R. *pimpinellifolia* 'Grandiflora' (R. 'Altaica') of gardens, since this was growing nearby. The dark wood and dainty foliage of R. *ecae* are repeated in this plant, but the flowers are larger and of bright pale yellow, 1½ ins across, slightly cupped. Early. Faintly fragrant. 7 feet.

'**Hidcote Gold**'. 1948. Apart from the fact that this plant has been growing for many years at Hidcote and was apparently raised there, I have no records of it. It is possibly a hybrid of R. *hugonis*, and the other parent is no doubt R. *sericea pteracantha*, since it bears conspicuous flattened prickles very like those of this species. It is a vigorous, graceful bush with long wand-like branches and drooping twigs studded with good, clear yellow, single, five-petalled flowers and plenty of small foliage. An attractive shrub combining the five petals of a yellow rose with the striking armature of R. *sericea pteracantha*. 7 feet by 7 feet. (Photograph, Plate 3).

Postscript, 1973 Edition

'**Golden Chersonese**'. Allen, 1963. 'Canary Bird' × R. *ecae*. This good hybrid inherits the fern-like prettiness of R. *ecae* and also its deep yellow colouring, coupled with the larger bloom of 'Canary Bird'. Like its parents it flowers delightfully, early in the season. Fragrant. Erect growth. 8 feet by 6 feet. Gault and Synge, plate 167.

8

The Japanese or Rugosa Roses

The Plant of Roses, though it be a shrub full of prickles yet
it had been more fit and convenient to have placed it with
the most glorious floures of the world than to insert the
same among base and thorny shrubs.

Gerard's *Herball*, 1597.

THIS NOBLE group of hardy floriferous shrubs has two major disadvantages. First, nearly everyone who hears the word *rugosa*
conjures up a mental image of the so-called 'R. *rugosa*' which is
used as an understock specially for standard roses, and which is a
hybrid of R. *rugosa*, and is otherwise practically worthless in the
garden; and, second, that *rugosa* varieties do not lend themselves
well for cutting and thereby lose a lot of publicity in shows and in
the home. They have on the other hand so many assets that these
few disadvantages are greatly outnumbered.

The species is a member of the group Cinnamomeae and is a
native of north-eastern Asia, of northern China, Korea, and
Japan, and was first recorded in Europe in a botanical way by
Thunberg in 1784. E. A. Bunyard relates how the Chinese in
particular portrayed this rose as far back as A.D. 1000, and the
China Rose even earlier. As it was also grown in Japan it was
understandable that it should reach us from those shores first, and
in 1796 it was introduced as a novelty by Lee and Kennedy of
Hammersmith, but did not prove very popular. It was scarcely a
type of rose that would have been given an honoured place then
for it brought no new colour to roses; the craze for Chinoiserie was
over, the day of the flowering shrub had not been thought of, and
the blooms were comparatively shapeless.

Looking at R. *rugosa* today we find a rose with few faults. It is

99

extremely hardy; it is bushy and it thrives on sandy and other soils, but it is not so successful on heavy clay and chalk. It flowers from the end of May onwards into autumn, bears heps, and gives autumn colour. It has a variety of colours and an excellent fragrance. From its petals the Chinese, so W. J. Bean records, made a kind of *pot-pourri*, and its heps have been used in Europe for making preserves. I have seen no disease on it or on its varieties, and pests do not make any impression on it. It would be very difficult to give a longer recital of merits to any other shrub, and yet this rose and its varieties can hardly be described as popular, although a definite trend towards increased favour has been noticed in the last ten years.

It grows freely enough and sets quantities of seeds which germinate well, and it hybridizes readily with almost any rose growing near by. Its disadvantages are its lack of form in the double varieties, though the singles are as beautiful as any; the short duration of each flower; its suckering proclivities and excessive prickliness. Unfortunately the last character is nearly always handed on—often with interest—to its progeny. On light soils the suckers can become a nuisance, but only to clumpy herbaceous plants and small shrubs which cannot stand being invaded. It is just a question of giving it enough room, and I can think of many shrubs that, in a given area, would not provide half so much enjoyment as one of the Rugosas.

The Rugosa Rose existed for the best part of a hundred years in Europe before much attention was paid to it. And then, when the transformation enacted among popular roses had begun to pall, rose-growers began to accord it some attention. Many crosses with popular garden roses were made and a few good hybrids cropped up, but there the matter stopped, for in the main the hybrids were sterile or incapable of handing on the tremendous vigour and scent of the parent. They were raised mostly in France and the United States.

During this century it has been given much more interest. It became recognized as a rose that could withstand extreme cold, and some of the varieties raised around the turn of the century in Germany have proved useful in central Europe; the same thing has happened in the northern United States and Canada, where many of the China Rose derivatives cannot stand the extreme weather.

One asset has not yet been exploited, that of its adaptability in sandy soils, and especially in maritime districts. My attention was called to a thriving, dense, suckering colony of it, which had been seen by Mrs C. C. Hurst on the shore at West Wittering; I have also noticed it established in sandy soil near Newmarket. It would be a wonderful rose for consolidating windbreaks on dunes, for it would, I imagine, make such dense growth, with a rootstock like a woody bracken, that it would be proof against wind-drift. It might perhaps be an unpleasantly prickly neighbour for a party of bathers, but the scent, wafting over the sun-warmed sand, would perhaps outweigh the inconvenience of an occasional scratch.

There are of course the big public parks in our coastal towns to be considered; R. *rugosa* is surely the right plant for them, a care-free bush that likes the sea air, flowers during the whole of the holiday season, and repels small children and dogs. It is un-doubtedly *the* park rose, and great quantities are grown annually in Europe for sale to municipal bodies.

The species is now well on the way to make history. A usually sterile hybrid, probably between R. *rugosa* and R. *wichuraiana*, named 'Max Graf', was raised in 1919 in the United States, and in the early 1940's, in the hands of Herr Wilhelm Kordes, a seedling from it spontaneously doubled its chromosomes and became fertile. Miss Ann Wylie wrote about this in the Royal Horti-cultural Society's *Journal*, February 1955, and went on to tell how Herr Kordes at once perceived his opportunity and has raised many hybrids from it. He crossed it with the Wichuraiana climber 'Golden Glow' and Floribundas, and has achieved a remarkably hardy disease-resistant race. They are, however, mainly climbers and do not concern us here.

Today the species and its hybrids present a mixed lot. This is inevitable, when breeders get busy, with any genus or species. I have already mentioned the understock *rugosa*, which is possibly a hybrid with 'Manetti', and is sometimes called 'Hollandica'. It is supposed to have originated in Holland and, in spite of its weak-ness, its suckers, and its comparatively short life, it is nowadays the most popular 'stem' with nurserymen, for 'standard' roses. It is best to get rid of this rose from our shrub category. It is never planted deliberately, but often a dense yet lanky thicket may be found in a garden where a budded scion has succumbed to its embrace. The nearly single, light mallow-pink flowers, produced throughout the growing season, could be tolerated, even enjoyed, if one could feel happier about the spreading root and the lanky stems. On some waste railway bank or gravel pit, or in some sooty backyard, its disadvantages may be forgiven, but the genus *Rosa*, and R. *rugosa* in particular, has better to offer.

R. *rugosa* varies considerably in nature, and a nearly related species, hybrid, or variety, R. *kamtschatica*, has been confused with it by writers during the years; it is not of much garden value. My laudatory remarks at the beginning of this chapter refer almost entirely to the forms and close hybrids of R. *r. typica*, which is usually considered as the normal wild type. Its natural colours make it a harmonious companion for Old Roses, and it starts flowering even in advance of these, usually by the end of May in Surrey, in all its forms.

The garden forms and hybrids fall fairly clearly into two groups: those which are actual forms or very near hybrids of R. *r. typica*; and big lusty hybrids with other roses. Together with a few others, including the prostrate R. ' Paulii ' and ' Max Graf ', all of them will be found in Chapter 14.

The following are all forms or such near hybrids that from a gardening point of view they are practically identical, except for their floral variety. They form dense rounded bushes, usually nearly as wide as high, covering the ground with many shoots, well set with large and small prickles and bristles, making them impenetrable; the leaves usually have seven or nine leaflets and are neatly shaped, glossy, deeply veined or corrugated, turning yellow in the autumn, and covering the bushes with a mantle of rich dark green. The flowers are borne singly or in small clusters on small shoots produced very freely early in the season; later, strong shoots appear bearing up to a dozen or so flowers. The singles and semi-doubles show creamy yellow stamens, much paler than in many species, and this colour assorts particularly well with the floral tones. The buds are beautiful, long and pointed with a mass of pale green bracts around the larger clusters. In fact the pale green wood, thorns, bracts, and calyces make excellent contrast to the flowers and leaves. The doubles are loosely knit, somewhat shapeless, open quickly from the bud, and are at their best the first day. In hot weather they last only two days, but a long succession is maintained. The scent is delicious, redolent of cloves, and carries well on the air. The heps retain their projecting calyx lobes and are very handsome, large, round, and shining.

Very little pruning is required; the plants grow bushy naturally, but if they become old and gaunt due to overcrowding they can be cut back severely. No rose benefits so much from being allowed plenty of space to create its naturally well-balanced, rounded shape. To ensure a long flowering season the doubles may be clipped over in early February. The singles may be treated likewise, but the formation of heps on them is inclined to prevent the formation of later crops of flowers, and a choice has to be made between flowers and heps.

They make splendid sturdy hedges and can be kept in shape by pruning or clipping to about 4 or 5 feet high by 3 or 4 feet wide, and for such a hedge they should be planted at 3 feet apart. Supports would be necessary on less fertile soils to take a hedge to greater heights. As suckers are part of the natural Rugosa traits, due consideration should be given to ultimate spread at the time of planting, particularly on light soil. Some plants may become 8 feet wide after six or more years of cultivation, and if suited there is no limit to what they can do. It will be understood therefore that unless some pruning of shoots and roots is contemplated they are not suitable for small borders.

RUGOSA TYPICA. *R. rugosa rugosa*. It is difficult to pin down one form as the type of so variable a species, but this is generally considered to have the normal colour for the species. When raised from seed it is variable. Vigorous growth, less upright than *R. rugosa alba* and 'Roseraie de l'Haÿ'; excellent foliage. Its only disadvantage is the unpleasant contrast between the violaceous carmine of the flowers and the bright tomato-red heps, which it produces freely. This wild type is the best for dune-planting especially as it is more often available on its own roots from nurseries. 5 feet.

Andrews, Plate 129. A magnificent drawing.

Lawrance, Plate 42. *R. ferox*; 'Hedgehog Rose'. *R. rugosa*.

Botanical Register, vol. v, t.420. *R. ferox*. *R. rugosa*; a good portrait.

Siebold, vol. i, t.28. Excellent.

RUGOSA 'Alba'. *R. r. albiflora*. Pure white single flowers, blush-tinted in the bud. The white in Rugosa varieties is much purer than in most other roses. An exceptionally vigorous form, very bushy and well covered with fresh dark-green leaves. Particularly effective in late summer when the crops of large, shining, orange-red heps appear, contrasting with the later flowers. 6 to 7 feet. When well grown will make a magnificent large rounded bush.

The Garden, vol. ix, p. 452. A very fine portrait.
Journal des Roses, Août 1906.
Strassheim, June 1907.
McFarland, *Roses of the World*, p. 237. With heps.

RUGOSA ALBO PLENA. A name covering double white forms.

RUGOSA ROSEA. A form recorded by Rehder, with light-coloured flowers. It might occur freely in nature or when seeds are raised from *R. rugosa typica* or *alba*. Botanically it covers all single pink forms, such as 'Fru Dagmar Hastrup'.

RUGOSA 'Rubra'. This is a splendid horticultural clone also known as *R. r.* 'Atropurpurea'. In growth and foliage and fruit it follows *R. r. typica*, but in colour it is wine-crimson against which richness the creamy stamens shew to advantage.

RUGOSA PLENA. This name covers double coloured forms not named otherwise. 'Roseraie de l'Haÿ' would be grouped here botanically.

L'Horticulteur Français, 1862, Plate 19. ⎫ Leaves too attenuated
Roses et Rosiers, Plate 44.   ⎬ and too few prickles;
                                            ⎭ probably a hybrid, or *R. kamtschatica*.

Step, vol. i, Plate 73.
Gartenflora, 1875, vol. xxiv, Plate 846. A garden form or hybrid. 'Kaiserin des Nordens.'

'Belle Poitevine'. Bruant, 1894. Although I have failed to find exact details of parentage, this is usually reported to be a hybrid of *R. rugosa*, raised by Georges Bruant. The foliage is not so glossy as the most typical forms like *R. r.* 'Alba' and 'Rubra', and the growth is not quite so lush. It does, however, make a similarly good bush. The flowers are loosely double, opening rather flat, four inches across, shewing creamy stamens; pale magenta or mallow-pink. Good heps. 5 feet by 5 feet. Park, Plate 189.

'Blanc Double de Coubert'. Cochet-Cochet, 1892. The parentage given, R. *rugosa* × 'Sombreuil', is very doubtful. Shews little trace of hybridity except that it is much less bushy and lush than R. *rugosa* ' Alba '. The pure white blooms are loosely semi-double, less flat than others of this group, slightly blush-tinted in the bud. 6 feet by 5 feet. The best-known rose in this group; those who have grown only this variety should try some of the others.
Journal des Roses, Février 1897.
Trechslin & Coggiattı.

'Calocarpa'. See Chapter 14.

'Delicata'. Cooling, 1898. An American, and probably a hybrid. The least vigorous and bushy of this group and seldom a satisfactory plant in the garden or in the nursery, where it seems very difficult to propagate. The flowers are semi-double, resembling 'Belle Poitevine' but of a delightful cool lilac-pink. Foliage fairly good. Perhaps 5 feet when growing well, though usually about 3 feet.

'Fru Dagmar Hastrup'. Hastrup, *c.* 1914. A seedling from R. *rugosa*. A most satisfactory plant, of compact growth, dark green foliage, and exquisite single flowers of clear, light pink entirely lacking the purplish shade of the others. Fortunately the heps are rich crimson, not the usual orange-red of the other singles, and as a consequence they harmonize with the flowers. The cream stamens are conspicuous, and the buds are rich deep pink. 5 feet by 5 feet. Its slightly lower and very compact growth make it one of the few ideal roses for hedges. (Plates III, heps; IV, flowers.)

'Hansa'. Schaum, 1905, at Iowa. A very tough, free-flowering bush with typical growth and foliage. It is greatly valued and planted in northern and central Europe, but I find it much less appealing than the little-known 'Roseraie de l'Haÿ'. The flowers are fully double, well formed, of deep crimson-purple of rather a harsh tone, and the foliage shews signs of hybridity. 5 feet by 4 feet.

Les Plus Belles Roses, page 182, has a portrait of 'Souvenir de Pièrre Leperdrieux', which I have not seen. This portrait with its excellent heps is very near to 'Hansa'.

'Roseraie de L'Haÿ'. Gravereaux, 1901. Reputed to be a sport from or hybrid of R. *rugosa rosea,* which is difficult to believe; it is of normal growth, slightly more erect than R. *rugosa* ' Alba ', but equally fresh and luxuriant, the lovely foliage densely covering the whole bush. The buds are particularly long and pointed, scrolled like a perfect ' Céleste ' or Hybrid Tea, and of dark purplish red; they open to 4½ inches wide, fairly full, glorious blooms of intense rich crimson-purple, with cream stamens lighting the centre, from which radiate folded petals. It is much looser, more velvety, and of brighter, richer colouring than ' Hansa '. Few heps. A superb rose, admirable with blue hydrangeas. 6 feet by 5 feet. (Plate IV.)

Journal des Roses, Août 1906.

Strassheim, June 1907.

Les Plus Belles Roses, p. 116. Somewhat exaggerated, but the true colour.

Park, Plate 191. Too pale.

'Scabrosa'. Prior to 1939. I have been unable to trace the origin of this splendid form, which is extra vigorous, bears large leaves, and makes a wide handsome bush, of typical appearance. The single flowers are also large, 5½ inches across, of violaceous crimson, with the usual cream stamens, and are followed by immense orange-red heps. Certainly the grossest development so far among the forms and near hybrids of the species, in leaf, flower, and fruit. 5 feet by 5 feet.

Park, Plate 190.

While I doubt if it applies, Andrews's Plate 129 is similar to this variety.

'Souvenir de Christophe Cochet'. Cochet-Cochet, 1894. Records state that this is R. *rugosa alba simplex* × 'Comte d'Épremesnil'; it is very similar to 'Belle Poitevine', but the foliage and flowers are less attractive. 'Comte d'Épremesnil' was a Rugosa seedling, which had double pinkish flowers, and bore fruits. 6 feet.

Journal des Roses, Septembre 1894. A grandiose portrait. Rather too bright.

Rosenzeitung, 1893.

'Souvenir de Philémon Cochet'. Cochet-Cochet, 1899. This was a sport from 'Blanc double de Coubert', and I have noticed it recurring from time to time in recent years. It differs in floral shape only, being very double, the mass of small central petals and wide outer petals producing a flower not unlike a double hollyhock. The faint blush tinting of the bud is usually preserved in the centre when the flower is full blown. 4 feet to 5 feet.

It is very difficult to decide, where learned botanists differ, how to group the Kamchatka Rose, by some treated as a distinct species, R. *kamtschatica*, and by others as a variety of R. *rugosa*. It is not important horticulturally, being inferior in value to R. *rugosa* in every way, but the many figures of it, to the exclusion of R. *rugosa*, in old books make me think that R. *rugosa* may sometimes have been depicted and captioned in error. It was introduced in 1770. Also known as R. *r. ventenatiana*.

Botanical Magazine, t.3149. R. *rugosa kamtschatica*.

Duhamel, vol. vii, Plate 10. R. *kamtschatica*.

Botanical Register, vol. x, t.419.

Redouté, vol. i, Plate 47. Probably R. *rugosa*.

Roses et Rosiers, Plate 44. Probably of this species.

Postscript 1980 Edition

Ramanas Rose. A term often used in conjunction with *Rosa rugosa*, without explanation. Mr Desmond Clarke, in editing *Rosa* for the Eighth Edition of Bean's *Trees & Shrubs*, suggests that it may be derived from the Japanese *Hamanashi*, or ' Shore pear '. R. *rugosa* is frequently found by the sea though its heps are rather far removed from a pear.

9

Some Strange Species and their Hybrids

Among all floures of the worlde the floure of the rose is
cheyf and beeryth ye pryse. And by cause of vertues and
swete smelle and savour. For by fayrnesse they fede the
syghte: and playseth the smelle by odour, the touche by
softe handlynge. And wythstondeth and socouryth by
vertue ayenst many syknesses and euylles.

Bartholomaeus Anglicus, *De Proprietatibus Rerum*,
translated by John de Trevisa, 1398.

THE HEPS of many roses are bristly but only a very few are actually
prickly, like those of a Horse Chestnut, though smaller. There are
three species in cultivation with this peculiarity. Two of these are
closely related, R. *stellata* and R. *mirifica*; in fact the latter is sometimes classed as a variety of the former. The other species, R.
roxburghii, also known as R. *microphylla*, is totally distinct. While
the first two are small wiry shrubs, R. *roxburghii* is a mighty plant,
and is placed separately by botanists in the sub-genus *Platyrhodon*,
while R. *stellata* is in the sub-genus *Hesperhodos*.

ROXBURGHII. The 'Burr' or 'Chestnut Rose' ('Rose
Châtaigne'). A native of China and Japan, and introduced to
cultivation in 1908. It makes a large rounded bush, the stiff
angular-branching stems having flaking, buff-coloured bark
which adds to its attraction in winter. It is a particularly
unpleasant rose to handle, being rigid and armed with pairs of
hooked thorns below the leaves. As many as 15 leaflets occur,

narrow and arranged in compact ladder-like fashion; the flowers
are variable in colour from nearly white to deep rose, and are
supported by stalks, calyx tube, and calyx all prickly and very
distinct. The resultant hep is an inch or more across, rounded,
with persistent, conspicuous, broad calyx lobes and covered
with stiff prickles. It so happens that the double form. R. r.
roxburghii, was introduced many years before the single wild
type, in 1824, and the figures in old books are naturally of this
double form. In consequence the forms are classed as follows:

ROXBURGHII NORMALIS. China, whence it was introduced in
1908. The single type of the 'Chestnut Rose'. The four-inch-
wide flowers are very beautiful, but evanescent and rather hide
themselves under the leaves. The value of this plant in gardens
is better gauged by its foliage, stance, and interest than by its
floral effect. In poor sandy soil it has attained some 9 feet in
height and width.

Botanical Magazine, t.6548. This shews the Japanese form R.
   roxburghii hirsuta or hirtula, whose leaves are pubescent
   beneath, thus differing from R. r. normalis, the Chinese form;
   introduced before 1880.
Iwasaki, Phonzo Soufou, vol. lxxxiv.
Gault and Synge, Plates 45 and 46, flowers and fruits.

ROXBURGHII ROXBURGHII. R. roxburghii plena, R. microphylla.
An ancient cultivated form of the 'Chestnut Rose' which is
presumably of Chinese origin. Miss Willmott tells us how its
portrait in a collection of Chinese drawings resulted in Lindley
mentioning it in his monograph, and it was found to exist in the
Calcutta Botanic Garden, whence it was introduced by Dr
Roxburgh from Canton. It flowered first in Britain in 1824.

In my experience it is not so vigorous as the single type,
although it might eventually attain a height equal to it. The
flowers have large, pale pink outer petals making a frame for the
mass of short central petals, which are of intense deep pink with
a lilac tint. Slightly scented. 4 feet.

Journal des Roses, Septembre 1874. R. microphylla, 'pourpre
   ancien'. A fanciful flower and colour.
Botanical Magazine, t.3490. A splendid portrait.
Willmott, Plate 135. Half-open flowers only.

Iwasaki, *Phonzo Soufou*, vol. lxxxiv.
Botanical Register, vol. xi, t.919. A flower of rather exaggerated perfection.
Reeves' Drawings of Chinese Plants. Very good.

The Chestnut Rose has given some hybrids which, while not in the front rank of garden value, are interesting, beautiful, and perhaps an indication of what may follow; they are 'Coryana', ' Jardin de la Croix ', ' Roxane ', and × *micrugosa*, which will be found in Chapter 14.

STELLATA. Western Texas to North Arizona. *Hesperhodos stellatus*. This dwarf plant is distinguished by having *only three* leaflets—hairy, deeply toothed and at first sight rather like those of a gooseberry—and minute stellate hairs on the stems. Grey-green stems, bearing short, sharp prickles of ivory colouring when young, form a wiry thicket up to about 2 feet; in flower it is silky like a cistus, the colour being a deep vinous pink of a subdued tone, with yellow stamens; it is in flower for a long time. Coming as it does from so far south, it needs all the sun we can give it and thrives best in a well-drained position against a south wall. The heps are rounded, of dull red colouring. I have not found it so vigorous as R. *s. mirifica*, but at Bayfordbury both are of equal vigour when raised from seed. Willmott, Plate 305.

STELLATA MIRIFICA. New Mexico. The 'Sacramento Rose', so called because of its growing in the Sacramento Mountains; closely related to R. *stellata* although sometimes classed as a separate species. It is perhaps of stronger growth and more readily adaptable to British garden conditions, forming a dense bush, filled with wiry, arching stems freely branching and set with small sharp thorns in the manner of R. *stellata*, but with smooth stems. The leaves usually have five leaflets and are more or less smooth. It is more free in flower and slightly longer in petal and of paler colouring, but is also silky and like a cistus.

Again it is reputed to love all the sun we can give it, and a well-drained soil, though in my own garden in poor sandy soil it has ascended to 4 feet on a wall, practically without any sunshine. This is a useful and unusual little rose of charm and

interest to the plantsman. No hybrids are known. (Fig. 4.)
Botanical Magazine, t.9070. A poor plate.
Mansfield, Plate 2.
American Rose Annual, 1932, photograph.

PERSICA. The remaining species to be considered is R.
persica, or, classified as it is now in a separate genus, *Hulthemia
persica* (*Lowea berberifolia*, *Rosa berberifolia*). It is a strange little
shrub, only a few inches high, succeeding best in extremely
warm, well-drained positions such as at Highdown, where it
spreads by underground runners, throwing up small shoots
bearing simple—not pinnate—grey-green leaves. The flowers
are a brilliant buttercup yellow with a scarlet blotch at the base
of each petal, reminiscent of a halimium. It is very difficult to
propagate and establish.

While some spontaneous hybrids have been reported from
the Soviet States, the only one I have come across is that now
known as *Hulthemosa hardii* (*Rosa hardii*), presumed to be a cross
between *Hulthemia persica* and *Rosa clinophylla*. The latter is
closely related to R. *laevigata*, and a far cry, botanically, from
H. *hardii*. It appeared in the Jardin de Luxembourg, Paris, in
1836, probably from seed of R. *persica*. The fact that it has
remained in cultivation for so long cannot be attributed to its
vigour as we know it, for it is notoriously difficult and short-
lived, though more tractable than H. *persica*. Its colour has
endeared it to us, for it has retained the brilliance of H. *persica*,
but has a larger flower, 2 inches across, and larger red blotches.
For many years a plant grew successfully in the University
Botanic Garden at Cambridge, but I expect the best one ever
grown was at Berkeley Castle, where, Captain Berkeley told
me, it achieved 9 feet by 9 feet, against a wall. There is no
doubt it is a spectacular plant when in full flower and as soon
as plants are available on their own roots it should be tried
in favoured places against sunny walls in the south-eastern
parts of England. As H. *persica* is a native of areas from Persia
to Afghanistan, both it and its hybrids are probably best suited
to the sunnier districts of England. Where they thrive R. *stellata*
and R. *mirifica* would also be expected to thrive.

It is a pleasant thought that J. A. Hardy, who was no doubt a keen plantsman and rosarian, should be commemorated in this remarkable plant, while his wife has to her credit the famous white Damask Rose 'Mme Hardy'. Neither are likely ever to go out of cultivation from popular neglect, so long as they retain vigour.

Botanical Magazine, t.7096. *Rosa persica*.
Duhamel, vol. vii, t.14. *R. berberifolia*. Poor.
Willmott, Plate 1. *R. persica*.
Botanical Register, vol. xv, t.1261. *Lowea berberifolia*.
Willmott, Plate 2. *R. hardii*.
Journal des Roses, Juin 1881. *Rosa hardii*.
Paxton's Magazine of Botany, vol. x, Fig. 195. *Rosa hardii*.

Postscript for 1980 Edition

Of late years Mr J. L. Harkness of Hitchin, Hertfordshire, has raised further hybrids with *R. persica*, but unfortunately all have proved to be sterile.

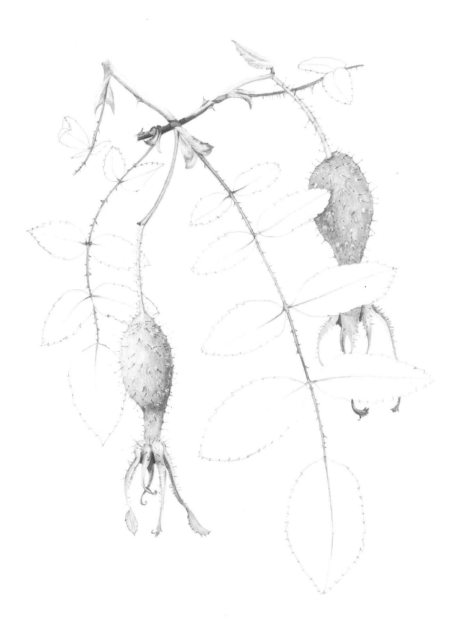

1. The fruits of R. *setipoda* develop in late summer.

2. R. *carolina* ' Plena '.

3. The rose ' D'Orsay ', an old rose, probably a hybrid of
R. *virginiana*. Rich pink, August flowering. See p. 77.

4. The rare ' Sacramento Rose ' from New Mexico
(R. *stellata mirifica*).

5. The blush pink 'Fimbriata' (1891), a R. *rugosa* derivative of earlier raising than the Grootendorst varieties.

6. ' Bloomfield Abundance ', showing the characteristic
    elongated calyx-lobes. See pages 148 and 151.

7. 'Cécile Brunner', a miniature bloom of great charm.

8. 'Nevada', one of the most magnificent of shrub roses,
derived from a form of R. *moyesii*.

Descriptions of Shrub Roses

PART 2

Shrub and other Roses
having Affinity to
the China Rose

10

China Roses

As this blind rose, no more than a whim of dust,
achieved her excellence without intent,
so man, the casual sport of time and lust,
plans wealth and war, and loves by accident.

Humbert Wolfe.

THE China Rose is the foundation species upon which all our modern roses are built, whether they be bedding roses or shrubs or perpetual-flowering climbers. Its influence in rose-breeding over a hundred years has been so great, so overwhelming, and so potent that it is difficult to see where we should have been without it. We are so used to thinking of roses in terms of Hybrid Teas and Floribundas that we are apt to forget that these are, comparatively, very new and specialized, and they owe more than half their success and *éclat* to the China Rose.

In 1891 William Paul thought very highly of China Roses and included in his twelve best roses for freedom, constancy of bloom, and for massing: 'Fabvier', 'Cramoisi Supérieur', 'Common (Old Blush) China ' and ' Fellenburg '. They still rank among our most free-flowering roses.

Rosa chinensis was the name given in 1768 to a pressed specimen in Gronovius's Herbarium, which in 1733 he had called 'Chineeshe Eglantier Roosen'. It was a crimson form. In 1751 the rose was seen growing in the gardens of the custom house at Canton by Peter Osbeck, a pupil of Linnaeus. The single-flowered wild species was not discovered until 1885, and thus our rose history in regard to this species really starts with four garden roses, possibly hybrids with the Tea Rose as recorded by Dr Hurst.[1]

---

[1] *The Old Shrub Roses*, page 74.

His 'four stud Chinas' were 'Slater's Crimson China' introduced in 1792, 'Parsons's Pink China' (1793), 'Hume's Blush Tea-scented China' (1809), and 'Parks's Yellow Tea-scented China' (1824). The first is a double crimson China Rose that may have been in cultivation in Italy since the middle of the seventeenth century. Thus was the initial work already done for us in China, and enthusiasts in Europe were thereby provided with *perpetual-flowering* roses ranging through pink to true dark crimson, salmon and pale yellow, for hybridizing. Nor was this all. I have already said how these roses flowered through summer and autumn; they also had a new shape, a new texture, a dwarf habit, and totally different leaves and twigs from any other in cultivation, and different fragrance. The wild *R. chinensis* (now called *R. c. spontanea* to distinguish it from garden forms or hybrids discovered previously) was found by Dr Augustine Henry in glens near Ichang in Central China. He devoted a long article to it in the *Gardeners' Chronicle* for 23 June 1902, describing it as a climber, growing like *R. banksiae*, with 3 to 5 leaflets, and solitary flowers (single), generally deep red but sometimes pink. As far as I know the wild species is not in cultivation. We have single-flowered China Roses such as *R. c.* ' Mutabilis ', ' Miss Lowe ', and ' Sanguinea ', but just what these are derived from we do not know. The fact that they, and all the double-flowered Chinas which we grow, are perpetually in flower proves that they are either sports or otherwise derived from ancient hydrids of *R. chinensis*. (Once-flowering climbing roses tend to produce perpetual-flowering dwarf sports as recorded by Hurst; ' Little White Pet ' and ' The Fairy ' are further examples. The reverse is also true sometimes.)

Our garden China Roses are shrubs of small to medium growth according to the local climate, and have smooth wood, reddish when young and sparsely set with small, handsome, dark red thorns. The leaves are also sparsely borne, with 3 to 5 pointed segments; they are smooth, richly tinted with red-brown when young, and contribute greatly to the general colour of the plants. (This leaf-colour is reproduced in its most intense richness in such roses as 'Donald Prior' and 'Rosemary Rose', both modern Floribundas.) The flowers have five or more rather limp petals of silky texture, making rather a shapeless flower after their first opening, especially in the singles. I have grown and seen China

Roses in different districts and in exposed open places; on poor soils they may barely reach 2 feet in height, while the same form or variety in good rich soil, away from ground frost or against a wall, may reach 9 or 10 feet.

'Old Blush'. For our present purpose we may take the 'Monthly Rose' as our standard for comparison. It is a well-known garden plant and may be identical to 'Parsons's Pink China', introduced in 1793. Being pink and with a plain China Rose scent and of compact habit, it may perhaps be nearly unadulterated R. *chinensis*, whereas probably all the coppery named forms are infused with the Tea Rose. There is a single-flowered pink sport.

There are few garden plants of so great value in cultivation today as the 'Old Blush', and it can well take its place with the winter jasmine, the forsythia, the lilac, and other favourites without which no garden is complete. It is a perfect bedding rose and needs little pruning, and in common with all China varieties it roots easily from cuttings. It seems to thrive in any soil, and will reach 10 feet on a sheltered wall, while for a dwarf flowering hedge of about 3 feet it is almost unequalled. The scent is like that of sweet peas and the petals are exquisitely veined. A noticeable character of all true China Roses is that the colour of the petals deepens as they age, instead of fading, as with all other species. Tom Smith, the famous nurseryman of Newry, Co. Down, used to claim this to be the 'Last Rose of Summer' of the Irish poet, Thomas Moore, and a plant often provides me with buds at Christmas, after a mild autumn.

Willmott, Plate 79. A splendid portrait.

Andrews, Plate 66. The 'Pale China Rose'. A rather poor portrait; exaggerated.

Lawrance, Plate 26. R. *semperflorens*. Bad.

Duhamel, vol. vii, Plate 18. R. *semperflorens*. Probably 'Old Blush'. Very poor.

Redouté, vol. i, Plate 51. R. *indica vulgaris*, 'Parsons's Pink China'.

'Slater's Crimson China' ('Semperflorens'). Similar to 'Old Blush' but of rich crimson colouring and open in growth; smaller, more richly tinted, pretty leaves and flowers, loosely open and delicately scented. It is not generally realized that true dark crimson was quite unknown among garden roses before the introduction of this plant. No Damask or Gallica rose was darker than light crimson, except where overclouded with purple or maroon. To this introduction, then, in 1792, we can trace back all our favourite dark red roses. This rose had been lost for many years, but has been traced and obtained from Bermuda. Dr Hurst found it to be a triploid. Mr Gordon Rowley found a similar but much dwarfer, diploid plant in a Hertfordshire garden (which also grows at Wisley), identical with the plate p. 89 in Willmott's *The Genus Rosa*.

Andrews, Plate 72.

Lawrance, Plate 28. Bad.

Step, vol. ii, Plate 80.

Jacquin, *Horti Schönbrunnensis*, vol. iii, Plate 281.

Drapiez, vol. vi, p. 418. 'Le Rosier du Bengale toujours fleuri.'

Botanical Magazine, t.284. Shows an unusually thorny stem for a China Rose.

'Hume's Blush Tea-scented China'. Introduced in 1809. Unfortunately this hybrid appears to be extinct in Europe, but its portrait confirms that it must have been a hybrid between *R. chinensis* and *R. gigantea*. It was probably not very hardy but it was an important ancestor of the Tea Roses. The names given by Andrews and Redouté are interesting, denoting the distinct fragrance derived from the Tea Rose. Dr Hurst recalls that 'special arrangements were made by both the British and French Admiralties for the safe transit of plants of this new Tea-scented China to the Empress Josephine at Malmaison, in spite of the fierce war that was raging between England and France at that time'. Thus does horticulture transcend the petty bickerings of mankind.

Andrews, Plate 77, *R. indica odorata*.

Redouté, vol. i, Plate 61. *R. indica fragrans*, 'Hume's Blush'.

Botanical Register, Vol. X, Plate 804.

'Parks's Yellow Tea-scented China'. Introduced in 1824. Probably of similar parentage to 'Hume's Blush', but leaning more towards the Tea Rose in colour and perhaps in scent, this is also unfortunately extinct so far as I can ascertain. It is possible that these two roses remain still in some forgotten garden in a climate more equable than that of Britain. By union with the Noisettes this rose became the ancestor of the famous yellow climbing Tea Roses such as 'Gloire de Dijon' and 'Maréchal Niel', which are often classed as Noisettes.

Redouté, 3rd edition, 1835, vol. iii. R. *indica sulphurea*, 'Parks's Yellow'. Poor.

In the Lindley Library of the Royal Horticultural Society there are some volumes of beautiful Chinese paintings collected by a Mr Reeves. Their probable date is 1812–31. In the second volume are the following Chinese roses: *semperflorens*; Double Dark Red Monthly; Monthly Blush; Indica double white. Plate 32 is possibly 'Parks's Yellow'.

The following may be considered as fairly typical forms of the China Rose, or near hybrids.

'Cramoisi Supérieur'. Cocquereau or Plantier, 1832. 'Agrippina.' The true deep crimson of 'Slater's Crimson China' pervades this beautiful free-flowering variety. It is *petite* in its growth, with small wiry twigs gradually building up into a small bush; dark green small leaves richly tinted when young, and cupped double blooms borne singly or in small clusters in summer and in large heads on the strong young shoots later. It is remontant and a glorious colour. Like all China Roses it does best in sunny, sheltered positions. 3 feet. The climbing form 'Cramoisi Supérieur Grimpante' is a magnificent plant for a sunny wall; Tom Smith mentioned in his catalogue for 1912 that he had 'seen the whole front of a two-storey house completely covered with the Climbing Cramoisi', whose flowers 'are continually produced all the season through'. I have not found it so perpetual as the bush form, but China Roses do not grow satisfactorily in my area. Not very fragrant.

Curtis, vol. ii, Plate 11. Good.
Jamain and Forney, Plate 54. Poor.
Journal des Roses, Août 1883. Good.

'Hermosa'. Marcheseau, 1840. 'Armosa', 'Setina', 'Mélanie Lemarié', 'Madame Neumann'. Occurred as a seedling with four different breeders between 1834 and 1841; Dr Hurst called this a China-reversion. In some works 'Hermosa' is classed as a Bourbon, but it is very near indeed to the 'Old Blush' in habit and other characters. It is of a particularly bland lilac-pink, much fuller of petals—which are rolled at the edges—than 'Old Blush'. It is also much more thorny, producing a round hep whereas 'Old Blush' has an oval hep. It is equally vigorous but usually rather more compact, and I generally observe that it is not quite so continuous. But a bunch of 'Hermosa' blooms leaves little to be desired; their form and colour are perfect, and it is fairly fragrant. As a rule the bush form does not exceed 3 feet.

There is a climbing form, known as 'Climbing Hermosa', which originated with Henderson in 1879, but like most climbing sports of free-flowering dwarfs, it is not so perpetual, few flowers being produced after the long first flush. 'Hermosa' used to be a great favourite. George Paul, writing in the Royal Horticultural Society's *Journal* in 1896, says it 'is *par excellence* the dwarf hedge rose'.

Choix des Plus Belles Roses, Plate 38.

Jamain and Forney, Plate 34, Poor.

Curtis, 1850, vol. i, Plate 7. 'Armosa.'

Thomas, G. C., p. 114.

'**Miss Lowe**'. This is a name given to a single crimson of good colour and shape but of a very small growth. It is free-flowering, growing in good soil perhaps to 4 feet, but with me is usually 18 inches. It is light crimson turning to dark crimson, with rather quilled petals.

The Garden, 1887, vol. ii, p. 128. An excellent portrait from a painting by Miss Lowe at Wimbledon.

'**Mutabilis**'. 'Tipo Ideale.' Writing in the *Revue Horticole* for 1934, page 60, Henri Correvon, the celebrated Swiss alpine gardener, stated that it was given to him forty years previously by Prince Gilberto Borromeo. Later he saw it growing in Milan, but as nobody appeared to have a name for it, M. Correvon called it, very aptly, *mutabilis*, although there had been a *sempervirens* variety of this name previously. E. A. Bunyard mentioned a portrait of it by Redouté in the Jardin des Plantes, Paris, but this portrait is of the Centifolia rose 'Unique

Blanche ', which is also called ' Mutabilis '. It is sometimes called R. ' Turkestanica ', which is a rose in the Pimpinellifoliae section and quite distinct.

It is a slender but vigorous and robust rose, with dark plum-coloured young wood, reddish thorns, and handsome coppery young foliage. In sheltered gardens where it really thrives, as at Kiftsgate Court, it is a magnificent shrub reaching 8 feet high and wide with stout stems an inch or more in diameter, in the open border. On sunny walls in Kent it is an equal success, but very often in lowland gardens it reaches only 3 feet in height and is more like a bedding rose.

The colour of the flowers is remarkable: they open from slender pointed buds of vivid orange, flame coloured where the sun strikes them; on opening they are of soft pale chamois-yellow within, while the flame of the bud continues to mark the outside. The second day, after pollinating, they change to soft coppery pink, and on the third day as they wrinkle and fall the colour deepens to coppery crimson. The colours are deepest in hot weather; the countless blossoms resemble flights of butterflies.

As a bedding rose this variety has great assets, particularly its long season of flowering, from early June until the autumn, and its varied tones which enable it to fit into almost any colour scheme. It flowers early enough to plant it with the blue hardy geraniums such as G. himalayense ' Alpinum ' and G. ' Johnson's Blue ', which create an especially good contrast. Its flame tones and coppery leaves assort well with combinations of red, orange, and yellow, while its general effect is soft enough to create a pleasing complement to grey foliage. Its possibilities are endless and it is so free that it might well find its way into our public parks as a bedding plant. (Plate VI.)

Willmott, Page 81. ' The variety known as Miss Willmott's indica is a garden form.' There is no further description and no particulars of origin. Although this does not shew all the variations of colour I consider it applies to R. chinensis ' Mutabilis '; at least it shews colouring fairly near to the orange-pink in the original painting.

Revue Horticole, 1934, p. 60. Excellent plate shewing all colours. Trechslin & Coggiatti. Good.

'**Sanguinea**' is perhaps the name of the single crimson variety which my colleague James Russell received from the South of France labelled 'Amourette' (which is a pink rose). It is a vigorous plant, probably growing to 5 feet in good soil, with stouter wood and larger, darker flowers than 'Miss Lowe'. 'Sanguinea' was a sport from R. *c. semperflorens*, but so far no reverse sport has occurred on my plants.

Old plates of such roses as these are as follows:

Andrews, Plate 69. R. *indica simplex*. Raised from seed sent from France in 1816.

Redouté, vol. i, Plate 49. R. *indica*.

'**Serratipetala**'. 'Oeillet de Saint Arquey.' Mr Roy Shepherd states that this rose was found in France in 1912 and is known under the above synonym. It is a vigorous bushy plant, considerably wider in growth than others of these more typical varieties, with widely branching angular stems building up into a good bush, but sparsely leaved. The leaves are of a leaden green, and the flowers small, long-lasting, borne freely in angular clusters or singly. Each petal is fringed like those of a pink. In hot weather it is a rich maroon-crimson but in cooler weather nearer to pink, especially on the smaller very fringed central petals. It is fairly double with little fragrance. Young shoots and leaves are plum coloured. 4 feet by 4 feet. It cannot be described as a striking garden rose, but more of a curiosity with some value for small bouquets, like the Green Rose. It is not as perpetual as the other China Roses, but produces a few late flowers. The leaves and flower colour denote close affinity with R. *chinensis*.

'**Viridiflora**' (R. 'Monstrosa'). The 'Green Rose'. With similar growth to 'Old Blush', this is a free-flowering and otherwise normal plant but has all its floral parts transformed into greenish scales. The result is a beautiful oval bud, quite small, of soft blue-green, and at that stage it is acceptable. Unfortunately, on opening, it becomes loose and tawdry, splashed with brown, and cannot be called beautiful. 3 to 4 feet. It is a curiosity, and demonstrates the extraordinary variability found in the China Rose. Mr Shepherd records that it was in cultivation as early as 1743; Mr August Jäger states

'Bambridge and Harrison, 1856', but the late Mr Geoffrey Taylor sent me a cutting as follows: 'There is a note in Henry Bright's *Year in a Lancashire Garden*, 1879, quoting a letter to the *Gardeners' Chronicle* from a Mr Buist of the Rosedale Nurseries, Philadelphia: "There appears to be some uncertainty in regard to the origin of this rose. It is a sport from *Rosa indica* (the China Rose of England and Daily Rose of America). It was caught in Charleston, S.C., about 1833, and came to Baltimore through Mr R. Halliday, from whom I obtained it, and presented two plants to my old friend Thomas Rivers in 1837".' I have been unable to trace Mr Buist's letter.

Flore des Serres, 1856, vol. xi, Plate 1136.

Roses et Rosiers, Plate 19.

Journal des Roses, Septembre 1908.

Rosenzeitung, June 1908.

L'Horticulteur Français, 1856, Plate 19.

Apart from R. *chinensis mutabilis*, which may be derived partly from the Tea Rose, the above seven varieties are of almost pure China derivation. Now, reverting to Dr Hurst's 'four stud Chinas', we can pass to the second two (presuming that the first two gave rise to the pink and red varieties); they are 'Hume's Blush Tea-scented China' and 'Parks's Yellow Tea-scented China'. Both were derived from R. *chinensis* crossed with R. *gigantea*, the Tea Rose, and may have arisen in Chinese gardens hundreds of years prior to their introduction to England.

While it cannot be proved that the following, which are usually classed as China Roses, were derived directly from these two Chinese hybrids, it is more than likely; they are far removed from other classes of roses which were being raised at the time and certainly are near to the Chinas in growth and many other characteristics, while showing also the influence of the Tea Rose in their colour and scent.

They all make twiggy, bushy plants with coppery-tinted young shoots and leaves, and bear loosely semi-double flowers with limp silky petals. I find they have a splendid habit of producing three main bursts of bloom, the first at the end of May and through June; then, after a pause, another in August; while from mid September onwards they are continually in flower until winter comes. As Hybrid Teas and Floribundas flower most profusely in July and September the happy way in which these Chinas fill in and keep the colour going can be easily perceived. It is worth noting that the yellowish varieties among the following roses fade as they mature, and therefore are markedly different from the purer China Rose varieties.

'**Comtesse du Cayla**'. Guillot, 1902. Brilliant coral-flame, fading to salmon pink, with yellow-tinted reverses to the petals; tea and sweet-pea scent. Young shoots and foliage bloomy purple. 4 feet.

'**Fabvier**'. Laffay, 1832. 'Mme Fabvier' or 'Colonel Fabvier'. A short-growing variety approaching the form of a Polyantha Rose, but with typical China Rose stems, thorns, leaves, and lack of scent. The small flowers are borne singly or a few together, and have rather more than a single row of brilliant scarlet-crimson petals, often shewing a white streak. It is a gay little plant, always in flower, but it is difficult to fit into the garden. It would be admirable in small formal Victorian beds, or can be given a place in front of modern roses. Leaves richly tinted when young, turning to dark leaden green. Almost scentless. 18 inches.
Komlosy. Very good.
Choix des Plus Belles Roses, Plate 21. Very good.

'**Némésis**' is another miniature variety; see Chapter 12.

'**Le Vésuve**'. Laffay, 1825. 'Lemesle.' (Not to be confused with 'Vesuvius', a single crimson Hybrid Tea.) I found this rose many years ago in the garden at Ronans, Bracknell, Berkshire, and it was named for me by Courtney Page and Walter Easlea. It shews the noteworthy habit of the China Rose in the deepening colour of the fading flowers. In my light Surrey soil it has never been much more than pink with a few richer tones on the outer petals, but at Ronans the great old bush that I knew had reached 5 feet in height and the older flowers had turned to a warm coppery carmine. On opening it has a peculiarly soft, creamy tone of pink, not far removed from the Redouté portrait of 'Hume's Blush'. The sturdy, very thorny plant gradually builds up into a criss-cross of branches bearing elegant, pointed, rather grey-green leaves. The flowers are fully double, of tea-shape, with rolled petals and delicious soft tea-scent. It is constantly in flower. There was a climbing sport recorded in 1904.

Journal des Roses, Mai 1891. Misleadingly rich colouring.

Les Plus Belles Roses, Plate 92. A poor portrait, but shewing the typical colour of the mature flower.

'Madame Eugène Résal'. Guillot, 1894. Vivid nasturtium red with yellow base, quickly fading to pink. A sport from 'Mme Laurette Messimy'. 4 feet.

Journal des Roses, Avril 1895.

'Madame Laurette Messimy'. Guillot Fils, 1887. ('Laurette Messimy.') 'Rival de Paestum' × 'Mme Falcot'. Clear bright salmon-pink, shaded copper and yellow and with yellow base, fading to dull salmon-pink. Young shoots glaucous. 4 feet.

The Garden, 24 October 1891, p. 378. Very good.

'Purpurea'. Chenault, 1930. A small bush, with fairly typical leaves and growth for a China Rose; indeed the flowers and general appearance conform to this group. But I cannot help thinking it must have been hybridized with a Gallica or Bourbon to produce this rich, glowing, purplish crimson colour. I had this rose in the late 1940's but have lost it and would like to acquire it again. 18 inches.

Andrews, Plate 80. *R. indica purpurea*. As the plant I describe above was raised in 1930, this cannot refer, but the constant striving after a blue rose is still with us, even from those early days. Andrews wrote: 'The purple variety is said to have been first imported from China about the year 1810, to the gardens of Lord Milford, under the appellation of the Blue Rose. . . . This rose of expectation, when its blooms unfolded, no heavenly blue disclosed, but a red purple, which as it faded off became paler, less brilliant, but of a bluer or colder purple, which gives to the fresh-opened blossoms a very different appearance contrasted with those retiring; and although the blue's celestial tint is wanting, it is nevertheless a graceful and very abundant flowering rose.' The portrait shews a pink rose, slightly flushed with lilac!

'Rival de Paestum'. G. Paul, prior to 1848. Young shoots, thorns, and leaves rich glaucous plum colour. Long creamy buds are borne erect, but nod to open into loose, semi-double, ivory-white blooms. Gracious and floriferous. Slight tea-scent. 4 feet.

Three other roses are related to the China Rose and sometimes grouped with it:

' **Fellenburg** '. Omitted from this book as I consider it fits better with various Noisette Roses.

'Gloire des Rosomanes'. Vibert, 1825. A China × Bourbon hybrid. Used extensively in California as an understock, where it is called 'Ragged Robin', and also as a hedging rose, 'Red Robin'. An historic rose, and one of the founders of the Hybrid Perpetual Roses. Not of great garden value today. Large, double, crimson, fragrant flowers borne in large and small clusters. 4 feet.

Choix des Plus Belles Roses, Plate 12.

'Gruss an Teplitz', see Chapter 14.

11

Hybrid Perpetual Roses

He who would have beautiful roses in his garden must
have beautiful roses in his heart.

Dean Hole, A Book about Roses, 1870.

THE OLD saying about 'not eating our cake and having it' does not
apply, among roses, to the Bourbons and the Portland Roses. For
they give us the lovely colours, scents, floral style, and vigorous
growth of the Old Roses coupled with the perpetual flowering
habit of the China Rose. They were derived from an initial cross
between the old pink Autumn Damask (*Rosa damascena bifera* or
'Quatre Saisons', which is still in cultivation as it was in the days
of the Romans and before) and 'Parsons's Pink China'. It has been
supposed that the Autumn Damask descended ultimately from
Rosa gallica × *R. moschata*, but *R. gallica* has kept the Bourbons
small and compact, while in the Noisettes, without this influence,
the Musk and the Tea Rose together encouraged the Noisettes to
be climbers, and to develop yellow colouring which is absent in
the Bourbons.

The name Bourbon was given to the race because the first plant
was a chance seedling found on the Île de Bourbon (Île de
Réunion) in 1817, growing in close proximity to both its parents.
It became known as 'Rose Edward' in the adjacent island of
Mauritius. Seeds were sent to Paris and presumably the best one
raised was called 'Le Rosier de l'Île Bourbon'. The full story is
told by Dr Hurst in my book *The Old Shrub Roses*, page 82. In its
second generation it was named and distributed in France around
1823, reaching England about two years later. Dr Hurst writes:
'Mendelian segregation had given it a double dose of the China

gene for continuous flowering, and it was a beautiful semi-double Rose with brilliant rose-coloured flowers, and nearly evergreen foliage. From its Damask grandparent it inherited a delicious fragrance which was particularly marked in the late autumn months.'

For about forty-five years the Bourbon Roses were very important in rose gardens. They provided a welcome change from the solely summer-flowering roses, and also from the varieties known as Hybrid China Roses. These were similar crosses which were named and put into commerce in quantity although they only flowered once. Mendelian laws were not understood in those days and these by-blows were therefore tolerated and even encouraged.

In 1825 'Gloire des Rosomanes' appeared. It was the first really rich red rose, and must have been a great acquisition at the time. It became the chief ancestor of the red Hybrid Perpetuals and carried with it through the breeding the rich Damask fragrance inherited from its original forbear. Its colour was no doubt derived from its China parent.

It is sad that so few, so very few of the older Bourbons have come down to us. The oldest authentic recurrent variety we have is 'Souvenir de la Malmaison', which, Mr Shepherd records, was named in honoured memory of the Empress by the Grand Duke of Russia who was visiting La Malmaison. He was so taken by the flowers that he obtained a plant for the Imperial Garden at St Petersburg. This rose was in more ways than one a fitting variety to be so named; it was for those times a very large rose—the flowers of the climbing form cannot be surpassed in mere width by any rose today—it was moreover perpetual and a good grower. It shewed considerable Tea Rose influence and was a prolific parent, producing among others 'Gloire de Dijon'. At Hidcote and elsewhere it flowers exceptionally well in the autumn, and was originally a bush; the climbing sport did not occur until 1893.

It is, however, 'Louise Odier' (1851) which I like to think of as a good original type. Here we surely have an old Damask Rose transformed by the China into a vigorous bush, perpetual-flowering, with practically no Tea Rose in its being. Until I went carefully into dates I always felt that this, 'Champion of the World' (1894), 'La Reine Victoria' (1872), and 'Mme Pierre Oger' (1878), together with 'Reine des Violettes' (1860), were all much of a group—'Old Roses' with just that bit of China in them to enable them to satisfy those who must 'eat their cake and have it'. But they were only scattered appearances in the long chain of Bourbons which came and went from the catalogues during the nineteenth century.

One character remains constant in all the above roses, except 'La Reine Victoria' and its sport, and it is inherited from the Autumn Damask Rose and is noticeable in the Portland Roses too. It is the character to which I referred when discussing the latter in *The Old Shrub Roses*—the 'high-shouldered' effect of the flowering shoots. The length of stem between each leaf decreases noticeably towards the flower bud with the result that there is quite a frill of foliage immediately below the flower. This is particularly so in 'Reine des Violettes' and is also found in some of the Damask Mosses, which points to the same parentage.

Some of the other Bourbons such as 'Mme Isaac Pereire' and its sport are obviously approaching what we now look back upon as Hybrid Perpetuals. On the other hand 'Commandant Beaurepaire' presumably is an old type with few repeat blooms and the prickly growth of the Autumn Damask.

Now let us retrace our steps a little. In Italy, where the China Rose had been treated as a hardy plant long before it was trusted outside in England, various Old Roses grew and it is thought that a special seedling of brilliant red colouring arose in the neighbourhood of Paestum. Legend has it that the Duchess of Portland obtained it, brought it to England, where it was much treasured on account of its vivid colouring, and it became known as the 'Portland Rose', or *Rosa Paestana* from its supposed origin in Italy. Redouté has a good figure of it (Plate 109, vol. i). I had seen this rose for years in several collections (notably in Mrs Fleischmann's garden; and at Blickling Hall and Spetchley Park) without realizing until recently what it was. Dr Hurst considered that 'Slater's Crimson China' must have been involved on account of its brilliant colour and dwarf habit. This rose eventually went to France and from it was subsequently raised in 1816 the 'Rose du Roi', which became famous for its influence in breeding. In later times breeders looking back on this rose dubbed it the first Hybrid Perpetual.

And so the Bourbons and the H.P.s arose at approximately the same time and ran a fairly parallel course for many years. The non-perpetual seedlings raised from both these groups were, as I have said, very numerous and were called Hybrid Chinas, and a lot of them no doubt went right back to the Old Rose types such as 'Cardinal de Richelieu', 'Tour de Malakoff', and 'Paul Ricault', which have unusually smooth leaves for their floral type. Probably in many instances the Bourbons and Hybrid Perpetuals were inter-married and their characters became merged, but whereas produc-tion along Bourbon lines eventually ceased, the Hybrid Per-petuals soared ahead. They incorporated all the best traits available in the China Rose hybrids over fifty years or so, to emerge later as a recognizable race. They took their place in horticultural history as the first race of roses to appear in quantity yearly from different raisers. The selection in those days, when the characters and colours were considerably limited and no National Rose Society Trials were held, must have been much more diffi-cult than now, when the same state has been reached by later groups.

By about 1845 the H.P.s had fairly come into their own, with large flowers and ever more brilliant colourings. Raisers had acquired enough knowledge to produce really repeat-flowering plants. Some had long flowering periods; others merely gave a few flowers in the autumn. 'Few resume their former glory in autumn', said Dean Hole in 1870. None that I grow today can really be called perpetual, i.e. flowering throughout the summer and into the autumn, and on the whole I think the French gave a better title to this group than we did: they called them Hybride Remontant, changing to this from 'Damas Perpetuelle'. William Paul states that his own breeding of Hybrid Perpetuals started with seedlings from the purplish 'Princesse Hélène', which itself was 'the first strongly marked divergence from the Damask Perpetuals from which it sprang'. In three years he had twenty varieties from its seed. This was in 1837. In 1863 he says 'now the number is legion and they take the same place in gardens as the French roses did twenty-five years ago'. By 1869 he was com-plaining of loss of vigour among the newer roses, no doubt due to too much China and Tea influence.

Until about the end of the century the H.P.s were all-powerful. Books and catalogues teem with names. In 1859 'Victor Verdier' appeared, and this has sometimes been called the first Hybrid Tea. From this and 'La France', raised in 1867, a small group of varieties was raised, carrying strong Tea influence into the Hybrid Perpetuals. 'La France' was H.P. 'Mme Victor Verdier' × Tea 'Mme Bravy'. By the turn of the century new roses called Hybrid Teas had taken command and the power of the Hybrid Perpetuals was broken.

Today there are very few of the thousands of H.P.s still in cultivation and perhaps it is as well, for many were undoubtedly only fit for the bonfire. George Paul, writing in the Royal Horticultural Society's *Journal* for 1896, emphasizes this: 'I will not weary you with the earlier H.P.s. They played their part and do not want recalling.' Even in 1890 the term 'Garden Roses' was used to designate the Gallicas and their relatives; so many Hybrid Perpetuals were fit for nothing but the greenhouse and show bench. Dean Hole and the Rev. Foster-Melliar mentioned this failing. ' Rose du Roi ', an original crimson hybrid originated in France in 1815, but was called ' Lee's Crimson Perpetual ' over here; ' Rose du Roi à fleur pourpre ' occurred in 1819. The next oldest to come down to us is ' Baronne Prévost ' (1839), and in 1852 the still famous ' Général Jacqueminot ' appeared, descended from the Bourbon ' Gloire des Rosomanes '; the Général ushered in a wonderful race of vivid red colouring. It is sad and inexplicable to me how such a famous pink rose as ' La Reine '·(1842) can have disappeared. In its heyday it was in every catalogue and its portrait was in every book. Perhaps it may yet be retrieved. It was figured in *Choix des Plus Belles Roses*, Plate 13, and in the *Journal des Roses*, Mars 1880.

It must have puzzled many why most of the rose names of the nineteenth century were French, for by that time the rose was well established as the English national emblem. Mrs Gore, in *The Rose Fancier's Manual*, 1838, makes the matter clear. 'The high price of fuel [in France] places the cultivation of the tender exotics (by which English amateurs are chiefly engrossed) almost out of the question; and as the French adhere to the wise custom of repairing to their country seats in May and quitting them in December, their attention and money are appropriated to the improvement of such plants as adorn the flower garden during the summer season. They care little for any that cannot be brought to perfection in the open air; and precisely the same motive which promotes the cultivation of the dahlia in England has brought the rose to greater perfection in France. The extent of importation is, however, a convincing proof that though the more opulent classes of our countrymen are induced to pass the midsummer days of the rose season in London, a sufficient number of amateurs remain in the country' [for the promotion of rose-growing]. The French at that time had a highly organized horticultural department. Mrs Gore adds that 'The Chamber of Peers . . . have lately rendered the rose school of the Luxembourg nursery secondary [only] to the school of vines'. The word in brackets is mine.

'Alfred Colomb'. Lacharme, 1865. A seedling from 'Général Jacqueminot'. A bushy, vigorous plant, leafy and producing a few autumn flowers. Flowers are globular when open, fully double, rich scarlet crimson with darker shadings and fading slightly towards purple. Very fragrant. Also known as 'Marshall P. Wilder'. There was a climbing sport in 1930. 4 to 5 feet. Hariot, Plate 19.

'Archiduchesse Élisabeth d'Autriche'. Robert et Moreau, 1881. Having grown 'Vick's Caprice' (often mis-spelt 'Wick's') for several years, a gift from Will Tillotson, I was disappointed to find it reverting to a lilac-pink rose, without the stripes. However, judge of my delight when I came across its portrait in the *Journal des Roses*, with the statement that it occurred in Mr Vick's garden in 1892, on a bush of 'Archiduchesse Élisabeth d'Autriche'. Thus was the name of this plain pink rose found; it is exactly like Vick's striped form, q.v., except in colour. Bushy, about 3 to 4 feet.

'Baron Girod de l'Ain'. Reverchon, 1897. It recurred in 1901 and was provisionally christened 'Royal Mondain'. By a strange coincidence I have this rose growing next to 'Eugène Fürst' and had noticed the similarity in everything except colour. And then, browsing through the *Journal des Roses*, I found a plate of the Baron's Rose, with a note that it was 'a sport from Eugène Fürst'. By such chances are we able to check nomenclature; the statement proves that both roses are correctly named—which is something one can never be too sure about with these ancient varieties. The 'Baron' is a fine upstanding bush with green wood and few prickles, bearing broad, rounded leaves, and is constantly in production in the summer, sparingly so in autumn. The flowers are a bright, true crimson, with white deckle edges; less richly coloured and marked than the better known 'Roger Lambelin' but a better grower. It has a pretty habit of retaining most of the petals in cup-formation and reflexing the outer ones; at that stage it is exceptionally handsome. 5 feet. (Photograph, Plate 5.)

Journal des Roses, Mars 1906. Very poor portrait.

Gault and Synge, plate 106.

'Baronne Prévost'. Desprez, 1842. 'Flowers clear, pale rose, glossy, very large and full; form, compact. Habit, erect; growth, robust. A superb kind. Raised by M. Desprez of Yèbles. One of the largest.' Thus William Paul catalogued this famous and unique rose in 1848. Like many another it was available in the United States and reached me from Will Tillotson, but it appeared to be extinct over here. It has grown well and is a free-flowerer and, being so very early in the Hybrid Perpetual tradition, retains the Old Rose form: the flat, wide bloom, the quartering and button eye which are so appealing. The blooms are often 4 inches across, of rich pink suffused lilac, produced throughout summer and autumn. I see no reason why it should not go on for another hundred years. 4 to 5 feet. There was a striped sport, carmine on bright rose, called 'Baronne Prévost Marbrée' (recorded in *The Florist and Pomologist*). Not seen, but I record it here in case it occurs again.

Curtis, vol. ii, Plate 9. Poor portrait.

Jamain and Forney, Plate 25. Poor portrait.

Journal des Roses, Octobre, 1879.

'Emotion'. There were two roses of this name, one raised by Guillot in 1862 and another raised by Fontaine in 1879 with a synonym 'Alice Fontaine'. I think mine is the latter, but the two were similar. Both were classed as Bourbons, though the growth of my plants is not as free as that of others in this group, but more nearly approximates that of an H.P. Has beautiful, well-formed flowers, opening from tight buds, cupped, reflexed, quartered, well filled with crinkled petals of flesh pink, becoming paler with age. The pale colour of the foliage makes a pleasing complement. Perhaps 4 feet.

'Empereur du Maroc'. Bertrand-Guinoisseau, 1858. A hybrid of 'Géant des Batailles'. At first sight this might be considered a weakling, with its small dark leaves and growth resembling an old Hybrid Tea, but it is a healthy, free-flowering plant. It is of historic interest, being as far as I can ascertain the first really dark red with no purple shadings. It is of intense dark carmine with velvety maroon flush, and no doubt inherits its rather spindly growth and gorgeous colouring from 'Slater's Crimson China' somewhere back in its pedigree. No Gallica is richer than 'Duc de Guiche' and no reliable rose had apparently been raised among Bourbons, Hybrid Chinas, and Hybrid Perpetuals of such magnificent colouring. Its petals are small, often quilled and quartered, arranged in flat array. Intense fragrance. 4 feet.

'Erinnerung an Brod'. Geschwind, 1886. 'Souvenir de Brod.' Brod is a town in Bosnia. Supposed to be a hybrid between R. *rubifolia* (R. *setigera*) and 'Génie de Châteaubriand'. I think it doubtful whether there is really any R. *setigera* in its parentage, and it is a fairly typical Hybrid Perpetual. Double flowers, of Old Rose style, quartered, pleated, opening flat, and with green pointel; any shade from cerise-pink to dark crimson-purple is found in each flower. Good, Old Rose fragrance. Vigorous, reaching 8 feet.
Journal des Roses, Octobre 1907. A fine plate.

'Eugène Fürst'. Soupert et Notting, 1875. 'Général Korolkov.' The original from which 'Baron Girod de l'Ain' sported in 1897, and of equal vigour and general garden value, making a good plant with good foliage. The short-petalled flowers are well-formed, cupped, with outer petals soon reflexing, and of intense carmine flushed with maroon, rich and velvety; reverses paler. Delicious fragrance. A hybrid of 'Baron de Bonstetten'. 5 feet.
Journal des Roses, Avril 1883.

'Ferdinand Pichard'. Tanne, 1921. I have been unable to ascertain whether this was raised from seed or occurred as a sport. A valuable repeat-flowering striped rose, which is supposed to be a Hybrid Perpetual, but as it is obviously closely related to 'Commandant Beaurepaire' I have dealt with it in my supplementary chapter in the 1961 revised edition of *The Old Shrub Roses*.

'Fisher Holmes'. Verdier, 1865. A hybrid of 'Maurice Bernardin'. A splendid old variety which I found at Kew, with a whole bed devoted to it. It is hard to beat as one of the better Hybrid Perpetuals, with its vigorous growth, good leaves, and recurrent blooms of velvety rich scarlet-lake, heavily shaded crimson, and borne on strong stalks. Good scent. William Paul placed 'Fisher Holmes' among his best twenty-five in 1868. 5 feet.

'Frau Karl Druschki'. Lambert, 1901. 'Reine des Neiges', 'Snow Queen', 'White American Beauty'. This has always been an indispensable white rose but its name has been against it, and thus names more euphonious to other tongues have been coined. Had it always been known as 'Schneekoenigin' ('Snow Queen') as was originally proposed, its popularity would have increased greatly. In many ways it is the most beautiful white rose ever raised, but lacks scent. It is a vigorous bush with good but coarse, light-green leaves and erect growth. Every stout shoot bears one or more superb high-centred blooms through the summer, with elegantly rolled petals; they are of purest white with a lemon flush at the heart and more or less carmine-tinted on the bud. 5 to 6 feet.

It has an interesting pedigree. On the seed-bearing side it probably owes existence far back to *R. centifolia* through 'La Reine'. Seed from this famous large silvery pink gave the blush 'Souvenir de la Reine d'Angleterre', and two progressively whiter sports produced 'Merveille de Lyon', which, crossed with 'Mme Caroline Testout', produced the 'Frau'. 'Mme Caroline Testout' was the result of 'Mme de Tartas', a Tea, crossed with 'Lady Mary Fitzwilliam', which again has a Tea ('Devoniensis') in its parentage together with a Hybrid Perpetual ('Victor Verdier'). Thus 'Frau Karl Druschki' is not a Hybrid Perpetual but a Hybrid Tea, but in general appearance it certainly conforms fairly well to our present group.

It is a wonderful rose for colour schemes in the garden or in the house, and its long, strong stems make it ideal for cutting and grouping with similar roses such as 'Conrad F. Meyer' and 'Mrs John Laing'.

Darlington, p. 138.

McFarland, *Roses of the World*, p. 87.

Journal des Roses, Août 1902.

Hoffmann, Plate 20.

'Général Jacqueminot'. Roussel, 1853. Possibly a hybrid between 'Gloire des Rosomanes' and 'Géant des Batailles'. Be this as it may, at its time of introduction this was a brilliant red rose. Nowadays I feel it is outclassed in form and colour. Rich crimson flowers, fully double, large and cabbagy, very fragrant, borne on good stems. The bush is vigorous with good, fresh green foliage. The main display is in the summer with a few blooms later. A famous plant and ancestor of 'Liberty', 'Richmond', 'Étoile de Holland', 'Crimson Glory', etc. Reaches 6 feet on good soils. Synonyms: 'La Brillante', 'Richard Smith', 'Triomphe d'Amiens', and 'Mrs Cleveland'.

McFarland, *Roses of the World*, p. 92.

Komlosy. Too dark.

Jamain and Forney, Plate 60. Fanciful.

Niedtner, p. 256.

'Georg Arends'. Hinner, 1910. 'Frau Karl Druschki' × 'La France'. In view of the parentage this should be classed as a Hybrid Tea. If it had been I think it would have been more often grown; Hybrid Perpetuals have a way of being neglected. For a Hybrid Tea it is a little on the coarse side, while as a Hybrid Perpetual it is of superlative beauty. I cannot improve on the description in my *Manual of Shrub Roses*: 'No other pink rose raised before or since has flowers of similar beauty; each petal rolls back in a beautiful way, and the flower, from the scrolled bud to the blown bloom, retains its clear strawberry-ice pink; the cream is mixed in the reverse of the petals. "Druschki" growth and foliage. Delicious scent.' Nearly thornless. 5 feet.

'Gloire de Chédane Guinoisseau'. Chédane and Pajotin, 1907.

A hybrid of 'Gloire de Ducher'. An extra handsome and vigorous variety with dull, dark-green leaves. The blooms are large, full, well-shaped, of very bright crimson-red, and are produced freely at midsummer, with a few later: sweetly scented. 5 to 6 feet.

'Gloire de Ducher'. Ducher, 1865. 'Germania.' A lanky grower best trained on a wall or pillar, or supported by other shrubs or pegged down. Apart from the summer flowers on side-shoots, great autumnal blooms are produced at the ends of vigorous new wood. They are of large size, rich and velvety, dark crimson-purple, with maroon shadings; some petals are quilled and folded, and there is usually a button eye, revealing the paler reverses of the petals. Well clothed in good foliage. 7 feet. Very fragrant. One of several good roses that were preserved by the late Mrs Constance Spry during the Second World War.
Jamain and Forney, Plate 43. Very poor.
Journal des Roses, Juillet 1881. Rather gross.

'Glory of Steinforth'. See 'Ruhm von Steinfurth'.

'Henry Nevard'. F. Cant, 1924. A good dark-red, full, shapely, very fragrant rose, with sturdy, erect growth and large, leathery, dark-green leaves. A handsome plant and flower. 4 to 5 feet.

'Hugh Dickson'. H. Dickson, 1905. Descended from 'Gruss an Teplitz', which is no doubt the source of its good colouring. An extraordinarily vigorous plant, for which reason people sometimes ask for 'Climbing Hugh Dickson'; a climbing sport was announced in California in 1914 but I have not seen it. However, the bush form has no difficulty in reaching 10 feet in good soil. Unfortunately these long shoots, which are exceptionally well clothed in bright-green leaves, unless pegged down flower only at their extremities. The flowers may be in clusters and should be disbudded; they are large, fully double, well shaped and high centred, of brilliant scarlet crimson, fairly fragrant. Its vigour is against it, but when suitably trained can give a magnificent show.
Darlington, Frontispiece.

'**John Hopper**'. Ward, 1862. 'Jules Margottin' × 'Mme Vidot'. Extra double flowers in the old style; well-serried ranks of rolled petals, but rather loose; vivid cerise-pink to light crimson, with mauve sheen on fading. Very fragrant. A vigorous healthy plant, bearing erect thorny wood with refined foliage. A few blooms in autumn. 5 feet. A real old 'cabbage' in its usually understood sense.
Floral Magazine, 1862, vol. ii, Plate 110.
Journal des Roses, Mai 1881.
Hariot, Plate 38. Magnificent.

'**Jules Margottin**'. Margottin, 1853. A great parent in the past, but not of much account now, as it is a coarse, thorny plant, and is not truly perpetual, nor very decisive in its colour. Extra double flowers, opening flat and somewhat quartered, of carmine rose. Not very fragrant. 6 feet.
Hariot, Plate 40. Very fine.
L'Horticulteur Français, 1853, Plate 18. Too bright.
Journal des Roses, Décembre 1880.

'**Mabel Morrison**'. 1878. Reported to be a sport from 'Baroness Rothschild', which was a sport from 'Souvenir de la Reine d'Angleterre'. Though classed as a Hybrid Perpetual it more closely resembles a Portland Rose, and I have accordingly included it in the 1961 edition of *The Old Shrub Roses*.
Jekyll ('White Baroness'), between pages 106 & 107.

'**Madame Gabriel Luizet**'. Liabaud, 1877. A hybrid of 'Jules Margottin'; vigorous, but not very recurrent. Large double blooms of bright silvery pink, paler at the edges and inclined to be cupped. Fragrant. 5 to 6 feet.

'**Marie Baumann**'. Baumann, 1863. 'Général Jacqueminot' × 'Victor Verdier'. I have not seen this rose, but it is occasionally listed. A globular carmine-red variety, vigorous.
The Garden, 1883, vol. i, Plate 516.
Hariot, Plate 50.

'**Mrs John Laing**'. Bennett, 1887. Ancestry includes 'La Reine'. Hundreds of pink roses have been raised and named since the appearance of this, but none has that bland, old-world, uniform tone of pink with its faint lilac flush. Nor have many roses so excellent a constitution, which enables it to thrive in poor sandy soils and to excel in good soils, where its upright habit and stiff flower-stalks provide some of the best blooms anyone could want on plants up to 6 feet. The flowers are large, fully double, with high outer petals, rather shorter within, opening from an exquisite bud to a well-filled cupped flower. It is one of the most satisfying roses to grow and cut, and has a glorious scent. Foliage plentiful, of soft, light green, dull and smooth. Nearly thornless. For one who was brought up smelling this rose—and even complaining of its ubiquity in a small garden—this is a conservative estimate of its attractions. Dean Hole was much more lavish: 'Not only in vigour, constancy, and abundance, but in form and features, Beauty's Queen.'

Darlington, p. 40. Shews the typical deeper colouring on the outer petals.

Journal des Roses, Mars 1914. Poor.

'**Paul Neyron**'. Levet, 1869. 'Victor Verdier' × 'Anna de Diesbach'. Another descendant of 'La Reine' and an extra vigorous plant up to 6 feet, with copious, large, glossy foliage in mid green. The stiff shoots bear truly enormous flowers rather like 'Peace' in size and shape, but flatter, sometimes quartered and more filled with petals; deep rosy pink with lilac flush, paler on the reverse. Of no special ornament in the garden, and of no attraction to the nose, but a luxury to cut. Big peonies are larger, but they are over by the time the rose appears, and it is remontant. Few thorns.

Jamain and Forney, Plate 19. Small and poor.

McFarland, *Roses of the World*, p. 204.

Illustrirte Rosengarten. A poor portrait and too dark.

Journal des Roses, Septembre 1877.

In the *Revue Horticole*, 1898, p. 288, is an astounding portrait entitled 'Panachée de Bordeaux', with the statement that M. Abel Chatenay considered this to be a sport of 'Paul Neyron'; I wish it would occur again.

'**Prince Camille de Rohan**'. E. Verdier, 1861. 'La Rosière', 'Souvenir d'Auguste Rivoire', 'Edouard Dufour'. Descended through 'Maurice Bernardin' from 'Général Jacqueminot'.

'Although not a full rose, possesses the qualities of distinctness in an eminent degree; the flowers are dark velvety maroon, shaded towards the circumference with blood red: it is not more than average size, but the colour is exceedingly rich and beautiful.' So wrote William Paul in 1863. I find it has a weak flower stem, but a bushy branching habit unlike many other H.P.s, and on good soils it is a splendid leafy bush. 'Roger Lambelin' is a sport from it. Prolific in flower through summer and again in autumn. 4 feet.
Hariot, Plate 55. Good.
Komlosy.

'Reine des Violettes'. Millet-Malet, 1860. Although this is always classed as a Hybrid Perpetual it has little connection with their accepted style. First, it makes a large graceful bush, often as wide as high, well covered with leaden-green leaves of smooth texture, and having the 'high-shouldered' effect under the blooms that I connect with the Autumn Damasks. Second, the blooms have the flat 'expanded' shape of the old Gallica Roses, well filled with rolled and quartered petals, and with button eye. Third, it partakes more nearly of the Old Rose mauve colouring than any other which I have seen having China parentage. There is nothing like it; it is the apotheosis of the Old Roses, with an invaluable habit of flowering through the summer and again, freely, in the autumn. On half opening to a deep cup from unpropitious buds, the blooms are of dark, soft grape purple. The next day they open widely and are paler but with still rich colouring; later they fade to softest parma violet, and at all times in the open flower the velvety upper surface contrasts with the lighter silky reverse of the petals. This is a rose to be treasured for all time. It needs a rich soil. 6 feet by 5 feet. (Plate II.)

'Roger Lambelin'. Schwartz, 1890. It occasionally sports back to its parent 'Prince Camille de Rohan' and, like the Prince, has a weak stalk and is only a success on good soils. I have seen bushes 5 feet high and wide, full of foliage and bloom on good soil as at Bayfordbury, but more often than not it is stunted and cankerous. And a poor flower is not worth having when one compares it with a first-class bloom; then the fairly full effect is of crimson-purple velvet of gorgeous quality, deckle-edged with white. As the blooms fade the crimson turns to maroon crimson. Much more bizarre than 'Baron Girod de l'Ain' but less sure. Very fragrant. McFarland, *Roses of the World*, p. 231. Rather fewer petals than normal. *Journal des Roses*, Mai 1895.

'Rose du Roi à Fleur Pourpre'. 1819. 'Mogador.' A sport from 'Rose du Roi', which was a descendant from the Autumn Damask through the Portland Rose, and is generally looked upon as the first of the Hybrid Perpetual Roses. It has not grown very high with me, but produces fairly constantly medium-sized blooms with surprisingly high centres for its period. They are shapely, of richest vinous crimson, fading to a wonderful purple tone in good conditions. Richly scented, small leaves. 3 feet. It was a gift, an heirloom, from Mr George Salmon of Dundrum; and the bloom he showed me was as remarkable as any I have seen.

Writing in 1950, Mr Salmon recorded that his mother obtained the stock from an old garden in Northern Ireland in 1893, and that he had never seen the variety elsewhere. He found it more or less perpetual.

The original 'Rose du Roi' was raised at Sèvres in 1819 and is figured in Jamain and Forney, Plate 58, shewing the typical 'high-shouldered' effect, with the top leaf immediately under the flower.

'Ruhm von Steinfurth'. Weigand, 1920. 'Red Druschki.' 'Frau Karl Druschki' × 'General McArthur'. A fine strong-growing rose with flowers similar to 'Mrs John Laing' but larger and more richly coloured. For some reason it has never found favour although it is really a Hybrid Tea. It certainly resembles the Hybrid Perpetuals and so I take the liberty of including it here. 4 to 5 feet.

'Souvenir d'Alphonse Lavallée'. Charles Verdier, 1884. A tall grower, with rather sparse, small foliage of mid green. Extra double blooms of beautiful shape, small, velvety, of intense dark maroon-crimson, with no hint of purple, but almost black shadings. The intensity of colouring in a half-open bloom is amazing. Very sweetly scented. Few thorns. It is a rose for good soils, where it will make strong shoots up to 7 feet or so; when these are pegged down, bearing blooms along their entire length, none can resist it, whether they are lovers of old or new roses.

Journal des Roses, Février 1901. Rather light in colour.

'Souvenir de Brod'. See 'Erinnerung an Brod'.

'Souvenir du Docteur Jamain'. 1865. 'Général Jacqueminot' × 'Charles Lefèbvre'. A somewhat temperamental plant needing good soil and an aspect away from the sun, or at least facing west, for the petals 'burn' and turn brown in hot sunshine. But it is worth all trouble to get those matchless, velvety, dark wine-coloured blooms clouded over with maroon-purple. Very fragrant, and flowers again in autumn. We owe the preservation of this remarkable rose to the Hon. V. Sackville-West, who found it at Hollamby's Nurseries, Groombridge, and generously distributed it. A great success on good soils, where it will attain 10 feet on a wall.

'Triomphe de l'Exposition'. Margottin, 1855. The foliage is pointed, dark green; the young leaves are yellowish. An attractive flower, well filled with petals, button-eyed, and quartered, opening fairly flat; light carmine-crimson with deeper shadings. An old type of rose, sweetly scented. 5 feet.

Journal des Roses, Mai 1884.

'Ulrich Brunner Fils'. Levet, 1882. One of the lusty, upright, smooth-leaved ordinary Hybrid Perpetuals, carrying rather vulgar, light-crimson, vivid cerise, or rosy-red flowers, flushed lilac. Rich fragrance. Often has foliaceous sepals. 8 feet. August Jäger says it is a seedling of 'Anna de Diesbach' but Max Singer states: 'issue de "Paul Neyron".'

McFarland, *Roses of the World*, p. 275. Rather dark.

Kingsley, p. 115. Very good.

Journal des Roses, Juillet 1888. A flattering colour.

Leroy, Plate 3.

'Vick's Caprice'. 1897. A sport from 'Archiduchesse (or

Impératrice) Élisabeth d'Autriche' which occurred in Mr Vick's garden at Rochester, New York. Its chief claim to preservation is that it freely produces soft 'old-rose'-pink flowers striped and flecked variously with white or palest pink, from dark-red buds. The blooms are fully double, like those of 'Mrs John Laing', but with shorter petals and shorter stalks, and very fragrant, produced on a compact leafy plant. Few thorns. Inclined to 'ball'. 3 to 4 feet.

Journal des Roses, Mars 1898. Flowers very good.

Gault and Synge, plate 117.

———

'La France'. Henderson 1893. There are many good portraits of this famous rose:-

Niedtner, Plate 96.

Hariot, Plate 41.

Journal des Roses, Mars, 1879.

Les Plus Belles Roses, p. 76.

Hoffmann, Plate 9.

Bois and Trechslin, Plate 5.

12

Poly-poms—an Interlude

Drest in your gown of blue brocade,
A rose upon each dainty shoe,
Lady in loveliness arrayed,
I'd love to dance with you.

Helen Taylor, 'To a Miniature'.

WHEN I started this book it did not occur to me that I should need to write a chapter, even though a short one, on the Poly-poms, or Dwarf Polyanthas, in order to complete it. It is yet a little early, I am told by Floribunda devotees, to make a song about the 'neglected Poly-poms' and dub them 'old fashioned' or 'dwarf shrubs', in order to find a corner for them in my collection. 'And', they might well add, 'be their last champion!' Writers of today about modern roses ignore them: they are overshadowed by the triumphant Floribundas, and nobody grows them. But are they outclassed? For continuous colour-giving coupled with a short growth they have never been surpassed. Their undoing has been brought about by their small scentless flowers, in the same way that their parent 'Crimson Rambler' and its breed have lost popularity among climbers. A rose must have a 'soul' if it is to survive, and to my mind these have none. Yet we have only to go to Blickling Hall, a National Trust garden in Norfolk, to find 'Locarno' (1926) and 'Paul Crampel' (1930) in a mixed planting creating as good a show of colour as could be desired. The plants sport back and forth, and a kaleidoscope of tints combines to give a richness that could not otherwise be achieved, and is just what is desired to offset the neighbouring beds of brightly coloured yellow and red herbaceous plants. Just occasionally, then, I find these dwarf roses are exactly right for certain schemes, and I hope that such as 'Cameo', 'Ideal', 'Yvonne Rabier', 'Paul Crampel', and several of the others may survive into the future.

But they cannot be called 'Shrub Roses', and I must now make some excuse for this chapter. The excuse is that the Poly-poms include a very few varieties which are exquisite and small (not weak) and need championing, and one of which needs a deal of clarifying. These few are outlying roses, we may say, on the fringe of the Poly-poms, but not really belonging to them, and as there is nothing like them in the world of horticulture, I feel that my excuse will be accepted. Nobody who has contemplated 'Cécile Brunner' could possibly let it become lost, and this is only one of them.

The first two Poly-poms were sister seedlings, the second generation from a hybrid between the Japanese R. *multiflora* and a Chinese Rose, as recorded by Dr Hurst; they were 'Paquerette' and 'Mignonette', and appeared in 1873, being distributed in 1875 and 1881 respectively. It is possible that the China Rose was the Dwarf Pink China which we now call R. *chinensis* ' Minima ' or ' Lawranceana ', and which had been raised in England in 1805 and is reputed to be R. *chinensis* × R. *gigantea*. So that ' Paquerette ' and ' Mignonette ' carried great potentiality in their parentage, and indeed the latter was the parent of many famous Poly-poms through several well known varieties; among them was 'Mme Norbert Levavasseur', whose name is always cropping up in rose ancestry. Since pinks and whites came apparently easily it is not surprising that a Tea Rose was pressed again into service in order to achieve yellow, having regard to what had happened in other, older groups of roses.

'Mme Falcot', a large double nankeen-yellow Tea, was therefore used for crossing one of the seedling Poly-poms, or R. *multiflora* itself, and 'Perle d'Or', the result, appeared in 1884. A pink Tea, 'Mme de Tartas', was used on a Poly-pom, and 'Cécile Brunner' was named in 1881. Thus 'Cécile Brunner' can claim to be the first Tea-Poly-pom, and after about eighty years of useful life is in danger of slipping quietly away. Instead of being allowed to go, others should be raised until we have a whole race of these quintessential varieties, which have never been surpassed, nor have they any rivals, because there is nothing like them except one extraordinary chance hybrid, 'Bloomfield Abundance'. They are small to medium bushes, quite healthy and vigorous, incessantly in flower, and every flower is a perfect miniature of a Covent Garden bloom of 'Lady Sylvia' or 'Mme Butterfly', with the same perfection of scrolled and sculptured bud and yet of a size to go into a thimble. Anything more finished, fragrant, and dainty, for buttonholes, corsages, and small sprays could not be imagined.

These are not roses for park bedding. They do not provide enough colour. But in small beds they are most attractive, especially where the scale of the rose garden is comparatively small, as at Abbotswood. There both 'Cécile Brunner' and 'Perle d'Or' achieve a high degree of continuity and are always admired. Is there not here a pointer: in the smaller garden of today does not the smaller flower, provided it is well-turned, have a new value? And is it too much to hope, therefore, that we may even yet have a race of these miniatures in all colours, including silvery mauve and maroon, white and orange and crimson, for the delight of what undoubtedly would be a large admiring public? The only good newcomer is 'Jenny Wren', a hybrid of 'Cécile Brunner', but, alas, considerably larger.

Here I must add a further paragraph to explain the difference between these roses and the tiny Lawranceanas that have been raised in such quantity during the last twenty years or more. The roses I am writing about are stalwart bushes, reaching to 2–4 feet, but with sprays of miniature blooms, and fit for general garden use; not fussy little pieces, to be set about with miniature rockeries, imitation lawns, trees, and gnomes. I leave these roses where they are most suited, in the greenhouse and on the show table.

'Cécile Brunner'. Ducher, 1881. A seedling Poly-pom × 'Mme de Tartas' (a pink Tea). Also called 'Mignon' (not 'Mignonette'), 'Mme Cécile Brunner', or 'The Sweetheart Rose' not 'Sweetheart', a climber). A small-wooded H.T. with small, dark-green, rather shiny leaves, and very few thorns. The tallest plants I have seen were about 4 feet in height, but it is usually nearer to 2 feet. Besides the small, leafy side-shoots, each bearing one bloom, it throws up, particularly in late summer, sturdy shoots bearing branching heads (not in an elongated panicle) containing up to about 12 blooms. These shoots are devoid of thorns. It should be noted that they are smooth, devoid of bracts, and that the calyx is short and *never extends into a leafy lobe* beyond the bud. The blooms are of beautiful Hybrid Tea shape, but less than two inches across when fully expanded, clear, pale silvery pink, warmer in the centre. It is constantly in flower and is the most shapely of all these little beauties (Fig. 7).

Journal des Roses, Février 1885.

Rosenzeitung, September 1886. ' Mme Cécile Brunner '; enlarged.

Trechslin & Coggiatti.

The late Mr Murray Hornibrook told me he had a lemon-white sport of 'Cécile Brunner' growing in his garden in France, and fortunately managed to send me material before he died. There is a climbing form, ' Climbing Cécile Brunner ', which is not so constantly in flower, and has been known as ' Fiteni's Maltese Rose ' and ' Climbing Bloomfield Abundance '.

'Mme Jules Thibaud'. A sport from 'Cécile Brunner' very near to it, but of peach colour rather than pink. I have been unable to trace its origin.

'Perle d'Or'. Dubreuil, 1883. R. *multiflora* (or dwarf form or hybrid) × 'Mme Falcot', a yellow Tea Rose. This is a more vigorous, leafy plant than 'Cécile Brunner', and old plants achieve 4 feet in height and width. I have seen particularly good ones in Cambridge Botanic Garden and in Walberswick churchyard, Suffolk. The wood is rather more thorny and more stout, the leaves rather richer in colour, the flower-heads have stouter stalks and more, larger flowers with more petals. In shape this rose does not quite equal 'Cécile Brunner' although it is exceedingly good. The buds have not quite the H.T. perfection of outline and the inner petals, of which there are many, are narrow and often folded. In colour the young bud is rich, warm yolk orange opening to a paler salmon shade heavily mixed with cream. Deliciously scented. The colour and the narrow central petals are the main distinguishing features from 'Cécile Brunner'.

Journal des Roses, Septembre 1887. Poor.
Rosenzeitung, January 1887. ' Perle d'Or ' and others. Poor.
Kingsley, p. 129.
Trechslin and Coggiatti.

'Bloomfield Abundance'. George C. Thomas, 1920. A hybrid
between 'Sylvia' (a hybrid Wichuraiana raised in 1912) and
'Dorothy Page Roberts'. Owing to its parentage this rose might
be classed with the Hybrid Musks, but its close resemblance to
'Cécile Brunner' makes its inclusion here imperative. There is
much confusion between them. The smallness of the flower
is no doubt inherited from 'Sylvia', while its shape is Hybrid
Tea.

'Bloomfield Abundance' as a young, or starved, plant, is much
like 'Cécile Brunner'; the flowers have less colour in a less-
filled centre, but have larger outer petals. The same beauty of
bud is apparent. When established the plant will throw up great
summer shoots perhaps 6 feet high, without leaves except on
the main stem; the wiry side branches are devoid of leaves but
have a few bracts, and make wonderful airy panicles, with one
flower at every extremity. The panicle may be 2 feet long and
1 foot wide, with perhaps two or three dozen flowers. There is
nothing like it. Apart from these airy sprays, flowers are
produced singly and in clusters from every old shoot, and the
plant on good soil can build itself up into a leafy bush 7 feet by
7 feet or more. Every flower has one or more calyx-lobes
elongated into a leafy blade beyond the bud, and these and the
airy sprays at once distinguish it from 'Cécile Brunner', with
which it is often confused. It is a thrifty garden plant and makes
a remarkable effect in the late summer months.

Huge bushes of 'Cécile Brunner' described by enthusiastic
cultivators always turn out to be 'Bloomfield Abundance'.
Both can be readily propagated by cuttings, and when a small
plant of 'Bloomfield Abundance' changes hands and is without
a name it is natural that someone should recognize it as 'Cécile
Brunner'.

Who knows but that 'Cécile' may be in the parentage of
'Abundance'? It is possible, but at any rate they are totally
distinct roses when grown well. I have been told that 'Abun-

dance' was a sport from 'Cécile'; that it actually occurred again in So-and-so's garden, but how sure are we that the original in that garden *was* 'Cécile'? The parentage is given boldly in McFarland, *Modern Roses*, and I think we must leave it at that until convincing proof occurs in contradiction. (Fig. 6.) See also page 151.

Though they are not related to the above roses, and not strictly Polypoms, I feel this is the place to mention the following:

'Clothilde Soupert'. Soupert et Notting, 1890. 'Mignonette' × 'Mme Damaizin'. This originally came to me from the Hon. Robert James of St Nicholas, Richmond, Yorks, and is mentioned under the name of 'Mme Hardy du Thé' on page 194 of *The Old Shrub Roses*. Mr James had received it from Miss Willmott, who claimed it was brought over from France by the *émigrés*. Neither this name nor an alternative, 'Mme Melon du Thé', have I ever traced in any publication. Judge of my delight therefore when I found the portrait of this little rose in the *Journal des Roses*, quite unmistakable, and at last we have an authentic name. The fact that it is a rose of little garden value does not matter; two bogies have been laid! It is quite an historic piece, for it is a hybrid between one of the two first Polyanthas and a Tea Rose. 'Mignonette' was a prolific parent.

This little free-flowering rose makes a compact bush up to about 18 inches in height and can bear charming circular blooms, 2 inches across, papery, filled with curved petals, creamy white with a depth of pink in their centres. That is what happens in warm summer weather. Very often the blooms are made worthless by wet weather. I should not like to convey that it is on a par with the other roses in this chapter, but merely include it to set matters right about its nomenclature. A climbing sport appeared in the United States in 1902, but I have not seen it.

Rosenzeitung, 1889.

Journal des Roses, Mars 1889. Appears to be a copy of the above.

'Improved Cécile Brunner'. Duerhsen, 1948. 'Rosy Morn.' 'Dainty Bess' × 'Double Gigantea'. Flowers 3 inches across. If breeders think *this* is the way to get beautiful roses, let them carry on; they may achieve victory some day. But why drag in the name of 'Cécile Brunner'?

'Little White Pet'. Henderson, 1879. 'White Pet.' This has nothing to do with China Roses or Poly-poms, but horticulturally fits in best here. It is a dwarf perpetual-flowering sport of 'Félicité et Perpétue', a Sempervirens Rambler raised at the Château Neuilly in 1827. The plant seldom reaches more than 2 feet high, is seldom without a cluster of its beautiful dense rosette-blooms, of creamy white touched with carmine in the bud. Possibly the most free-flowering rose apart from the Chinas.

Garten-Zeitung, 1880, t.28.

'Némésis'. 1836. A dwarf pompon-type of China Rose, which fits best in this group. Dainty small leaves on a dwarf twiggy bush. The flowers are double, quite small, of rich plum crimson with coppery shadings, borne in small clusters early in the summer and in great heads on the strong young shoots later. Not much scent. 2 to 3 feet.

'Opal Brunner'. Marshall, *c.* 1948. Classed as a climbing Floribunda, this has the colouring of the Hybrid Musk 'Cornelia', slightly richer, but with smaller flowers and prettier buds. Though certainly not a China Rose, it is mentioned here to keep the 'Brunner' varieties together; at the same time, as with 'Improved Cécile Brunner', I feel it is an insult to link it with that variety. Parentage unknown.

As one browses through rose books it is amazing how often one comes across some odd rose which has survived through sheer beauty for many years, although it may never have become popular, for the simple reason that it did not conform to the accepted standard. Such a one is ' **Gruss an Aachen** ', which has 'Frau Karl Druschki' and other famous roses of Tea ancestry in its bloodstream. Raised in 1909 it is now classed as a Floribunda, a name given to a group evolved many years later. It can hold its own in floriferousness and size of bloom with any today, is deliciously fragrant, and a healthy dwarf plant. The flowers are 4 to 6 inches across, of creamy, pale apricot pink, fading to creamy white, well filled with petals and of the flat Old Rose shape. It bears no resemblance to any of the other roses in this chapter but I mention it as I feel it has great garden value and is little known. A few discerning gardeners knew it and grew it, like Major Lawrence Johnston at Hidcote, where it still gives to the White Garden an air of distinction, beauty, and fragrance. One day I want to plant it mixed with 'Magenta'. It is illustrated well in the *Journal des Roses* for August 1912, and in Strassheim's *Rosenzeitung* for March 1912. Climbing and pink sports have occurred.

Postscript, 1973 Edition

An article in the Royal National Rose Society's Annual, 1972, by Capt. C. A. E. Stanfield, R.N., seems to prove conclusively that 'Bloomfield Abundance' is in reality a sport from 'Cécile Brunner'.

Postscript, 1980 Edition

In support of Captain Stanfield's findings are two photographs of the original 'Bloomfield Abundance' in the *American Rose Annual* for 1920 and 1928, and another in colour in McFarland, p. 24, conclusively proving that our present 'Bloomfield Abundance' is not entitled to the name. Mrs Léonie P. Bell of Pennsylvania kindly brought these illustrations to my notice.

13

Hybrid Musk Roses

... Rose of the World; th' embroidered Tuscany;
The scented Cabbage, and the Damascene;
Sweet Briar, lovelier named the eglantine;
But above all the Musk
With classic names, Thisbe, Penelope,
Whose nectarous load grows heavier with the dusk
And like a grape too sweetly muscadine.

V. Sackville-West, *The Garden*, 1946.

IN 1904 Peter Lambert, a German nurseryman, put upon the market a rose called 'Trier' which was destined to be the forerunner of a new group of roses. It was descended from a seedling of 'Aglaia', reputedly crossed with 'Mrs R. G. Sharman-Crawford', but genetical research suggests that the fusion with the latter did not take place. 'Aglaia' was a rambler or loose shrub which Lambert had introduced in 1896. It is rather similar to the well-known rambler 'Goldfinch' but considerably more refined, and although it does not flower so freely, it retains its pale yellow colouring better. One still comes across it, hanging over old garden walls. 'Aglaia' has as parents R. *multiflora* and 'Rêve d'Or'; the latter was a Noisette raised in 1860, with considerable Tea influence, and with R. *moschata* some way back in its pedigree, through the older Noisettes.

'Trier' has so little Musk Rose influence that the group of roses we are about to discuss has very little claim to be called Hybrid Musks, or hybrids of R. *moschata*, but that is the name they have been given and will no doubt, through long usage, keep. Their parentage from 'Trier' backwards contains strains of all garden races, and the actual crosses which produced the Hybrid Musks were mainly with Hybrid Teas, but most of them contained 'Trier' or something near it. They are in fact a thoroughly mixed bag and the title is rather far fetched.

Be that as it may, certain very fine garden shrubs have come to us along these lines and from several sources, and they have, strangely enough, sufficient similarity to bind them together in a horticultural group. Most of them are remarkably fragrant. 'Trier' is deliciously scented, and it is a scent derived I am sure from R. *multiflora*; this Japanese species, to my nose, is powerfully and richly fragrant with a fruity odour, as are so many of its relatives. Moreover, it is considered a complementary species to the great Musk Rose chain which extends in a line over almost the whole of the Old World from Madeira to Japan, with R. *brunonii* and allied species through the Himalaya and China. Yet again this scent is especially 'free in the air', as Francis Bacon describes it; and some of the Hybrid Musks can be 'savoured' far off on warm, damp days. This is indeed a wonderful attribute; their scent can be detected yards away, a glorious perfume and a tremendous asset to any garden. The blend at that time of the year with the fragrance of 'Mock Orange' or philadelphus can be sublime; and fortunately the mock-oranges provide good white flowers, so valuable in any grouping of shrub roses. The Hybrid Musks are indeed splendid types for our new ideal: perpetual-flowering, fragrant, large-flowered, vigorous shrub roses. But let us look further into their development.

Lambert had been growing 'Trier' for only a year or two before he crossed it with other roses, and from 1909 until 1922 he produced a small series which became known as the 'Lambertiana' roses. Only one of these is not connected with 'Trier', and in one 'Aglaia' was used instead, but they make a fairly uniform collection. They are more rightly described as recurrent, small-flowered (Poly-pom) pillar-roses or semi-climbers rather than shrubs; they made loose bushes 6 to 8 feet high. Their foliage was also of the Poly-pom style. I grew them all at one time, but discarded the lot as they were neither large in flower nor decisive—some were not even beautiful in colour, and they lacked personality. Possibly they had some other attribute, such as greater hardiness, which would have appealed to a German raiser. In the following pages I have given a list of all the varieties I have grown, for the purpose of recording this step towards the perpetual-flowering shrub roses.

Meanwhile the Rev. Joseph Pemberton had been busy in his garden at Havering-atte-Bower, a village in Essex where Queen Elizabeth I had a 'locked garden of trees, grass and sweet herbs'. In the extremely mixed group he produced it is difficult to see any definite plan of hybridizing if the parentage given in the records available is correct, but he evidently had a high regard for scent, and probably discarded all seedlings which were unworthy in this respect. A total of two dozen roses was named by Pemberton and put on the market by J. A. Bentall. Of these, nine have practically disappeared (these I should like to acquire), six are just in cultivation, and a further nine have taken their place in the forefront of roses, and indeed of flowering shrubs. After Pemberton's death Bentall carried on and produced six more varieties, only two of which still linger in cultivation. This was quite a remarkable memorial to the two raisers, but at the time I doubt if many realized what actually had been achieved. The few excellent swans were overwhelmed by the geese and also by popular opinion, which was still rabidly doting on Hybrid Teas and dwarf Polyanthas; the achievement was also somewhat overshadowed later by the Poulsen group. The Hybrid Musks received a place in many catalogues but the demand was small, and they had not found their niche in the gardening world.

Coloured plates of Hybrid Musk Roses are conspicuous by their absence. Apart from one poor picture of an over-coloured 'Felicia' in the National Rose Society's *Annual* I have found no good portrait other than that recorded for 'Danaë'. This almost complete absence helps to show how much too soon they were evolved—before anyone was really looking for shrub roses.

After the Second World War they soon became more appreciated and are now indispensable for creating fragrance and colour in shrub and mixed borders in July and onwards. For they flower when the species and the old roses are fading, and thus open at a useful time from the garden planning point of view, spilling their bounty to the eye and nose with the deutzias and philadelphuses, weigelas and escallonias and all the shrubs of their kind which burst forth at midsummer. That at least is what they do in Surrey;

and after their first glorious display is over, the new shoots continually push and produce later blooms until cold weather finally calls a halt. In fact 'Vanity' has received both its awards from the Royal Horticultural Society in the month of October, at which time no shrub has so much beauty and scent.

A further claim to garden value is made by a few varieties, particularly 'Penelope' and 'Wilhelm', together with its sport 'Will Scarlet': these retain their heps through the winter, or at least until a long spell of arctic conditions spoils them. The heps are produced in such quantity that they create a rich glow of colour over the bushes. I have lost stock of the following varieties and should like to hear from any reader who could spare a few cuttings: 'Aurora', 'Belinda', 'Ceres', 'Clytemnestra', 'Daphne', 'Fortuna', 'Galatea', 'Havering', 'Sea Spray'.

Let us first glance through the Lambertiana group; they are chronologically first, and a resting place on the way to ultimate perfection, but are no longer grown in Britain.

LAMBERTIANA ROSES

'Arndt'. 1913. 'Hélène' × 'Gustav Grünerwald'. An open-growing bush or semi-climber with dark burnished coppery foliage and dark brown wood. The flowers are small and double, borne in Poly-pom style in summer and again in autumn; the bud is well coloured with red and orange, opening to subdued flesh pink. Sweetly scented. 'Hélène' and 'Aglaia' in its immediate ancestry, also 'Crimson Rambler'. 6 feet.

'Chamisso'. 1922. 'Geheimrat Dr Mittweg' × 'Tip Top'. Descended from 'Trier' through both its parents. Similar in general appearance and value to 'Arndt', of clearer pink, centre yellowish white. Dark foliage, recurrent bloom. 8 to 10 feet.

'Excellenz von Schubert'. 1909. 'Mme Norbert Levavasseur' × 'Frau Karl Druschki'. Richly coloured foliage; small dark pink or light crimson flowers in Poly-pom clusters. Recurrent, vigorous.

'Heinrich Conrad Söth'. 1919. 'Trier' is a quarter-parent. A pretty, shrubby rambler with small, dark, glossy leaves. Flowers in large pyramidal trusses, small, single, pink with white eye. Recurrent. 6 feet.

'Hoffmann von Fallersleben'. 1917. 'Geheimrat Dr Mittweg' × 'Tip-Top'; both parents are descended from 'Trier'. Deep salmon pink, yellowish shadings, in small or large clusters. Vigorous.

'Lessing'. 1914. 'Trier' × 'Entente Cordiale'. Light green leaves and trusses of small, single Poly-pom flowers, blush-rose, yellow-centred, and sometimes having white streaks.

'Trier'. 1904. 'Aglaia' seedling × 'Mrs R. G. Sharman-Crawford'. A fairly erect bush or climber with small leaves, and tiny, nearly single flowers of light creamy yellow, pink flushed. 6 to 8 feet. An important parent, but uninteresting horticulturally. Rosenzeitung, August 1907. Flattering.
Amateur Gardening, 4th June 1910.

'Von Liliencron'. 1916. 'Geheimrat Dr Mittweg' × 'Mrs Aaron Ward'. Dark glossy leaves; small double flowers, light yellowish rose, deeper reverse. Seldom flowers much after the summer crop. 'Trier' is once again in the ancestry.

HYBRID MUSK ROSES
(*mostly raised by the Rev. Joseph Pemberton*)

'Aurora'. 1928. 'Danaë' × 'Miriam'. Nearly single, canary yellow passing to milky white. Not very tall-growing but produces large sprays.

'Autumn Delight'. 1933. Foliage fresh dark green, rather dull and leathery, practically thornless. The buds are pointed, apricot yellow, opening to a nearly single flower of extreme beauty of soft creamy buff-yellow. In hot weather they fade to creamy white but in cool autumn are especially good, always retaining a cupped shape. Beautiful stamens. A good display in summer from side-shoots and magnificent heads of blossom in autumn. 5 feet by 4 feet. A delightful cool-coloured effect and admirable for giving lightness to a grouping of 'hot' floribundas.

'**Ballerina**'. 1937. Large clusters of small flowers, of clear pink, single, with white eyes. 4 feet.

'**Belinda**'. 1936. A vigorous plant producing large clusters of soft pink flowers. 4 to 5 feet.

'**Bishop Darlington**'. Raised in California by Captain G. C. Thomas in 1926. 'Aviateur Blériot' × 'Moonlight'. A new rose sent to me by Mrs Stemler of Will Tillotson's Roses, California, and a pleasant addition to the group, with the true musk fragrance. Large, semi-double, creamy flesh-coloured flowers, opening from shapely coral-coloured buds. The large zone of yellow at the base of the petals lights the whole flower. Not yet fully tested, but full of promise. Perhaps 5 feet.

'**Buff Beauty**'. No record has come my way of the parentage of this rose, but it was introduced in 1939. It has an excellent habit, with arching branches gradually building up into a good graceful bush; more sturdy and compact than 'Pax' but similar in general growth. Very good dark green, broad leaves, bronzy when young. The flowers, as in all others, are borne singly or in small clusters at midsummer, but in long panicles as the strong new shoots produce them in late summer and autumn. They are large, shapely, fully double, rich apricot yellow fading slightly, tinted coral in the bud, with a most delicious scent, leaning towards the Tea Rose quality. Red-brown young stems. The whole plant is excellent and it is continuous-flowering; admirable as a 6-foot by 6-foot shrub or trained on a wall, when it will grow higher in good soil. (Plate VI.)

'**Callisto**'. 1920. A seedling from 'William Allen Richardson', selfed. Greenish-brown stems and thorns and mid-green crinkled leaves. It is very near in general appearance to 'Cornelia', with similarly shaped flowers and truss, but the colour is soft, warm buttery yellow from small, round, deep-yellow buds touched with apricot, fading to near white. Rich fragrance of oranges. 3 to 4 feet or higher.

'**Ceres**'. 1914. A semi-double fairly vigorous rose in creamy white, with conspicuous stamens. I have not seen this variety.

'**Charmi**'. 1929. Small 'polyantha' leaves, dark wood, and

thorns with fringed stipules and glandular pedicels. Single pink
flowers, with the usual yellow stamens. Fresh scent of apples.
Rather lacking in character. Probably 4 feet.

'Clytemnestra'. 1915. 'Trier' × 'Liberty'. Deep coppery-salmon
buds open to small, crinkled, salmon-yellow flowers, fading to
chamois, excellent in autumn. Dark leathery leaves. An
attractive, richly coloured variety. Spreading, bushy. 3 to 4 feet.

'Cornelia'. 1925. Parentage unrecorded, but it so well conforms
to the accepted style of these roses that we may presume 'Trier'
or 'Aglaia' is in its ancestry, if only on account of its scent,
which is pronouncedly soft, rich, and musky. A splendid,
vigorous bush, with shining, dark green, smallish leaves. Even
the small, summer flower sprays arch gracefully, bearing tight,
unattractive buds developing into small rosette blooms with
yellow stamens, of soft coppery apricot fading to creamy pink.
The big sprays which appear late in the growing season are
particularly good in bud, being of rich, warm, coppery coral,
and a far better colour when open than in the summer. These
autumnal sprays may be 18 inches long and are superlative for
cutting. 5 feet by 7 feet as a bush, higher if trained on a wall.
The scent is especially pervasive. (Plate 11.)

'Danaë'. 1913. Reputedly 'Trier' × 'Gloire de Chédane
Guinoisseau', but it is more probably 'Trier' selfed. Rich green,
shining foliage, mahogany-tinted when young. When opening
the flowers are of deep yolk yellow, fading to ivory in hot
weather. So far this has not made a large bush with me, but is
quite healthy. 4 feet by 3 feet.
The Garden, 1913, p. 254. Rather heavily coloured but a splendid
portrait.

'Daphne'. 1912. A semi-double blush-pink variety. I have not
grown this.

'Daybreak'. 1918. 'Trier' × 'Liberty'. Chocolate-brown stalks
and stems with dark red-brown young foliage turning later to
dark green. Rich yellow buds opening to loosely double or
semi-double light yellow flowers with dark golden stamens.
Rich musk fragrance. 3 to 4 feet.

'Eva'. 1933. 'Robin Hood' × 'J. C. Thornton'. The first parent was a Pemberton Hybrid Musk, with a Polyantha in its ancestry, and this variety may well be likened to an immense Polyantha, with stout stems bearing heads of single flowers like 'American Pillar'. Showy, but it has never appealed to me as a garden plant. Good foliage. Fairly fragrant. 6 feet. It was the first tetraploid to occur in this group and in consequence it was speedily used to good effect by its raiser, Herr Wilhelm Kordes, to produce various strong-growing shrub roses, many of which are Floribundas.

'Felicia'. 1928. 'Trier' × 'Ophelia'. This is in every way an ideal plant. It is compact and bushy, with good broad foliage, and can be pruned suitably for bedding, when it can rival any Floribunda of its colouring in general display. But lest comparison with Floribundas may be taken in disparagement I must add that if left to itself it builds up into a fine bushy plant and is admirable for hedging. The flowers inherit some of 'Lady Sylvia's' beautiful shape and colouring, being warm apricot-pink in the bud, opening to tones of silvery pink, most charmingly blended. This seems to me the perfect shrub rose for beauty and continuous display. Some plants about ten years old at Sunningdale are about 5 feet high and 9 feet through and are so smothered with bloom in July that no other shrub can surpass them for effect.

'Fortuna'. 1927. 'Lady Pirrie' × 'Nur Mahal'. A compact plant with nearly single flowers of rose-pink becoming paler, with conspicuous anthers. Rich fragrance. 3 feet. I have no experience of this variety.

'Francesca'. 1922. 'Danaë' × 'Sunburst'. Dark red-brown wood and thorns, with glossy, long, dark green leaves, creating a fine, luxuriant, leafy bush of graceful habit and inclined to Tea influence in leaf, flower, and scent, but quite hardy and vigorous. The arching, but not weak, stems support loose, nodding, apricot-yellow blooms, of long shape in the bud, fading in hot sun to butter colour. At all times beautiful and richly Tea-scented. Has very much the air of a Noisette or early Tea Rose, and is a valuable garden shrub. 6 feet by 6 feet.

'**Galatea**'. 1914. Flowers in rosette shape, small, soft, buff-white edged pink, borne in clusters. This and 'Havering' are not in my collection.

'**Hamburg**'. 1935. 'Eva' × 'Daily Mail Scented'. Leaves of typical H.T. quality, and erect growth, rather spindly compared with many of the varieties. It has sacrificed bushiness for the sake of its intense red colouring, the equal of any H.T. The flowers are borne in small clusters, with shapely buds of maroon-red with a few broad, flat petals, contrasting well with the yellow anthers, remaining in cupped shape. Slight musk fragrance. Not very free, nor is it a graceful bush. 5 feet by 3 feet.

'**Havering**'. 1937. Borne in small clusters, the flowers are of soft pink, large and semi-double. Sturdy upright growth. About 3 feet.

'**Kathleen**'. 1922. 'Daphne' × 'Perle des Jardins' (?). A very vigorous, branching shrub with long-stemmed clusters of small, single, blush-pink flowers from apricot buds. Coppery young shoots and leaves, turning to green; narrow leaflets. Pronounced musk scent. The petals unfortunately suffer from 'spotting' after rain. 5 feet by 4 feet.

'**Moonlight**'. 1913. 'Trier' × 'Sulphurea'. Dark-brownish wood, with reddish thorns, supporting a mass of branches, clothed with upturned, small, dark, shining leaves. In summer, multitudes of flowers are borne in small sprays; cream buds, opening white, small, semi-double, and with their yellow stamens making a splendid contrast to the foliage. In the autumn on the great new shoots, I have had heads 18 inches across, containing many dozens of flowers, rivalling in effect 'Vanity' itself. 'Trier' has certainly had abundant influence with this rose, for it is musk-scented as well. It is an excellent rose for garden effect, shrubby yet graceful, and can be used as a pillar rose or allowed to ramble through low trees or over hedges, since its branches will reach 10 feet or more in length if allowed.

'**Nur Mahal**'. 1923. 'Château de Clos Vougeot' × seedling. Plentiful leathery, dark leaves on a compact, low-branching, sturdy bush, resembling 'Penelope' in growth and in the semi-double, wide-open flowers. The colour is soft dark carmine-red in the bud, becoming a soft, light mauve-crimson, with showy stamens. This is one of the most satisfactory of the Hybrid Musks, suitable for hedging or as a shrub or, suitably pruned, for bedding. Its colour is rather subdued but just what is wanted to act as a connection between the 'old' roses and the musks. Musk fragrance, but not very strong. 4 feet by 5 feet.

'**Pax**'. 1918. 'Trier' × 'Sunburst'. The most lax in growth of all the Hybrid Musks, making a large, arching bush which is laden with drooping masses of bloom, borne in small clusters in summer and in later months in long sprays. Creamy yellow pointed buds develop into loose, semi-double, creamy-white, wide flowers with pronounced dark golden stamens; the petals are shapely, rolled at the edges, making a beautiful flower. The foliage is dark green and the stems dark brown in effective contrast. Musk and Tea-scent richly blended. Equally good when trained over an arch or hedgerow or allowed to achieve shrub dimensions by the gradual building up of the arching stems; 6 to 8 feet high. (Plate V.)

'**Penelope**'. 1924. 'Ophelia' × seedling. The excellent bushy growth and broad, ribbed leaves at once put this rose into the front rank. In flower it is as free as any, bearing wide, semi-double blooms in small and large clusters. The buds are salmon orange, quickly losing their bright colour on opening, but making a delightful contrast on the half-open spray; on expanding in cool weather the colour remains a delicate creamy pink, fading nearly to white in full sunshine. Good stamens. Magnificent trusses appear in autumn. This is one of the very best roses for creating a white effect without being white, and grown with grey foliage and pale-coloured flowers, particularly pale blue, it can be really exquisite. Rich, musky fragrance. I have seen it 8 feet high in special conditions, but it is usually about 5 feet by 4 feet.

By late November the heps develop their soft colouring; it is a delightful diversion from the usual red, glossy berries of most shrubs to find these heps are dull and bloom-covered, and change from cool green to coral pink slowly. The warmer the autumn the more highly coloured they become, and last for many weeks. I know of no other shrubs with berries approaching this soft colour. (Plate III, heps only.)

'Pink Prosperity'. 1931. I doubt whether this was a sport from 'Prosperity'; it was more likely a seedling. Green wood; fresh, rich green foliage often folded upwards, on an erect plant like a very large Polyantha, and bearing flowers rather in the same style. They are, however, larger than those of the average Polyantha, each one being a perfect, double rosette of warm, clear pink. Small summer trusses are followed by heavier ones in autumn. Highly fragrant. 6 feet by 4 feet.

'Prosperity'. 1919. 'Marie Jeanne' × 'Perle des Jardins' (?). A fine, upstanding bush with glossy, dark leaves, but like 'Pink Prosperity' more of a giant Polyantha than a true-to-type Hybrid Musk. The trusses of bloom cover the bush and after opening become ivory white, with a lemon flush in the centre, losing their creamy-pink bud tint. A very effective garden plant, and sweetly scented. 6 feet by 4 feet.

'Robin Hood'. 1927. Seedling × 'Edith Cavell'. A vigorous plant, like a Polyantha, in cherry red, with small double flowers in large clusters. This is not a favourite of mine, being dusky and dusty in tone, rather soulless and scentless, but it has played its part well in rose-breeding, being very fertile and a parent of 'Eva' and 'Wilhelm'. 4 feet by 3 feet.

'Rosaleen'. 1933. Large clusters of small, double, dark-red flowers. Unknown to me.

'Sammy'. 1921. A hybrid of 'Gruss an Teplitz', the seed being borne by a 'Trier' hybrid. A glossy-leaved plant producing pleasing, large Polyantha clusters of light carmine, semi-double blooms. Thornless. 4 feet. Rather too near to a Poly-pom to be effective as a shrub.

'Sea Spray'. 1923. Clusters of ivory white, flushed pink.

'Thisbe'. 1918. 'Marie Jeanne' × 'Perle des Jardins' (?). It is fortunate that this variety has such a pronounced Musk fragrance, otherwise in spite of its colour I should be inclined to neglect it. Semi-double rosette blooms open from rich buff-yellow buds, fading later to creamy buff, enclosing rich golden stamens. Erect growth and light green leaves, the later sprays of bloom resemble 'Cornelia's' in shape. This is near to the Lambertiana group but on account of its fragrance should never be forgotten. 4 feet by 4 feet.

'**Vanity**'. 1920. 'Château de Clos Vougeot' × seedling. A most remarkable plant, but not suitable for a small garden. One plant will put up a fair display but will probably be ill-balanced and shapeless. It is essentially a rose for growing several together, planted about 3 feet apart, when the long, angular shoots will interlace and compensate for the open habit, and create a great thicket. In summer it will cover its widely spaced leaflets with short trusses of bloom, and later the 5-foot autumnal shoots will arise. Their stalks are glaucous green and support branching heads perhaps 2 feet across, open and leafless, but displaying the flowers to advantage, like a flight of butterflies. They emerge from pointed crimson buds, are almost single and of good size, of clear rose pink with a tuft of yellow anthers. Rather a harsh colour in high summer but softer with the approach of cooler weather; this is because its China Rose ancestry causes the petals to deepen in hot sunshine. Their scent is sweet-pea-like, very sweet and strong. A wonderful shrub, continually in bloom, reaching 8 feet in height and width on good soils. (Plate V.)

'**Wilhelm**'. Kordes, 1934. Known as 'Skyrocket' in the United States. 'Robin Hood' × 'J. C. Thornton' (H.T.). A sister seedling of 'Eva'; similarly a tetraploid and useful as a parent. This splendid, vigorous, and showy shrub rose has one disadvantage: it is very slightly scented. To some eyes—the eyes of a modern rose-lover—it also has a disadvantage in its colouring, which is a deep crimson with plum shadings. But we do not all want flaming scarlets and I find 'Wilhelm' satisfying to a great degree; it gives a mass of rich colour which is heavier in tone than most other shrub roses, and is sumptuous when used with pink and light colours. The flowers are semi-double, opening from intense maroon, pointed buds, and borne in large and small trusses. Around the yellow stamens is a lighter zone, paling to lilac-pink. A faded flower is dark mauve-crimson. It is one of the few comparatively new shrub roses which can be used as a meeting point between the 'old' roses and the moderns.

As a shrub it leaves nothing to be desired; stalwart, bushy, with few thorns on the great green shoots and handsome dark-green leaves in plenty. The bright orange-red heps with persistent grey calyces do not colour before November and last through the winter. As a pillar rose, and with suitable pruning, it could be taken up to 10 feet or so. Usually 6 feet by 5 feet.

'Will Scarlet'. A sport which occurred on a plant of 'Wilhelm' under my care in 1947 and was introduced in 1950. It is identical to its parent in all respects except colour and scent and brings to the Hybrid Musk group a splash of real scarlet in some lights. The tone of the petals is pale in the centre, brightening to vivid rose and true 'hunting pink' on the freshly open flower, emerging from brilliant scarlet buds. In hot weather a faint suffusion of lilac appears in the centre. It presents a dazzling display and may well be used to link the shrub roses to the Floribundas. Equally valuable to 'Wilhelm' for its winter display of glossy orange-red heps. Delicate fragrance. 6 feet by 5 feet.

Postscript, 1973 Edition

Those wishing for further information on the Reverend Joseph Pemberton, his house and his roses, may like to turn to my article in the Royal National Rose Society's Annual, 1968.

14

Shrub Roses of the Twentieth Century

Rose, shut your heart against the bee.
Why should you heed his minstrelsy?
Refuse your urgent lover, rose,
He does but drink the heart and goes.

Humbert Wolfe.

In this chapter are grouped varieties which in the main are comparatively new and do not owe their derivation directly to the Old Shrub Roses. That is the only general claim I can make about them; their parentage and characters are extremely diverse. Most of them have been the results of deliberate crosses, and it is interesting to find that few of the yellowish ones owe their colour to modern Hybrid Teas or Floribundas, but to R. *foetida* and R. *spinosissima* directly. R. *rugosa*, being the fecund parent that it is, is concerned in the ancestry of a great number. A learner may find it disconcerting to be confronted with such a heterogeneous collection, so I will do my best to arrange them into groups, having more regard to horticulture than to botany.

First, there are the once-flowering shrubs which are mostly pink or white and assort well with the Old Shrub Roses. There is the renowned 'Complicata' itself, which I described in my first book, together with the taller R. 'Dupontii'. Similar but sprawling types, suitable for wild gardening, banks, ground cover, or flinging over stumps, bushes, and hedgerows, are R. × *polliniana*; 'Macrantha' and its forms or hybrids, 'Daisy Hill', 'Harry Maasz', 'Raubritter', and 'Dusterlohe'; 'Lady Curzon',

'Schneelicht', 'Paulii' and 'Paulii Rosea', with 'Max Graf' the most prostrate of the lot, and nearly as prostrate as R. *wichuraiana* itself.

I am never sure about the placing in the garden of the three modern-coloured Moss Roses, 'Gabrielle Noyelle', 'Golden Moss', and 'Robert Leopold'; their colours are upsetting among the Old Roses—though they possess some of their fragrance—and they are not reliably recurrent.

Some of the most substantial shrubs—descended as might be expected from R. *rugosa*—are R. × *micrugosa* and its relatives, the 'Grootendorst' varieties and 'Schneezwerg'; similarly fine shrubs are 'Adam Messerich', 'Fritz Nobis', 'Zigeuner Knabe'; with them we must remember the Hybrid Musks in Chapter 13. 'Nevada' and its sport remain unchallenged as perpetual-flowering shrub roses of the largest size. To this category we might add 'Golden Wings' and 'Aloha'; no doubt others will materialize in the future.

For the back of the border, so that their gaunt lower growths become hidden, I would choose the tall 'Refulgence', 'Conrad F. Meyer', and 'Nova Zembla', 'Sarah van Fleet' and 'Mme Georges Bruant'.

Famous early-flowering roses are the several 'Frühlings' varieties, a series of Burnet Rose crosses, among which 'Frühlingsgold' stands out as a really splendid shrub for spring display; all of these have a tendency towards yellow, likewise the *rugosa* hybrid 'Agnes'. I am watching the performance of some of the newer crosses in this colour, such as 'Gold Bush', 'Claus Groth', 'Oratam', and the *rugosa* hybrid 'Vanguard'.

Now, taking them more botanically, we find that R. *rugosa* provides a rich assembly. While they do not resemble very much the forms of the species described in Chapter 8, most of them have the unmistakable stamp of R. *rugosa*, particularly in its thorny wood. Few can be called refined; 'Schneezwerg' has charm and also 'Fimbriata', while the flowers of 'Dr Eckener', 'Sarah van Fleet', and 'Mme Georges Bruant' approach the shape of a Hybrid Tea. In the garden I find that 'Agnes', 'Carmen', 'Fimbriata', 'New Century', 'Mrs Anthony Waterer', 'Mme Georges Bruant', 'Sarah van Fleet', and 'Schneezwerg' all inherit, with the

Grootendorst varieties, something of the round, bushy habit of R. *rugosa*, although very inferior to it. 'Ruskin' and 'Dr Eckener' are almost uncontrollable, the latter in particular because of its excessive prickliness. It may be asked therefore why these roses are still grown. Certainly they have few real assets and I do not think our gardens would be much poorer without them. They are, however, fairly productive; some, like 'Schneezwerg', 'Fimbriata', and the Grootendorst varieties, are charming and constantly in flower. And then it comes back to scent; all except the 'Grootendorsts' are fragrant, some exceedingly so; in addition many are very hardy owing to their R. *rugosa* ancestry.

It is difficult to discern any real trend in the above hybrid production. Some were probably the opposite of what was expected, but were considered to be too good to discard. Several species have entered the lists, apart from the hybrids recorded earlier in this book, and important crosses resulting in attractive roses are 'Cerise Bouquet' (R. *multibracteata* hybrid); 'Auguste Roussel' (R. *macrophylla*); 'Fritz Nobis' (R. *rubiginosa*); 'Moyesii Superba' (R. *moyesii*); 'Scarlet Fire' (R. *gallica*); and finally 'Golden Wings', 'Claus Groth', and the 'Frühlings' varieties (R. *spinosissima*).

Among the progeny of Hybrid Teas and Floribundas crossed with roses of Hybrid Musk and Sweet Brier derivation—mostly raised by Herr Wilhelm Kordes—a striving after hardy big shrubs with shapely Hybrid Tea-style blooms is more apparent. Even these, I suspect, will give way in due course to something more floriferous and shapely. There are some good plants among the extra vigorous Floribundas such as 'Chinatown' (large, yellow), 'Escapade' (rosy lilac, white centre), 'Frensham' (dark red), 'Iceberg' (white); some which are more dwarf but which still do not conform to a Floribunda style are 'Gruss an Aachen' (Chapter 12), 'Magenta', and 'Morning Stars', all exceedingly fragrant.

A few Hybrid Teas can be classed as Shrub Roses when well grown. For back planting, where its gawky stems are covered by lower bushes, 'President Herbert Hoover', raised in 1930, cannot be beaten as a free-flowering plant up to 6 or 8 feet, loaded with bloom at midsummer and again later. It can be seen all over the country, tall enough to show over garden fences, a rich blend of flame, pink, and orange, while its equally vigorous sport in coppery rose, 'Texas Centennial', has never become popular. Among vigorous varieties are 'Buccaneer', 'Fred Howard' (both 1952), 'Helen Traubel' (1951), and 'Uncle Walter' (1963). Looking at the bulk of roses in this chapter as a group, while there are some superlative roses among them, we must realize that they do not compare with the true Rugosas and 'Nevada' in growth and floriferousness. 'Nevada', though not so free as the true R. *rugosa*, is a landmark in shrub rose hybridization, but is unfortunately sterile. It occupies the same position among shrubs as that other splendid sterile rose 'Mermaid' does among climbers. Taken altogether, they present an interesting array, and I think we may conclude that some progress has been made towards perpetual-flowering shrub roses with fragrance and with all modern colours, though much has yet to be done.

'Adam Messerich'. Lambert, 1920. 'Frau Oberhofgärtner Singer' crossed with a hybrid between a 'Louise Odier' seedling and 'Louis Philippe'. The last was a purplish Centifolia. The result is a fine, upstanding bush with stout, green wood bearing few thorns, and leaves of modern appearance. The flowers are semi-double, cupped, silky, retaining their warm, deep-pink colouring well, produced in a heavy summer crop and intermittently later. Rich raspberry fragrance. Supposed to be a Bourbon, but fits better here. 6 feet by 5 feet.

'Agnes'. Saunders, 1922. Raised at Ottawa. R. *rugosa* × R. *foetida* 'Persiana'. A fairly erect bush gracefully spraying its thorny twigs outwards, heavily covered with small parsley-green leaves which in general characters are between the two parents. Early in the season a great crop of flowers appears, strongly reminiscent in shape and colour to the 'Persian Yellow'; fully double, even crowded in the centre with a mass of small petals, of rich butter yellow tinted with amber. It usually produces a second crop of flowers in late summer. Bristly receptacle. Unusual and delicious scent. 6 feet by 4 feet. (Photograph, Plate 9.)

Although it is effective at a distance when in full flower, this rose should be enjoyed at close quarters to appreciate its rich, intriguing scent and old-world shape.

Sitwell and Russell, p. 24. A poor representation.
McFarland, *Roses of the World*, p. 2.

'À Parfum de l'Haÿ'. Gravereaux, 1903. R. *damascena* ×
'Général Jacqueminot'. For some reason, probably because of
its name and association, this rose has become renowned for its
scent, but I have never discovered anything exceptional about
it, finding it just fairly well scented when comparing it with
other Rugosas and allied roses. It is undoubtedly a good rose in
hot climates, and is liked in California. With me it is a second-
rate rose as far as quality of bloom is concerned, producing on
weak stalks clusters of cupped, semi-double flowers of light
crimson, distinctly lilac flushed. The plant is thorny, and set
fairly freely with leaves of modern appearance. 5 feet.
Journal des Roses, Février 1903.
Revue Horticole, 1902, p. 64. Pale colour.
Trechslin & Coggiatti. Exaggerated.

'Aloha'. Boerner, 1949. 'Mercédès Gallart' × 'New Dawn'.
Although classed as a Hybrid Tea this has never made more
than a sturdy upright bush or pillar rose with me. The foliage
is dark and glossy and the main mass of blooms is succeeded
by many later crops. Each flower is full of petals—really
crammed—of good rose pink with deeper reverses and a warm
shading of orange-pink in the centre. Fragrant. Perhaps 7
feet by 4 feet.

'Altissimo'. Delbard-Chabert, 1967. Usually classed as a
climber, but with pruning it can be kept as a large shrub, up to
about 7 feet. Single blazing scarlet flowers are borne repeti-
tively over good foliage. Little scent.

'Auguste Roussel'. Barbier, 1913. R. *macrophylla* × 'Papa
Gontier'. This unusual cross seems to have led nowhere,
though the result is elegant and free-flowering. Imagine an
open-growing, arching bush with leaves and growth rather
like its first parent, and bearing pretty, semi-double to nearly
double, sophisticated blooms in clear, light pink with well-
formed broad petals. They are borne in clusters at midsummer
only and are sweetly scented. 6 feet by 8 feet.

'**Berlin**'. Kordes, 1949. 'Eva' × 'Peace'. A rose of rather modern appearance, as might be expected from the parentage, with large red thorns and handsome, dark, leathery leaves. The flowers are single, of blazing orange-red with a pale almost white centre, turning pink after pollinating; yellow stamens. Petals thick and leathery. Although sometimes classed as a Hybrid Musk I think this is very misleading. It has no character in common with the established members of that group, and is best considered as a strong-growing Floribunda. 4 feet by 3 feet.

'**Black Boy**'. Kordes, 1958. 'World's Fair' × 'Nuits de Young'. Bushy, thorny; mid-green leaves. So far the double flowers with mossy buds have revealed only crimson-purple tones, without the richness of 'Nuits de Young'. Large, loosely double flowers; Old Rose fragrance. 6 feet.

'**Blue Boy**'. Kordes, 1958. 'Louis Gimard' × 'Independence'. A small plant, with smooth leaves of distinctly greyish tone. So far the flowers have been lilac-pink, with an occasionally good bloom of intense dark purple-maroon, flecked with cerise and cerise reverse, fading to slate-purple. Petals broad and reflexing; handsome centre. Fragrant. 5 feet.

'**Bonn**'. Kordes, 1950. 'Hamburg' × 'Independence'. Large, rich green, glossy leaves on a rather sparse, upright bush. Loose, semi-double, orange-scarlet flowers fading to cerise-scarlet with lilac tones. Yellow stamens. Rounded, dark-red heps. Derives some vigour from the Hybrid Musk group through 'Hamburg' but in no way qualifies for inclusion in that group. Sweet-pea fragrance. 5 feet by 4 feet.

'**Calocarpa**'. Bruant, 1895. R. *rugosa* × R. *chinensis*. A perpetual-flowering hybrid which also bears a handsome lot of heps. Large, single flowers of rich lilac-crimson, with creamy yellow stamens. Perhaps a useful shrub but not an improvement on either parent; nearly pure R. *rugosa*. 4 feet.
Willmott, Plate 189. Good.
Journal des Roses, Août 1906. Depicts a double rose.
The Garden, 1897, p. 384. A good picture by H. G. Moon, but doubtful.

Rosenzeitung, June 1907. Depicts a double rose.

'Carmen'. Lambert, 1907. R. *rugosa rosea* × 'Princesse de Béarn', which was a red H.P. As a young plant this has some charm, especially in its pure dark crimson single flowers with their cream stamens. Unfortunately its foliage has a diseased appearance, and it seldom flowers after midsummer. 6 feet by 4 feet. Strassheim, October 1906.

'Cerise Bouquet'. Kordes, 1958. R. *multibracteata* × 'Crimson Glory'. From R. *multibracteata* it derives a strong, graceful, arching habit, small greyish leaves, and lots of grey-green bracts. The large flowers, which are borne in clusters, are derived more from its other parent; they are of intense crimson in the tightly scrolled, shapely bud, opening to fairly flat, nearly double blooms, brilliant cerise-crimson, offset by the yellow stamens. A rich raspberry fragrance contributes to what is a splendid and interesting addition to summer-flowering shrub roses. 9 feet by 12 feet. Plate I; photograph, Plate 15.)

'Chianti'. Austin; Sunningdale, 1966. R. 'Macrantha' × 'Vanity'. A modern shrub rose with good foliage and growth and velvety flowers of intense rich wine-purple, full of petals and a lovely shape. A useful fragrant addition for midsummer. 5 feet by 5 feet.

'Claus Groth'. Tantau, 1951. 'R.M.S. Queen Mary' × R. *spinosissima*. Richly tinted young growth, leaves turning to dark leaden-green, covering well the dense bush; dark twigs and thorns. In the spring the young shoots contrast well with the pointed red buds, which are striped with yellow. Large, loose, semi-double flowers, apricot-yellow fading to cream-pink. Rich scent of R. *foetida*. About 4 feet by 3 feet; very early flowering.

'Complicata'. I mentioned this rose in *The Old Shrub Roses* and have been unable to find out any more about it. In the light sandy soil in my garden, in close competition with a privet hedge, it has succeeded with a little help in climbing up to 10 feet into an apple-tree, and creates a superb display every season. It should be in every garden where shrubs are grown, and will make a handsome, solid bush if left to its own devices. Flowers 5 inches across, single, shapely, of bright, clear pink, borne on large arching sprays. When in full flower no shrub is more spectacular. Normally about 5 feet high and 8 feet wide.

'Conrad Ferdinand Meyer'. Muller, 1899. A hybrid between 'Gloire de Dijon' and 'Duc de Rohan' crossed with R. *rugosa* 'Germanica'. This is one of the most popular of the R. *rugosa* derivatives, and deservedly so, for it is vigorous and produces, in common with its sport 'Nova Zembla', fine, large flowers of good shape. The plant is very thorny, making a gaunt, upright plant frequently bare of branches for 4 feet, which can scarcely be called a shrub. Above this the good, large foliage is borne, and a huge crop of blooms appears in early summer and again in September. Most attractive, red-thorned, stout stalks support the big blooms, too rounded and filled to be called H.T.s, but a credit to the more substantial H.P.s, of soft silvery pink, with petals rolled at the edges and opening beautifully, revealing a 'muddled' centre. Glorious scent. The blooms of the later crop are usually superb. On account of its growth it is best grown well behind good bushy roses or shrubs up to 4 feet or even 5 feet. 8 to 9 feet by 4 feet.
Kingsley, p. 46.
Journal des Roses, Mai 1902.

'Constance Spry'. 1961. Raised by Mr David C. H. Austin of Wolverhampton; a cross between 'Belle Isis' (Gallica) and 'Dainty Maid' (Floribunda). An interesting and beautiful hybrid which my friend David Austin and I think is worthy to be named after one who did so much for the Old Roses. It is a vigorous plant, probably reaching 7 feet high and wide, well covered in good dark green leaves. The flowers are double, of clear, bright rose pink, cupped at first and opening to 5 inches in width when well grown. A magnificent bloom, in the grand Centifolia tradition, filled with petals and with a sweet fragrance of myrrh. This vigorous arching rose is best supported by hedge, fence or wall. (Photograph, Plate 6.)

'Coryana'. 1939. A seedling of R. *roxburghii* probably hybridized with R. *macrophylla*, raised from open-pollinated seed from Kew by Dr C. C. Hurst at Cambridge in 1926. This has many good points, but inherits from its first parent the unfortunate habit of hiding its flowers among its leaves. The growth is vigorous, stiff, and rather horizontal, with copious rich-green fern-like leaves, and the plant when fully grown is usually wider than high and densely branched to the ground. The deep rose-pink flowers have the perpendicular poise of R. *macrophylla*, and are wide and flat like R. *roxburghii*. Bright yellow stamens. Little scent. 8 feet by 10 feet. The bark peels as in R. *roxburghii*.

'De la Grifferaie'. Vibert, 1846. Possibly a hybrid of R. *multiflora* with one of the 'old' roses, bearing clusters of fully double, pompon-like, magenta-cerise blooms fading to lilac-white, deliciously scented, on long thornless arching branches.

This is one of the most usual 'old' roses to be sent in for naming. It is a thrifty old hybrid and, having been used for many years as an understock, often survives long after the scion has died. The colouring is certainly reminiscent of the Gallica Roses, but its frayed stipules and coarse, rounded leaves soon identify it. It is not to be despised for the show it puts up, and is useful for adding height to a border of old French Roses. Nearly thornless. 6 feet by 5 feet.

'Dr Eckener'. Berger, 1930. 'Golden Emblem' × a seedling of R. *rugosa*. Appallingly but handsomely prickly. Shoots growing 10 feet long in a season branch the following year and bear blooms much like a semi-double H.T. in light yellow, flushed pink or flame in the bud. It is not worth the space it needs in districts where most roses are hardy, but it may be a boon to gardeners in very cold countries. H.T. fragrance.

'Dr E. M. Mills'. Van Fleet, 1926. A hybrid of R. *hugonis*, but the other parent is not stated; it could possibly be R. *rugosa*. A free-growing bush with neat, small leaves, light green, and the whole plant is inclined to be downy. Semi-double palest yellow or ivory-white flowers, suffused pink in the bud, which do not open properly. I have not found it a worthwhile garden plant. 6 feet by 6 feet.

'Dupontii'. Raised prior to 1817 by M. Dupont, the founder of the rose-garden at Luxembourg, whom the Empress Josephine commissioned to help her assemble her collection at La Mal-

maison. It is a shrub of extreme beauty, nearly thornless, bearing pale grey-green, dull leaves which tone beautifully with the blush-tinted milk white of the flowers. These are borne singly or in clusters along the arching stems, and are of perfect, rounded outline. It has a rich fragrance of bananas, and bears a few orange-coloured, slender heps. The chromosome count does not confirm the suggested parentage, i.e. R. *moschata* × R. *damascena* or *gallica*. 7 feet by 7 feet.
Botanical Register, t.861. R. *moschata nivea*.
Willmott, Plate 43. Excellent.
The Garden, 1895, page 62. Poor.

'Düsterlohe'. Kordes, after 1931. The present plant was derived from 'Dance of Joy' × 'Daisy Hill' and is not a hybrid of R. *venusta pendula*, as is sometimes stated. A thorny, sprawling rose, with neat, dark green leaves. The flowers are borne singly and in clusters all along the arching branches, semi-double, of 'Tudor' shape, each petal raised and distinct from the others, of bright, clear rose pink with paler centre and yellow stamens. Can be a very showy garden plant at midsummer. The large pear-shaped heps are bright orange with persistent calyx, and are conspicuous through the winter. Not very fragrant. 4 feet by 8 feet. (Photograph, Plate 13.)

'Elmshorn'. Kordes. 1950. 'Hamburg' × 'Verdun'. Glossy, pointed leaves of mid green. Clusters of double cherry-red flowers, small, scentless, and soulless. Can be a showy plant at midsummer and again when the big, new shoots arrive later. 5 feet by 4 feet.

'Erfurt'. Kordes, 1939. 'Eva' × 'Réveil Dijonnais'. Vigorous, building up slowly from a low, bushy plant with plentiful, attractive foliage, richly tinted when young. The arching, branching stems bear large, wide-open flowers singly and in clusters, from beautiful long rosy-red buds; semi-double, lemon-white around the yellow stamens, deeply flushed with brilliant pink. One of the best of the newer perpetual Shrub Roses, giving a splendid effect of clear pink in the garden. Old Rose scent. 5 feet by 6 feet. (Plate VII.)

'**Fimbriata**'. Morlet, 1891. R. *rugosa* × 'Mme Alfred Carrière'. It seems that R. *rugosa* has a tendency to produce flowers with fringed petals, when one considers also the Grootendorst varieties, which have different parentage. The Noisette rose, 'Mme Alfred Carrière', has had little effect on R. *rugosa* in the production of this rose; it is a fairly good shrub with slightly rugose foliage, but in general is rather sparsely branched and leaved. Besides being known under the above name, it is sometimes found under the Irish name of 'Phoebe's Frilled Pink'; also 'Dianthiflora'. 'Phoebe' was Miss Phoebe Newton, who remembered an old plant growing at Killinure House. I have been unable to ascertain whether the word 'Pink' refers to the colour or the shape of the flower, but 'Dianthiflora' leaves us in no doubt, and indeed the flowers are much like those of a carnation or pink. They are not very double but the petals are shorter in the centre, and the edges of all are serrated, or fringed. It is a rose to grow for intimate use, scarcely for garden effect, although I remember a conspicuous bush of it in Miss Freeman's garden at Leixlip, which was covered with flowers; there, in rich soil and a moist climate, it had grown well. In hot dry Surrey it is not so successful. It is fragrant and occasionally has a few rounded, red heps. 5 feet. (Fig. 5.)
Journal des Roses, Septembre 1896.

'**F. J. Grootendorst**'. De Goey, 1918. R. *rugosa rubra* × 'Mme Norbert Levavasseur' (a Poly-pom rose whose ancestry is strongly Multiflora, through 'Crimson Rambler' and 'Gloire des Polyanthas'). Like its sports 'Pink Grootendorst' and 'Grootendorst Supreme' it has no scent and is therefore for ever damned by some people, and I must agree that this is a great disadvantage for which the cheap prettiness of the flowers and their unpleasant contrast with the foliage do nothing to compensate.

On the other hand it makes a bushy, prickly plant, healthy and vigorous, well covered with leaves somewhat in the Rugosa tradition, and bears bunch after bunch, large and small, of flowers throughout summer and autumn. These are small, fringed like those of a pink, and well swathed in light green bracts. The colour is a dull crimson-red, fading to magenta-crimson. 5 to 8 feet by 5 feet. I do not think it would be grown where other roses are hardy, except for the pretty fringed effect and its prolificity, for it is seldom out of flower.

'Fritz Nobis'. Kordes, 1940. 'Joanna Hill' × 'Magnifica'. Undoubtedly a valuable garden rose, and the most likely to achieve popularity among the three results of the cross, the other two being 'Max Haufe' and 'Josef Rothmund'. It inherits great vigour.from both parents, 'Joanna Hill' being a H.T. which grows up to 6 feet even on poor soil at Wisley, and from this plant also come the beautifully shaped semi-double flowers, opening from 'Ophelia'-like buds. They are clear pink in two tones, and reveal a few yellow stamens, and are deliciously scented of cloves. The strong zigzag stems have a splendid lot of broad, dark green leaves. An exceptionally fine shrub up to some 6 feet high and wide and of wonderful beauty at midsummer. Round, dull-reddish heps, which last into the winter.

'Frühlingsanfang'. Kordes, 1950. 'Joanna Hill' (H.T.) × R. *spinosissima* 'Grandiflora'. Very few of the newer shrub roses, or the species themselves, make such a luxuriant shrub as this; the copious leaves create a mantle of dark greenery against which the spring display of flowers is conspicuous. The flowers are single, sumptuous, and open wide and flat, but lack purity, being of a yellowish 'off-white'. In the autumn handsome maroon-red heps are produced, at which time the leaves usually turn to rich colours. 6 feet by 6 feet.

'Frühlingsduft'. Kordes, 1949. 'Joanna Hill' (H.T.) × R. *spinosissima* 'Grandiflora'. This is the only one of the set that has fully double, almost modern H.T. flowers, having inherited these and much of their colour from 'Joanna Hill'. They are shapely, with rolled petals, of a strange lemon-creamy-white, flushed with pink, with deeper apricot tones in the centre. An extremely rich fragrance is its proudest possession. Makes a vigorous leafy bush, 6 feet by 6 feet.

'Frühlingsgold'. Kordes, 1937. 'Joanna Hill' × R. *spinosissima* 'Hispida'. There is no doubt that in this rose we have a superlative plant which can hold its own in charm, fragrance, freedom of flowering, and growth with any flowering shrub. At the peak of its flowering period there is nothing more lovely in the garden and fortunately it thrives in any soil. Its great arching branches, freely but not densely set with leaves, carry along their length large, nearly single flowers of warm butter yellow, with richly coloured stamens, fading in hot weather to creamy white. It has a glorious, far-carrying fragrance. In some seasons it produces a September crop of flowers, but is usually only spring-flowering. Its spiny stems recall its *R. s. hispida* parentage. 7 feet by 7 feet. (Photograph, Plate 8.)

'**Frühlingsmorgen**'. Kordes, 1941. A hybrid of 'E. G. Hill' × ' Cathrine Kordes ' crossed with *R. spinosissima* ' Grandiflora '. I hesitate to claim that this is the most beautiful of all single roses: there are so many claimants. But appraising a flowering spray can easily suggest that here is a rare example of the breeder's art which equals if it does not eclipse nature's best efforts. Apart from the beauty of the clear rose-pink large petals which pass to clear, pale yellow in the centre, the flowers have the incomparable attraction of maroon-coloured filaments and anthers. It usually gives a crop of flowers in late summer as well as the generous mass in the spring. The bush is on the sparse side, leaves leaden-green. 6 feet by 5 feet. A few large, maroon-red heps are produced.

'**Frühlingsschnee**'. Kordes, 1954. 'Golden Glow'×*R. spinosissima* ' Grandiflora '. This has not developed strongly with me; the foliage is of a slightly greyish tinge, borne freely on arching branches. Beautifully scrolled buds of creamy yellow open to large, loosely semi-double, nearly white flowers. Fragrant. 5 feet.

'**Frühlingstag**'. Kordes, 1949. 'McGredy's Wonder' ×'Frühlingsgold'. This has not impressed me. The clusters of semi-double, golden yellow flowers are produced in early summer. Very fragrant.

'**Frühlingszauber**'. Kordes, 1941. The same parentage as 'Frühlingsmorgen', but of less good growth; with me, it is weak and awkward, never making a shrub, but creates a vivid though somewhat vulgar display in flower. The blooms are 3–4 inches across, semi-double to nearly single, of a flashy cerise scarlet with yellow centre on opening, fading to pink. A few large maroon-red heps. 6 feet.

'Gabrielle Noyelle'. Buatois, 1933. 'Salet' × 'Souvenir de Mme Krüger'. The first, in alphabetical order, of three yellowish Moss roses; the others are 'Golden Moss' and 'Robert Leopold'. Bright flesh pink to deep salmon is in the shapely small buds; they open to rich, creamy salmon with yellow base; semi-double, of starry shape. Free-flowering and showy. Attractive foliage. 5 feet by 4 feet.

'George Will'. Skinner, 1939. R. *rugosa* × R. *acicularis* × garden roses. Neat foliage, small for a *rugosa* hybrid, on thorny stems, making a fairly dense, rather upright bush. Semi-double flowers in clusters, from dainty buds, opening flat, of warm lilac pink. Fairly fragrant. So far this has not impressed me. 4 feet?

'Gold Bush'. Kordes, 1954. 'Goldbusch'. 'Golden Glow' × R. *rubiginosa* hybrid. This is making a freely branching, low bush, and has light, yellowish green leaves assorting well with the well-formed, deep peach-yellow flowers, semi-double to double, shewing yellow stamens. The shapely buds are coral-coloured. Rich Tea fragrance. Produces a good second crop, and may reach 5 feet in height, 9 feet in width. Full of beauty. (Photograph, Plate 16.)

'Golden Moss'. Dot, 1932. All strains of modern roses, apart from Floribundas and Poly-poms, are gathered together in this 'Blanche Moreau' hybrid. A lanky bush with dark green leaves, dark brown-red moss. The apricot buds open to well-filled, rather flat flowers of canary-yellow, fading paler, and with peach tones in the centre. 6 feet by 4 feet.

'Golden Wings'. Shepherd, 1956. An interesting and beautiful hybrid raised by Mr Roy Shepherd. R. *spinosissima* and the nearly related form or hybrid of it, 'Ormiston Roy', unite in the parentage with 'Soeur Thérèse', which is Hybrid Perpetual combined with Pernetiana. The result is a free-flowering and perpetual plant, no doubt of considerable hardiness; free-branching, compact habit; light green leaves of Hybrid Tea persuasion but not glossy. The blooms are borne singly or in clusters, with five to ten shapely petals making an exquisite large bloom. Clear, light canary yellow, fading slightly, contrasted by mahogany-amber stamens. Long, pointed buds. Deliciously scented. I have been highly impressed with its continuous performance, colour, and fragrance. 6 feet by 5 feet. (Plate VII.) McFarland, *Modern Roses* v, frontispiece.

'Grandmaster'. Kordes, 1952. 'Sangerhausen' × 'Sunmist'. When cut and exhibited in a fresh, unpollinated state this flower has lovely qualities. It is apricot-red in bud opening to amber-tinted lemon with apricot shadings and yellow stamens. Unfortunately the flowers fade, the stamens turn dirty after pollinating, and in addition it is not a good grower. Little scent. Sometimes classed as a Hybrid Musk without qualification.

'Grootendorst Supreme'. Grootendorst, 1936. This originated as a sport from 'F. J. Grootendorst', and at first sight is a more pleasing plant. The flower colour, a very dark garnet red, contrasts well with the light green hue of the leaves. But the plant is less vigorous and healthy than its parent, the foliage is often sickly, and the flowers are smaller. As a plant which does not look healthy is seldom a success in the garden, I discard this variety in preference to the original. 4 feet.

'Gruss an Teplitz'. Lambert, 1897. ('Sir Joseph Paxton' × ' Fellenberg ') × (' Papa Gontier ' × ' Gloire des Rosomanes '). Owing to this fine battle of names in its parentage this rose does not fit well into any group. From a horticultural point of view it may be classed as a Bourbon. The dark crimson flowers often shew intensification of colour after hot sunshine, which confirms the considerable amount of China Rose in it. The flowers are borne in small clusters at midsummer, but the strong, arching shoots later in the season may bear up to a dozen nodding blooms. Purplish young foliage becoming green, on a strong bush, reaching up to 6 feet or so, or 12 feet with support. Rich spicy fragrance. Perpetual. An admirable rose for many purposes, assorting well with new or old varieties, and useful for informal hedges.

Strassheim, 1899.
Journal des Roses, Septembre 1899. 'Salut à Teplitz'. Poor.
Hoffmann, Plate 19.

'Harry Maasz'. Kordes, 1939. ' Barcelona ' (H.T.)×R. ' Macrantha Daisy Hill '. In garden effect this may be described as a crimson-flowered variant of R. ' Macrantha '. The yellow stamens show up beautifully against the paler centre of the light crimson flower, which deepens in colour towards the edges of the petals, emerging from pointed, dark crimson buds. These flowers are borne along the trailing stems and create a vivid display. The foliage is dull, dark leaden-green. It would be superb trailing through some grey-leaved shrub. Shoots 10 feet long are produced in a season, and it is less bushy than R. *macrantha* and so is suitable for training on fences, over hedges, into low trees, etc. Well scented.

'Heidelberg'. Kordes, 1958. 'Sparrieshoop'×'World's Fair'. Throws up immense shoots crowned with large heads of brilliant flowers, large, double, of good shape, a glowing crimson-scarlet, overshot flame. The foliage is dark green, leathery, and glossy. It is fairly recurrent but does not make a bushy plant and is somewhat tender. 6 to 7 feet.
Park, Plate 192.

'Hon. Lady Lindsay'. Hansen, 1938. 'New Dawn'×'Rev. Page Roberts'. This might be described as the first shrub rose raised with H. T. flowers. It has plum red thorns and handsome growth, glossy dark leathery leaves of medium size, on a branching plant usually wider than high. The blooms have a 'Chatenay' freshness, double but showing stamens, of a delightful, two-toned, pale salmon pink; darker on the reverse of the petals. *Wichuraiana* scent, tempered with Tea. I find this a fairly good grower, and a free flowerer in hot summers. 4 feet.

'Jardin de la Croix' was raised at Roseraie de l'Haÿ in 1901, and one parent was R. *roxburghii*. A very interesting hybrid showing unmistakably the influence of this species. It grows well and has good foliage, and many buds have formed, but so far have not opened, in my collection. At the Roseraie the double pink flowers were good. This rose seems to be extinct.

'Josef Rothmund'. Kordes, 1940. 'Joanna Hill' × 'Magnifica'. An extra vigorous shrub with good, fresh green leaves and clusters of small salmon-pink, semi-double flowers of rather poor quality. 8 to 9 feet.

'Karl Foerster'. Kordes, 1931. 'Frau Karl Druschki' × R. *spinosissima* ' Grandiflora '. A most interesting cross, making a strong bush with medium-sized green leaves. The scentless, double, white flowers inherited from ' Frau Karl ' are shapely in the bud and when open. Effective in the garden. Recurrent. 5 feet by 4 feet when growing well.

'Kassel'. Kordes, 1957. 'Obergärtner Wiebicke' × 'Independence'. Classed as a climber, but makes a good arching shrub with plentiful, dark, glossy leaves. Vivid flowers in the 'Bonn' persuasion, but brighter and of better form. Brilliant cherry-red, with cinnabar-red and flame overtones, large, semi-double; profuse at midsummer, and intermittently later. Probably 12 feet on a wall but about 7 feet as a shrub. Rather gawky, needs support. Some fragrance.

'Kathleen Ferrier'. Buisman, 1952. 'Gartenstolz' × 'Shot Silk'. Rather open-growing, but producing large and small heads of semi-double flowers of deep pink, sweetly scented of raspberries and bananas. Makes a rather open shrub, but is fairly recurrent. 5 feet by 4 feet.

'Lady Curzon'. Turner, 1901. An exceptionally vigorous, prolific hybrid between R. *rugosa rubra* and R. ' Macrantha '; if left to itself it makes a mound of tangled branches some 8 feet high and wide, but its prickly, far-reaching, and arching growths can climb through bushes and low trees. The dark green, rough foliage shews signs of both parents. The single, crinkled, light pink, wide-open flowers are produced in the utmost profusion, completely smothering the branches for a few weeks. Beautiful stamens; good scent. I remember my first sight of this at Nymans, where its branches were interlaced with the tiny violet-purple flowers of the Rambler ' Violette '.
Gault and Synge, plate 174.

'Lafter' ('Laughter'). Brownell, 1948. 'Général Jacqueminot' and 'Dr van Fleet' are in its parentage, mixed up with modern roses. Of sufficient vigour and grace to be included here though classed as a Floribunda. Starts flowering late in the season and has successive crops; the clusters of semi-double flowers on arching shoots have brilliance and charm. They are of medium size, loosely cupped shape, semi-double, rich salmon-flame fading to salmon rose, with apricot reverse, yellow base, and yellow stamens. The light green leaves and red thorns complete a pleasing picture. Growth vigorous and will probably attain 5 feet by 4 feet. Rich *wichuraiana* scent of green apples and lemon.

'**Macrantha**'. One of the most prolific and thrifty of shrubs, making an intricate tangle of arching branches, set with small thorns, and bearing neat leaves. The flowers are borne in small clusters and are large, single, of cream pink fading to nearly white from a pink bud, with conspicuous stamens. In full flower it is an arresting sight and deliciously scented. It is, being procumbent and arching, an ideal shrub for foreground planting, clothing banks, stumps, and hedgerows. The round, red heps create a display later. 5 feet by 10 feet. This rose of uncertain garden origin is sometimes made a variety of R. *waitziana*, the name for the cross between R. *canina* and *gallica*; but if that is so our present plant is some generations removed from the original cross.

Willmott, Plate 403.

Revue Horticole, 1901, p. 548. Poor.
The Garden, 1897. p. 464.

'**Macrantha Daisy Hill**'. William Paul, 1906. Similar in all respects to R. ' Macrantha ', of which it is supposedly a hybrid, but with an extra two or three petals. This results in the flowers remaining open better in dull weather. Conspicuous in flower and later when bearing round, red heps. A thoroughly satisfactory garden shrub, mounding itself into a large dense mass, and exceedingly fragrant. Herr Kordes has used this freely as a parent. 5 feet by 12 feet.

'**Magenta**'. Kordes, 1954. Yellow Floribunda seedling × 'Lavender Pinocchio'. A beautiful rose, in effect a tall Floribunda with old-style flowers. The far-away connection with the Hybrid Musk group may be the reason for the excellent foliage, resembling that of 'Penelope'. Red thorns. Trusses of double flowers, opening from beautifully coiled lilac-pink buds to coppery lilac-pink with cerise shadings. Full-petalled, often quartered. Delicious scent of myrrh. 4 feet.

'Maigold'. Kordes, 1953. 'McGredy's Wonder' × 'Frühlings-gold'. Something between a climber and a shrub, this rose has really excellent foliage, rich, glossy and profuse. The flowers appear at the beginning of the rose season, of deep buff yellow, reddish in the bud, semi-double, shewing a bunch of golden stamens. Powerful, delicious fragrance. Repeats occasionally in late summer on tips of new shoots. As a shrub, about 5 feet by 10 feet.

'Märchenland'. Tantau, 1951. 'Swantje' × 'Hamburg'. 'Swantje' has 'Joanna Hill' in its parentage, a very vigorous Hybrid Tea, and 'Hamburg' has a slender connection with the Hybrid Musks. A strong-growing Floribunda with large, semi-double, salmon-rose flowers in clusters. Fragrant. 4 feet.

'Marguerite Hilling'. Sleet, 1959. A sport from 'Nevada' which occurred about 1954. The same colour form occurred at the Sunningdale Nurseries some years previously and also in Mrs Steen's garden in New Zealand in 1958. It promises to make as good a plant as 'Nevada' and the colour is a pleasing deep flesh-pink.

'Max Graf'. Bowditch, 1919. R. *rugosa* × R. *wichuraiana*. 'Lady Duncan' was of similar parentage. For many years lingering in obscurity, this rose has now sprung into the limelight for two reasons. First, because it spontaneously produced tetraploid seeds, the progeny qualifying for specific status as R. *kordesii*. It had been sterile for years but the fertile tetraploid has been the ancestor of many new roses raised by Herr Kordes. Secondly, because we now welcome roses that are satisfactory, attractive, weed-smothering ground covers. It makes a dense mat of trailing branches, seldom reaching above 2 feet until thoroughly mounded up with its own growths, and well covered with bright green leaves; I have grown two forms, presumably sister-seedlings, one with rather dull leaves and the other with more glossy leaves of darker green: the two would appear to lean toward either parent in this respect. Although they flower only once, it is a very long season, and the contrast of the nearly single pink blooms with white centres and yellow stamens over the greenery is pleasing, and they are sweetly scented of green apples.

It is a most valuable plant, rooting as it goes and creating a dense mantle over the ground; presumably with unlimited scope there would be no stopping it, for its subsidiary layers would ever produce new and vigorous plants. No weeds come through it. It is ideal for the fronts of shrub borders, for clothing banks and for hanging down walls, and no doubt could also be trained upwards, on banks and fences.

'Max Haufe'. Kordes, 1939. 'Joanna Hill' × 'Magnifica'. A lusty shrub or semi-climber, with good, broad foliage. Medium-sized, semi-double, pink flowers, wide open, shewing yellow stamens. Not free-flowering. Few thorns. 8 to 10 feet.

'Mechtilde von Neuerburg'. Bodin, 1920. A vigorous shrub, reported to reach 10 feet high and wide, and a hybrid of R. *rubiginosa*. The pink flowers are medium sized, single or with an extra petal or two, borne in clusters; nothing out of the ordinary. Fragrant. The fruits have yet to justify the plant's existence.

× MICRUGOSA. Raised prior to 1905; R. *rugosa* × R. *roxburghii* (R. *microphylla*). R. *vilmoriniana*, R. *wilsonii*. This combines the very bushy habit of both parents, leaning towards R. *rugosa* in its thorns and crisp foliage, while the flowers are single and flat, similar to R. *roxburghii*, and held in a similar way among the leaves, but do not last long. It is a very dense bush, and would make an excellent impenetrable hedge. Will probably exceed 5 feet by 6 feet. Heps rounded, bristly, orange-green. The thorny bark does not peel.

Gartenflora, vol. lix, Plate 1581. Unrecognizable.

Revue Horticole, 1905, p. 144. Fruits, very fine.

× MICRUGOSA 'Alba'. Raised by Dr C.C. Hurst at Cambridge; a second generation from the original cross. Slightly more erect in growth, with lighter green leaves and white flowers. Heps similar. The flowers are more fragrant than in the pink type, and successive crops are produced.

'Mme Georges Bruant'. Bruant, 1887. R. *rugosa* × 'Sombreuil', which was a creamy-white Tea Rose, and the result is what one would expect from such a cross: a big, strong, prickly, upright bush with glossy yet slightly rugose foliage in rich green. The flowers emerge from very shapely Tea Rose buds, creamy white, fading to white, fairly double and silky, scented, shewing yellow stamens. They are borne singly and in clusters, in great profusion at midsummer and in autumn, and intermittently meanwhile. It creates a specially good contrast of floral and foliage colours; seen against a dark yew hedge, as at Spetchley Park, it can be magnificent. Unfortunately the flowers are often poorly shaped. 6 feet by 4 feet.
Rosenzeitung, October 1906.

' Morletii '. Morlet, 1883. R. *inermis morlettii*. Also found under the name of R. *pendulina plena*, which is of doubtful authenticity. It is beautiful in spring, with richly tinted young foliage, which later becomes greyish green with reddish veins and stalks. Early in the flowering season it produces many clusters of double, small to medium-sized, magenta blooms. Densely glandular calyx and smooth receptacle. Dark, plum-coloured wood, devoid of thorns, making an elegant arching shrub. Foliage develops prolonged autumn colour, coppery-orange and red tones predominating. In spite of its lack of scent, this is one of the best shrub roses for continued effect, giving as it does colour in spring and autumn as well as at flowering time. Has been listed as R. *pendulina plena*. 5 feet by 5 feet.

' Moyesii Superba '. Van Rossem. A dusky beauty with the elegant growth of R. *moyesii*, but much more compact. Dark green foliage; plum-coloured stems, calyx and receptacle. Flowers are semi-double, in the R. *moyesii* persuasion, but of very dark maroon-crimson. It unfortunately has no scent and does not produce heps. My plants are yet young but a large bush should create an impressive sight, and may reach 7 feet in height. Reported to be R. *moyesii* × 'Gustav Grünerwald', but the chromosome count does not support the inclusion of the Hybrid Tea rose.

'**Morning Stars**'. Jacobus, 1949. With 'Autumn Bouquet', 'Inspiration', and a double dose of 'New Dawn' in its being this is a fresh-looking, small shrub with glossy, dark green leaves, and produces lemon-white, semi-double, modern flowers singly or in clusters through the season, shewing yellow stamens. Delicious penetrating lemon scent. Will probably reach 5 feet by 4 feet.

'**Mrs Anthony Waterer**'. Waterer, 1898. 'Général Jacqueminot' × hybrid of R. *rugosa*. A vigorous, arching, prickly bush with red thorns, and dull, dark green leaves, making usually a mound of arching growths. In early summer a luxuriant crop of flowers is produced, and a few later, but in my experience it does not have an effective autumn crop. The flowers are loosely double or semi-double, cupped, of rich, bright crimson flushed with purple, borne usually in small clusters or singly. Richly scented. This rose was given a special bed at Kew and was a splendid sight every summer; on a bright day the flowers fade, but the blend of colour over the bed is always satisfying. 4 feet by 7 feet.

'**Mrs Oakley Fisher**'. Cant, 1921. In the gardens of those who admire single-flowered roses, in constant flower through the season, borne on a large shrub, this exquisite variety is not overlooked. Shapely buds open into 5-petalled blooms of soft buff yellow, deliciously fragrant. At Sissinghurst it achieves some 6 feet by 6 feet. Strictly a Hybrid Tea but it fits well with roses in this chapter, providing much needed yellow, or would assort with Hybrid Musks.

'**München**'. Kordes, 1940. 'Eva' × 'Réveil Dijonnais'. One of the several perpetual-flowering shrub roses which have a distant connection, through 'Eva', with the Hybrid Musks; the influence of R. *foetida*, through 'Réveil Dijonnais', is not noticeable. It is a robust shrub with good, dark, glossy green leaves. The flowers, borne in clusters, are loosely semi-double from pointed maroon buds and are of intense dark garnet red, with an occasional white streak, but little scent. Large greenish heps with persistent calyx. A sister seedling to 'Erfurt', and valuable for the depth of tone it imparts to any collection. 8 feet by 5 feet.

'**Nevada**'. Dot, 1927. 'La Giralda' × a tetraploid relative of R. *moyesii*. 'La Giralda' was a cross between 'Frau Karl Druschki' and 'Mme Édouard Herriot', and the result is about what one might expect from a fusion of the H.T. type and R. *moyesii*. From the latter are inherited the great spraying branches flowering along their length; the leaves are light green, midway between the parents; the flowers are 4 inches across, nearly single, creamy white with blush tints, emerging from reddish buds. In hot weather the colour becomes more pink with sometimes a red splash.

This is one of the most spectacular of all flowering shrubs when in bloom, hundreds of flowers being littered all over the bush, almost obscuring the foliage, at early midsummer; later in August if the weather be warm a smaller crop matures; in good weather subsequent flowers appear until autumn. In dull summers a lack of continuity is noticeable and the colour fades nearly to white. It flowers with the Rugosa roses, and with them makes a large, rounded shrub some 7 feet high and even wider, shoots sometimes of 8 feet in length being studded with flowers for their entire length.

Doubts by leading geneticists have been cast on the published parentage of this rose since R. *moyesii* itself is a hexaploid; possibly one of the tetraploid forms or related species, such as R. *moyesii* 'Fargesii' or R. *holodonta*, was used. Trying to visualize a hybrid between one of these and a Hybrid Tea, I do not think that 'Nevada' is by any means an impossible result. (Fig. 8; photograph, Plate 12.) Pink sports have occurred and one has been named 'Marguerite Hilling' q.v. (Page 183.)

'**New Century**'. Van Fleet, 1900. R. *rugosa* 'Alba' × 'Clothilde Soupert'. This and 'Sir Thomas Lipton' were raised from the same cross, but have little in common. 'New Century' makes a fine bush, rather in the Rugosa tradition, but less prickly and with smoother leaves. The flowers are saucer-shaped, with several rows of petals of cool lilac-pink fading at the edges, and having a heart of creamy stamens. Very fragrant. At times the blooms have the fullness and shape of R. *centifolia*. 4 feet by 4 feet.

'Nova Zembla'. Mees, 1907. A sport which appeared in 1907 on 'Conrad F. Meyer'. It is in all respects identical except for the colour of the flowers, which are nearly white, with a delicate pink flush. Like 'Conrad Meyer' it produces its best blooms in early autumn, and at that time few flowers can touch it for shape, purity, and exquisite tint. Sweetly scented. 8 to 9 feet by 4 feet.

'Nymphenburg'. Kordes, 1954. 'Sangerhausen' × 'Sunmist'. A shrub rose of great promise. Vigorous, semi-climbing stems fork freely but do not make a good bush. Foliage large, glossy, dark green. The flowers are nearly double, of warm salmon-pink shaded cerise-pink and orange, with yellow bases to the petals, emerging from apricot buds. Extremely delicious green-apple scent, of penetrating intensity. Recurrent bloom until autumn. After the hot summer of 1959 the plants were resplendent in autumn with large turbinate heps of orange red. Probably 6 by 8 feet. (Plates III, heps; VIII, flowers.)

'Nyveldt's White'. Nyveldt, 1955. R. *rugosa rubra* × R. *cinnamomea* crossed with R. *nitida*. This shows most affinity to R. *rugosa* and makes a large arching shrub with fresh green leaves. The flowers are borne in clusters, single, of cold, pure white; recurrent. Fragrant. Heps orange-red.

'Oratam'. Jacobus, 1939. R. *damascena* × 'Souvenir de Claudius Pernet'. An unexpected rose to have Damask parentage. It has dark, broad, glossy leaves and fully double luxurious flowers, salmon, with yellowish reverse and centre. A rather vulgar rose, and one which I find rather difficult to assess for garden value, but it may well be useful among the modern shrub roses. Resembles the Rugosa hybrid 'Vanguard'. 5 feet by 4 feet.

'Park Jewel'. See 1961 edition of *The Old Shrub Roses*.

'Paulii'. George Paul—prior to 1903. R. *rugosa* × R. *arvensis*. R. *rugosa repens alba*. Excessively thorny, with *rugosa*-like foliage and flowers. The vigour and trailing habit of R. *arvensis* have added to the characters which are otherwise near to those of R. *rugosa*. The shoots grow up to about 12 feet long and lie flat on the ground, successive shoots gradually mounding up to 3 feet in height, but it is at all times a vigorous, dense ground cover and very thrifty. Flowers slightly clove-scented, like those of R. *rugosa*; petals deeply notched, crinkled, with a bunch of yellow stamens; many pale green bracts.

This trailer, with 'Max Graf', the R. *macrantha* forms, and R. *wichuraiana* itself, are the best ground-covering roses, and of them all R. *paulii* is the most thorny and dense. When in flower it looks like a clematis.

'Paulii Rosea'. Prior to 1912. Rather less vigorous than the all-conquering white type, this has a beauty of flower unexcelled by other single pink roses. The petals are deeply notched, pleated, silky, of clear and beautiful pink, but white around the yellow stamens, giving each bloom a very fresh appearance. I have heard of R. 'Paulii' producing a pink sport, and there-fore conclude that this form was originally a sport from R. *paulii*. Equally fragrant. *Les Plus Belles Roses*, p. 44. R. *gallica* × *rugosa*: unmistakably 'Paulii Rosea'.
Trechslin & Coggiatti. Very good.

'Pike's Peak'. Gunter, 1940. R. *acicularis* × 'Hollywood'. Coarsely toothed leaves; wide, semi-double flowers of bright cherry pink, paler in the centre around the yellow stamens. Fresh fragrance.

'Pink Grootendorst'. Grootendorst, 1923. Like 'Grootendorst Supreme' this was a sport from 'F. J. Grootendorst' and, in spite of its chocolate-box prettiness and complete lack of scent, it is a favourite with many. It resembles in every way its parent, and is seldom out of flower during the summer and autumn. The bunches of flowers are of brilliant, light cerise pink in marked contrast to the leaves, and create a good effect in the garden. It is excellent for cutting and adds 'point' to many a bowl of mixed roses. It is curious that both the sports are less vigorous and healthy than the original; a darker variant is often less vigorous than a pale rose, but here both of them are decidedly inferior to 'F. J. Grootendorst' in vigour and foliage. McFarland, *Roses of the World*, p. 211. Rather exaggerated; a good colour photograph.
Park, Plate 203. A good photograph.
Bois and Trechslin, Plate 9.

× POLLINIANA. Cultivated since 1820, this is a hybrid between R. *arvensis* and R. *gallica*. No doubt it has occurred many times— and both colour and habit would vary—but this particular clone seems well known in horticulture and is accurately portrayed by Miss Willmott. It is a low, sprawling shrub, gradually making a mound about 10 feet wide and 4 feet high, with prickly shoots which would climb through shrubs and into trees. Small olive-green leaves; the whole plant is decorated for a short period by the small clusters of large, single roses, clear rose pink in the dainty buds.and opening to blush, with yellow stamens and delicious scent. Young twigs are purplish coloured, with coppery leaves, partaking of R. *arvensis*.
Willmott, Plate 333.

'Poulsen's Park Rose'. Poulsen, 1953. 'Great Western' (a Bourbon) × 'Karen Poulsen'. Stout, reddish, prickly stems make a fine, big shrub with two great bursts of blooms, of high quality in dry, warm weather. The petals are rather thin, and are not resistant to rain. Large and small clusters of blooms, long-pointed in the bud, opening to shapely, nearly double blooms, of Hybrid Tea quality; soft pink. Fragrant. 4 feet by 5 feet.

'Queen Elizabeth'. Lammerts, 1954. 'Charlotte Armstrong' × 'Floradora'. This vigorous, upright-growing 'Grandiflora' rose is sufficiently large in growth to be included here. Its only faults, as I see it, are that it is of erect habit, not making a pleasing rounded bush and therefore needing other shorter Floribundas around it, and that it is not particularly fragrant. Shapely H.T. flowers of clear pink, borne singly and in clusters. Very free-flowering. 6 feet by 3 feet.

'Raubritter'. Kordes, 1936. R. 'Macrantha Daisy Hill' × 'So-larium' (rambler). A pretty, sprawling shrub for foreground and bank planting, eventually mounding itself into a hummock about 7 feet across, 3 feet high, with somewhat thorny, inter-lacing branches and small dark leaves. The flowers are borne in clusters, of clear, fresh pink, semi-double, but remaining prettily incurved, recalling the old Bourbon Roses. Each bloom stays in beauty for a week and the plants are beautiful for several weeks at midsummer. No other rose that I have met has such irresistible charm, with its low branches laden with ball-like blooms. Beautiful with all purple flowered plants and grey foliage. Liable to mildew. (Photograph, Plate 14.)

'Refulgence'. W. Paul, 1909. A big, gaunt plant descended from *R. rubiginosa*, with strong, thorny shoots 8 feet high, sparsely leaved but bearing refulgent scarlet-crimson, semi-double flowers. A showy plant which is best placed behind others to cover its ugly growth below. A few round to oval heps.

'Robert Leopold'. Buatois, 1941. Very vigorous Moss Rose hybrid with bright green leaves and dark thorns and 'moss'. The shapely, brilliant apricot buds open to coppery apricot, loosely double flowers of rounded outline fading to lilac-rose in full sun. Sweetly scented. 5 feet by 3 feet.

'Rosenwunder'. Kordes, 1934. 'W. E. Chaplin' × 'Magnifica'. A lax bush with richly coloured reddish twigs, nearly thornless; pretty, coppery young foliage; good, glossy summer leaves and attractive flowers followed by red heps. The flowers are loosely semi-double, cupped, coppery light crimson, with a rich scent of ripe gooseberries. 6 feet by 6 feet.

'Roxane'. Raised by Sir Frederick Stern, the result of crossing *R. roxburghii* with *R. sinowilsonii*. At Highdown this has reached about five feet in height. It has pleasant foliage of light green and flat, deep pink flowers, both more reminiscent of *R. roxburghii* than the other parent. Green prickly heps.

'Ruskin'. Van Fleet, 1928. *R. rugosa* × 'Victor Hugo' (H.P.). This is a coarse, unmanageable hybrid making very thorny shoots 10 feet or more long, and bearing plentiful good foliage of rough texture. Like the little girl in the nursery rhyme— 'when she was good she was very, very good, but when she was bad she was horrid'—the blooms can be sumptuous, of H.P. fullness and of a gorgeous crimson scarlet and with delicious scent. Sometimes, more often than not, one only has the scent. It can be made into a reasonable bush by pruning, or can be pegged down, or trained on wall or fence, and is very free-flowering at midsummer, with a few blooms later.

'**Rustica**'. Barbier, 1929. 'Mme Édouard Herriot' × 'Harison's Yellow'. In both parents is a strain of R. *foetida*, and this rose certainly leans towards them in its smooth brown wood and grey thorns, rich green leaves, wide receptacle and peculiar fragrance. The flowers are fully double though loose, coral- or salmon-tinted yellow. It flowers early in the season and is a beautiful plant when well grown, its arching branches being in flower for their whole length. 4 feet by 4 feet.

'**Sarah Van Fleet**'. Van Fleet, 1926. R. *rugosa* × 'My Maryland' (H.T.). Few flowering shrubs of any kind make such a dense mass of erect stems; they are covered with good leaves except at the base. It is ideal for a tall screen, or for planting at the back of the border, and is always in flower, creating a massed effect at midsummer; the September crop appears on longer stems with elegant prickles and foliage. The flowers are in clusters, with two or three rows of petals, opening from pointed buds to shallow cups of cool pink with a hint of lilac. Young foliage and shoots are bronze-tinted. Suitable for the largest plantings. 8 feet by 5 feet.

'**Scarlet Fire**'. Kordes, 1952. 'Scharlachglut'. 'Poinsettia' × R. *gallica* 'Grandiflora'. A great arching shrub with smooth brown wood and thorns and plenty of normal green leaves. During its one flowering season, which is long, it is a most spectacular plant. Each flower—and they are borne in clusters all along the branches—is well shaped, 3 inches across, composed of five perfect, lustrous, velvety petals of intense blazing scarlet-crimson, lightened by a neat centre of yellow stamens. Large, long-lasting, pear-shaped red heps with persistent calyx. A really splendid shrub of large dimensions, probably 7 feet by 7 feet or wider, which takes time to build itself into a firm bush. A colour photograph appeared as Plate VII in my first book, *The Old Shrub Roses* (Photograph, Plate 7).

'**Schneelicht**'. Geschwind, 1896. Reported to be R. *rugosa* × R. *phoenicea*. Good foliage, fairly typical of R. *rugosa*, of rich dark green, which shews up the pure white flowers, opening from pointed, blush-white buds; they are single with yellow stamens. The bush is composed of many arching branches, and the flowers are borne rambler-fashion all along the branches in clusters. Good, fairly light green foliage. Makes a really splendid mound comparable to R. ' Paulii ', less prostrate, but with better flowers, 5 feet by 8 feet. (Photograph, Plate 10.)

'Schneezwerg'. Lambert, 1912. R. *rugosa* hybrid. A most pleasing bush, of good shape, fairly dense and twiggy, bearing pairs of grey thorns, and dark, shining green, rugose foliage. The creamy buds are perfect, likewise the flowers—opening flat like an anemone, and with two or three rows of pure white petals and creamy-yellow stamens; they are produced without stint through the season, and the later crops coincide delightfully with the small orange-red heps. I have never clipped it, but think it would respond well and make a good hedge. One of the few hybrids of R. *rugosa* that approach the first-class category. 7 feet by 5 feet. It was originally reported to be R. *rugosa* × R. *bracteata* and this seems quite possible from its appearance.

' Scintillation '. Austin; Sunningdale, 1966. R. ' Macrantha ' × 'Vanity'. Decorated by yellow stamens, the scintillating mass of petals from the clusters of semi-double blush-pink flowers creates an effect at midsummer which one cannot forget. It is a vigorous sprawler for covering stumps and hedges and for climbing into small trees. Leaden green foliage. Very fragrant. 5 feet by 10 feet.

' Sir Thomas Lipton '. Van Fleet, 1900. R. *rugosa* ' Alba ' × 'Clothilde Soupert'. Although of different parentage, it is a similar large bush to 'Mme Georges Bruant', with green young wood and fairly good foliage. The blooms are creamy white, borne singly or in clusters, in early summer and intermittently onwards, semi-double to fully double. When a good one appears it can be as shapely as a camellia. 6 feet by 4 feet.

'Soleil d'Or'. Pernet-Ducher, 1900. 'Antoine Ducher' × 'Persian Yellow'. This cannot be described as a shrub rose, but it is such an historic piece that I feel I must mention it. The bulk of our flame and orange modern roses have this rose in their ancestry, for it was the first 'Pernetiana' rose; unfortunately it is a martyr to 'black spot'. Double, rich orange-yellow; the influence of R. *foetida* is found in its scent and foliage.

Revue de l'Horticulture Belge, 1900, Plate 109; also 1905, Plate 13.
Journal des Roses, Juin 1900.

'Sonnenlicht'. Kruger, 1910. 'Lady Mary Fitzwilliam' ×
'Harison's Yellow'. A vigorous plant, with foliage and growth
similar to the second parent, but coarser. The flowers are borne
singly along the branches, supported by a wide receptacle.
Many petals are contained in tight, greenish buds which do not
always open properly; clear canary yellow when full blown,
and rich R. *foetida* fragrance. Beloved by the late Mrs Constance
Spry for its lime-yellow tints. An arching plant that needs some
support, and flowers early in the season. 5 feet by 5 feet.

'Sparrieshoop'. Kordes, 1952. Arises from a cross between
Floribundas and the Sweet Brier known as 'Magnifica'. Deep
coppery-brown young shoots, thorns, and foliage; leaves
glossy and handsome, turning to dark green. Single flowers all
with one extra petal, leathery, crinkled, and slighty lobed; clear,
warm, rosy salmon pink, with lighter centre around the yellow
stamens; fading to pale pink. Sweetly fragrant. 5 feet by 4 feet.

'Till Uhlenspiegel'. Kordes, 1950. 'Holstein' × 'Magnifica'. A
very strong sprawling shrub, with dark plum-coloured new
shoots, thorns and young foliage, which later turns to mid
green. A great display of crimson-red single flowers appears in
summer. The flowers have white centres, and give an effect
reminiscent of 'American Pillar' but are more richly coloured.
Shoots 8 to 10 feet long; suitable for clothing banks, walls,
fences, or hedges.

'Vanguard'. Stevens, 1932. A hybrid between R. *wichuraiana* and
R. *rugosa* ' Alba ' was crossed with ' Eldorado ', an H.T. of Pernetiana descent from 'Mme Édouard Herriot'. This remarkable
hybrid is in a way a foretaste of the *kordesii* roses. It is a vigorous
plant, making stout wood and bearing large, shining, green
leaves, with large orange-salmon flowers, rather shapeless but
fully double. It can be treated as a bush or a pillar rose, but is
very upsetting in the garden except among roses of its own
colouring. 5 feet by 5 feet. I have lost this plant and wish to
acquire it again.

McFarland, *Roses of the World*, page 276. A good representation.

'Wadei'. 1919. R. *rugosa* × R. *moyesii*. A peculiar little sprawling shrub, whose yellowish, rough leaves always look sickly. Single pink flowers. Of little garden value.

'Zigeuner Knabe'. Lambert, 1909. 'Gipsy Boy'. A seedling of 'Russelliana', which is possibly descended from R. *setigera*. One of the most thrifty roses in my collection, making dense, graceful bushes 5 feet high and nearly twice as wide, composed of arching, prickly stems. Both stems and foliage are reminiscent of R. *rugosa*. It creates a magnificent effect in flower at midsummer, when it is covered with small clusters of fair-sized blooms, semi-double, flat and reflexing, of intense crimson purple, white towards the centre. Rather lacking in quality as a flower, but splendid as a shrub. Orange-red heps. A little fragrance.
Park, Plate 177.

Postscript 1980 Edition

In the search for weed-defeating ground-cover, three roses other than those mentioned on pp. 34 and 165 have recently come to the fore.

'**Nozomi**'. A Japanese hybrid (1968) has small, single pearly pink flowers in large trusses at midsummer. Dense, trailing habit, small neat leaves. 2 feet × 8 feet.

'**Snow Carpet**'. McGredy; Mattock, 1980. Fully double, small, white, rosette flowers in trusses, Rambler-style, over a dense carpet of trailing shoots set with small leaves. Owing to its repeat flowering habit, this bids fair to be an important plant. 1 foot × 4 feet?

'**Temple Bells**'. Morey; McGredy, 1974. Single white flowers with conspicuous yellow stamens borne in sprays at midsummer; fragrant. Small, glossy, dark green foliage; vigorous spreading habit; 1 foot × 10 feet? Related to R. *wichuraiana*.

15

Key to the Major Groups
of Cultivated Roses

with a list of double-flowered mutants

by GORDON D. ROWLEY

(*Formerly Keeper, National Rose Species Collection, John Innes Institute*)

THIS KEY is designed to cover only the main groups of garden rose in broad outline. It is well known that the system of classifying roses according to ancestry has many drawbacks, especially today when the lines of descent are complicated and interwoven. An artificial system of breakdown into classes based on habit, flower size and grouping, function, and general garden utility is badly needed to replace it, but has not been forthcoming. Hence the old categories are here retained. In addition to the main groups there are of course others—the side-branches of the rose family tree. There are the off-beat hybrids like 'Cantab' derived from *Rosa nutkana*, and 'Cerise Bouquet' from *multibracteata* and Kordes's Hybrid Spinosissimas. Other anomalies are roses bridging gaps between existing groups: 'Gloire des Rosomanes' (Bourbon × China), 'Cécile Brunner' (Tea × *multiflora*), and so on.

It is not practical to attempt to make a key for the identification of individual rose varieties. Apart from their enormous numbers, the very means of producing them by shuffling and reshuffling the same sets of genes in all possible combinations precludes a simple breakdown into groups. How, then, is one to name an old rose that has lost its label? Unlike the wild species they cannot be re-collected in the type locality or run down in a local flora. The only means is a search of the literature in the hopes of finding a description or plate to match: a task which has occupied Mr Thomas for many years now, with conspicuous success. It speaks much for his labours that the names of so many delightful old roses are back in circulation again after falling into neglect, or after the plants were thought to be extinct. It has been a pleasure to assist him botanically in his good work by drawing up the following key, and also by contributing the list of double-flowered mutants and the genealogies of hybrid *spinosissimas* and *rubiginosas*, which I hope may add to the usefulness of the book.

A Flowers quite single, with (4 to) 5 equal petals and numerous normal stamens.[1] — **WILD ROSES AND THEIR HYBRIDS** (Species and varieties)

AA Flowers full, double or semi-double, or at least with a few petaloid staminodes or small accessory petals. — **GARDEN ROSES** (Cultivars)

B Plants climbing or rambling, with long sprawling or arching shoots tapering towards the tips (i.e. with leaves of progressively smaller size).

C Stipules with long, free tips, early deciduous. Flowers very small, 1 (to 1½) inches in diameter. — BANKSIANS

CC Stipules with short, free tips, not deciduous. Flowers larger, at least above 1 inch diameter.

D Leaflets bright green, glossy, leathery and sub-evergreen. — HYBRID WICHURAIANAS

DD Leaflets dull green or flushed red, not (or scarcely) glossy, thin, deciduous.

E Stipules fringed. — CLIMBING POLYANTHAS

EE Stipules not fringed, at most gland-edged.

F Plants almost or quite unarmed, with red, glaucous branches. — BOURSAULTS

FF Plants prickly.

[1] Except for 'Frühlingsmorgen', 'Mermaid', 'Nevada', and a few large-flowered backcrosses of garden roses to species.

For a key to the wild species of *Rosa*, see B. O. Mulligan in R.H.S. *Dictionary of Gardening*, iv, 1951, 1810–11.

G Strong climbers   AYRSHIRES,
or arching shrubs   NOISETTES AND
with small to   TEAS
medium blooms.
GG Stiffly erect pil-   CLIMBING H.T.s
lar roses or
weakly climbing
bushes with large,
exhibition - type
blooms.
BB Plants not markedly climbing or
rambling; leaves not diminishing
towards the apices of the shoots.
H Flowering season short, in early   **OLD SHRUB ROSES**
summer, with at best occasional
blooms only in the autumn.
I Tall shrubs with hooked
prickles only.
J Leaflets grey, scentless.   ALBAS
JJ Leaflets green, sweet-   SWEET BRIERS
brier scented.
II Medium to small shrubs with
straight prickles and/or
bristles only.
K Leaflets small, numerous,   SCOTCH ROSES
7 to 11
KK Leaflets large, few, 5 to 7.
L Low shrubs with more
or less doubly toothed
glandular leaves; flow-
ers dark pink, light
crimson, purple or
maroon (rarely white).
M Leaflets dark olive   GALLICAS
green, leathery,
waxy; flowers held
erect, mostly crim-
son or purple.
MM Leaflets light green,
thin, rarely slightly
waxy; flowers nod-
ding, mostly pink.
N Buds covered in   MOSSES
mossy resin-
scented glands.
NN Buds not so.   CENTIFOLIAS
LL Medium, erect shrubs   DAMASKS
with simply-toothed
leaves, greyish, without
glands; flowers white
or pink; heps usually
narrow and elongated.

HH Flowering season long or with
    a marked resurgence in
    autumn.

    O Dwarf shrublets 6 inches to   POLY-POMS AND FAIRY
        1½ feet.   ROSES

    OO Medium bushes 2 to 5 feet.

        P Flowers large to very
           large, solitary or few
           per stem.

           Q Flowers flat or
              cupped,   many-
              petalled,   from
              short-conical   or
              squat buds.

              R Flowers deeply   PORTLANDS
                 set among the
                 foliage on short
                 stalks.

              RR Flowers longer-   BOURBONS AND
                 stalked and held   HYBRID
                 clear of the leaf   PERPETUALS
                 canopy.

           QQ Flowers high-cent-   HYBRID TEAS
              red, few-petalled,
              from narrow, con-
              ical buds.

        PP Flowers medium to   HYBRID POLYANTHAS
           small, numerous, borne   AND FLORIBUNDAS
           in trusses.

    OOO Large sprawling sucker-
         ing shrubs.

        S Sparingly armed with   HYBRID MUSKS
          scattered,   conical
          often curved prickles.

        SS Densely armed with   HYBRID RUGOSAS
          straight   slender
          prickles.

ROSE SPECIES FOR WHICH DOUBLE-FLOWERED MUTANTS HAVE BEEN RECORDED

CINNAMOMEAE
Rosa *beggerana*
californica
carolina
cinnamomea
pendulina
rugosa
webbiana
GALLICANAE
Rosa *gallica*
PIMPINELLIFOLIAE
Rosa *foetida*
hugonis
rapinii (= *hemisphaerica*)
spinosissima
xanthina
INDICAE
Rosa *chinensis*
BRACTEATAE
Rosa *bracteata*
clinophylla

LAEVIGATAE
Rosa *laevigata*
BANKSIANAE
Rosa *banksiae*
SYNSTYLAE
Rosa *arvensis*
henryi
moschata
multiflora
sempervirens
setigera
PLATYRHODON
Rosa *roxburghii*
virginiana
CANINAE
Rosa *canina*
rubiginosa
tomentosa

A number of other alleged doubles (as RR. *anemoneflora, pomifera, rapa*) are omitted as of hybrid origin, and some of the above are suspect, although it is difficult to be certain.

ORIGIN OF KORDES'S HYBRID RUBIGINOSAS

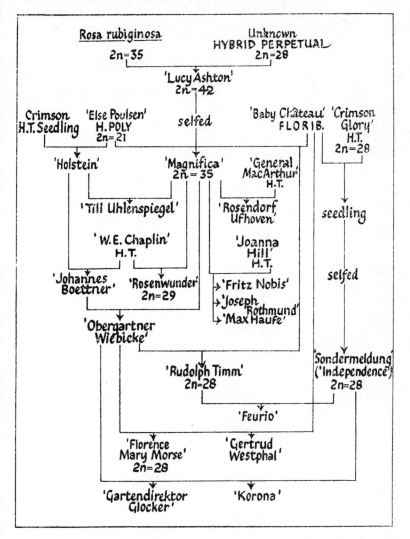

(*After Wylie 1955, redrawn and extended*) G.D.R. 1960

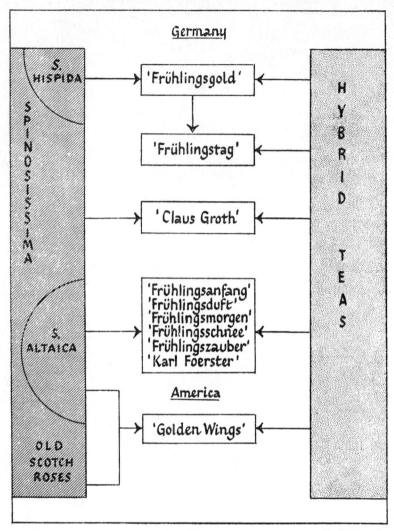

G. D. Rowley

Note for diagram opposite

From chromosome counts taken since this figure was drawn, Mr Rowley tells me that the Boursault roses are unlikely to have been derived from R. *pendulina*, but most probably from R. *blanda*.

G.S.T. 1980

SIMPLIFIED GENEALOGY OF THE MAIN
GROUPS OF GARDEN ROSES

*by Gordon D. Rowley, after Hurst, 1941 (reprinted from The Old
Shrub Roses)*

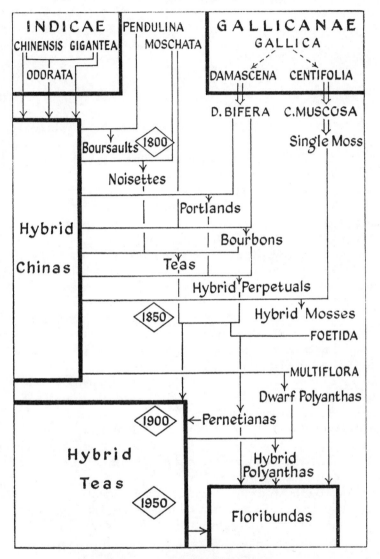

A single line indicates hybridization.
A double line indicates sporting.
A dotted line indicates possible relationship.

16

Fragrance

'BECAUSE THE breath of flowers is far sweeter in the air (whence it comes and goes, like the warbling of music), than in the hand, therefore nothing is more fit for delight, than to know what be the flowers and plants that do best perfume the air. Roses, damask and red, are fast flowers of their smells; so that you may walk by a whole row of them, and find nothing of their sweetness; yea though it be in a morning's dew. . . . That which, above all others, yields the sweetest smell in the air, is the violet, especially the white double violet, which comes twice a year. . . . Next to that is the musk-rose; then the strawberry leaves dying . . . then sweet-brier, then wallflowers . . . pinks, gilliflowers . . . the lime trees, honeysuckles. But those which perfume the air most delightfully . . . being trodden upon and crushed are . . . burnet, wild thyme, and water-mints; therefore, you are to set whole alleys of them, to have the pleasure when you walk or tread.' So Francis Bacon in his essay, 'Of Gardens', 1625.

In 1673 Sir Robert Boyle told of walking in a garden with a friend who could not bear the smell of Damask roses in an alley where there were some Red Roses (*R. gallica*). Although the alley was wide and the bushes not very near, 'he abruptly broke off the discourse we were engag'd in, to complain of the harm the Perfume did to his Head, and desired me to pass into a Walk that had no roses growing near it'.

These two extracts are conflicting. No doubt some of us have a much more developed sense of smell than others, and I can detect a fragrance in the air from a group of Old Roses myself, although it does not approach the volume of the scent given off by the Musk Rose or Sweet Brier.

If we can accept as a fact that scent is the main cause of the popularity of the rose, it may be as well to trace the development of fragrance from the Old Roses onwards.

I do not think anyone will dispute the claim of the Old Roses, headed by R. *gallica*, to pre-eminence in fragrance among hybridized groups. Their only competitors are the Noisettes and their close relatives the Hybrid Musks, and the difference in these groups is one not only of a different scent, but also the freedom of it in the air. But a bowl of Gallicas or Damasks or others of their type can hold their own indoors with members of any group.

Compared with them the China Roses are almost devoid of scent, and the Tea Rose is only delicately perfumed. It is evident that when these two new groups became fused with the old groups the volume of scent decreased in the new hybrids and became altered in quality. There were exceptions; most of the Bourbons which remain today are as fragrant as any of the Old Roses, but as in shape of bloom various seedlings approached the old or new styles, so no doubt the scent followed first one parent and then another.

Judging by the various writings of the nineteenth century I think we can say that most of the Hybrid Perpetuals were not as fragrant as the Old Roses. They were bred for size of bloom, for exhibition, and for the new colours and recurrent habit of flowering, and towards the close of the century became more and more plants which would produce large, brilliant blooms for the show bench under the care of expert head gardeners. Thus the old 'Garden Roses', as they were called even then, became relegated to the less progressive gardens. But many of the old, richly coloured Hybrid Perpetuals did retain much of the Damask fragrance. As the Tea Roses brought their refining influence gradually into this group, giving rise to the Hybrid Teas, the scent gradually altered again, sharpening and yet thickening as the first few Pernetianas appeared. Today a bunch of Hybrid Teas of assorted colours picked at random will give a wonderful variety of scents. If selected varieties are picked, noted for their fragrance, I do not think anyone could be dissatisfied.

Unfortunately the trend towards the fusion of Hybrid Teas and Floribundas is not likely to improve scent. There is little fragrance inherent in the descendants of the Poly-poms, and only gradually have a few Floribundas appeared which are really fragrant. This does not augur well for the immediate future.

What extremes we have been through can be visualized by recalling 'Paul Neyron' (1869), 'Frau Karl Druschki' (1906), and 'Covent Garden' (1919), all scentless but good roses otherwise. 'Reine des Violettes' (1860), 'Madame Abel Chatenay' (1895), and 'General MacArthur' (1905) are noted for their fragrance; in fact, to my senses at least, 'Mme Abel Chatenay' stands apart from all roses for its intense piercing fragrance.

The reason why these different species and groups of roses vary so much—not only in quantity but quality of scent—is because scent varies as much as colour or any other factor in each individual. In an extremely complex group like the Hybrid Teas almost anything may be obtained from a pod of seed, with extremes of variation except where the parentage has been suitably controlled.

Rose scent itself is a highly complex oily substance composed mainly of geraniol, but also including up to a dozen other foreign or allied substances, all contributing in some way to the fragrance of each flower. Scent is produced mainly in the petals and is given forth when the growth of the flower and the atmospheric conditions are right. From this it will be seen why double roses have more volume of scent than singles, except for the Musk group of species, whose scent is apparently in the stamens. We all know that scent is especially apparent in most flowers when the air is neither too cold nor too hot; in fact what is normal for us is normal for plants of the same latitude. In extreme conditions, such as wilting, extra scent may be released, although, I believe, it is not yet known what causes the release. Tiny globules of oily, fragrant substances can readily be seen with the naked eye in the skin of an orange, and also in a leaf of bog myrtle or magnolia, but a flower-petal being the flimsy thing it is, the scent-chambers are minute and cannot be seen without high magnification. Usually the best fragrance is obtained from a newly opened flower growing on a healthy, well-established plant on a windless day when growth is exuberant; since most fragrant plants inhabit the areas of the earth where humans thrive, rather than the tops of mountains where there is too much wind or deserts where it is too dry, we may expect fragrance to be at its best on a day when the air is

warm and moist rather than dry, when the plant will be function-
ing well. It is not that the moist air conveys scent better than dry,
but that the plant is giving it forth in greatest quantity.

We are at a disadvantage in discussing scent. So far as I am
aware there is nothing corresponding to the rainbow or spectrum
to help us to measure and classify the sensations we experience in
sniffing fragrance, and yet we depend upon it so much in our
daily lives. Even our palate—which can distinguish only the four
'primary qualities', sour, salt, sweet, and bitter—depends upon
the nose for all its finer assessment of flavours. (How useful it is,
for instance, to be able to pinch one's nose during the taking of
unpalatable medicine!) I find it very difficult to describe scents to
anyone. We all have a different set of values and associations. If
only one had been able to play with the principal scents in little
bottles at school, sampling them and mixing them as one did
water-colours, all might be different. As it is we only have a
vocabulary arrived at through association; while much the same
may be true at least of colours these are so obvious that their
vocabulary has become part of one's general education. For I am
convinced that the development of one's powers of smelling can
be an education; if one deliberately smells every flower and leaf,
one soon acquires a sense of values and identification 'marks', as
it were, learning to distinguish groups of plants quite easily.
While the smell of a crushed oak leaf or a bracken frond may be
instantly detected, the multitudinous combinations of an involved
group like hybrid roses may be a very different matter.

It is natural that we should acquire a standard for comparison
of rose scents from the ancestral Old Roses which grew around
the Mediterranean, and some of which form such an important
industry in Bulgaria. If the fragrance of these roses be called
typical, then we have several species with other and widely
different scents. Most noted and accepted is the fragrance of the
Tea Rose. I have often been asked why they are called Tea Roses
and whether they make tea from the leaves in China. This is not
the answer. The flowers smell of a freshly opened packet of tea,
preferably what is known as 'slightly tarry', not the tarry Lap-
sang. This delicious odour can easily be detected in several Tea
Hybrids, particularly in 'Lady Hillingdon'.

The next most accepted term is 'Musk'. although the rose

scent to which this generally refers is not really true musk but somehow became attached to the English Musk rose, which is thought to have been R. *arvensis*. And yet in books this species is described as scentless; I always find it delicious. This Musk fragrance to me seems to merge imperceptibly through all sorts of fine fruity odours including lemon and orange and heavier ones to the Austrian Briar's peculiar odour. I am not sufficiently educated in 'musk' to be able to appreciate where the one leaves off and the other begins. I have however made some attempt in this book and also in *The Manual of Shrub Roses* [1] to indicate the amount of variety and possible pleasure to be obtained from making even a cursory examination of rose scents.

'Polyantha Grandiflora is orange to me; R. *bracteata* and 'Morning Stars' nearly pure lemon; 'Adam Messerich' raspberry and 'Vanity' sweet peas. 'Ayrshire Splendens', 'Belle Amour', 'Magenta', and 'Constance Spry' are redolent of myrrh, while the typical Rugosas, 'Souvenir de St Anne's' and 'Fritz Nobis', remind me of cloves; R. *wichuraiana* hybrids like 'La Perle' are as fresh as green apples, 'Gerbe Rose' as peonies. 'Lavender Lassie' smells exactly like lilac. There is an absorbing study in rose scents alone. Without doubt the most valuable rose scent is that of the R. *moschata* group, which carries for yards in the air; on warm days a planting of such as R. *longicuspis*, R. *multiflora*, and 'Polyantha Grandiflora' can be detected a hundred yards away. Their scent is as all-pervading as the philadelphuses which flower with them. In the narrow confines of modern gardens great species like these, and still greater ones like R. *brunonii*, cannot be given room, but this quality of floating fragrance is also fortunately in several Hybrid Musks, particularly 'Cornelia', 'Felicia', and 'Penelope'.

There is no doubt that scent in the garden air is a precious addition to our careful plantings for colour, flower and leaf, and form of growth. Yet I have never heard of gardens of scent except for the blind, as if it were an attribute not appreciated by those blessed with vision. I see no reason why scent should not act as a complement to the exploitation of the visual arts. There are many plants whose scent is carried on the air apart from these two great examples the Musk Roses and the philadelphus or 'Mock

[1] Sunningdale Nurseries, 3*s*. post free.

1. R. *californica* *'Plena'*, a free-flowering and graceful shrub.

2. 'Abbotswood' (1954), a semi-double seedling of R. *canina*.

3. The original plant of 'Hidcote Gold' at Hidcote.

4. A fine shrub of 'Headleyensis' in a garden at Pewsey. Pale yellow.

5. A Hybrid Perpetual rose, 'Baron Girod de l'Ain' (1897); crimson with white edges.

6. The myrrh-scented 'Constance Spry' (1961), reminiscent of the old Centifolias.

7. The blazing scarlet blooms of 'Scarlet Fire' (1952) produce large heps in autumn.

8. A late-spring flowering, yellow shrub rose of excellence; 'Frühlingsgold' (1937), deliciously scented.

9. A well-flowered bush of the yellow Rugosa Hybrid 'Agnes' (1922).

10. 'Schneelicht', an excellent white ground-covering rose.

11. A good group of the Hybrid Musk rose 'Cornelia' (1925) with appropriate ground cover

12. 'Nevada', a six-year-old shrub in the author's garden.

13. A sprawling shrub rose 'Düsterlohe', whose pink flowers produce orange heps in autumn.

4. 'Raubritter' (1936), admirable as a ground-cover or for growing through other shrubs or into small trees, over stumps, etc.

15. A new hybrid of R. *multibracteata*, the rich-coloured 'Cerise Bouquet' (1958).

16. 'Gold bush' (1954), a Sweet Brier hybrid with soft golden blooms.

Orange'. Early in the year we have the Winter Sweet *Chimonan-thus praecox, Berberis sargentii,* and *sarcococcas; Prunus mume* 'Beni-chidori ', a Japanese apricot which anticipates a breath of hya-cinths; wallflowers, heliotrope; stocks—both bedding strains and the 'Night Scented'; pinks of all kinds and *Lilium candidum*; mag-nolias of the later-flowering species, especially *M.* × *thompsonii, grandiflora, obovata,* and the hybrid *M.* × *watsonii*; certain azaleas and rhododendrons; *Viburnum carlesii* and its near relatives and hybrids; *Humea elegans* and Tobacco Flowers, laburnum, lime, wistaria, and many more. They are the very breath of the garden, its life and joy, and as the scent comes and goes on each varying eddy, so it varies too in intensity and quality. With these flowers that give so much there are some leaves to note, equally free of their scent: the Douglas Fir, Sweet Brier or *Rosa rubiginosa, Hebe cupressoides*; Balsam Poplar in early spring, and in October the fallen leaves of *Cercidiphyllum japonicum,* which spread a subtle aroma of ripe strawberries. From the fields come wafts of beans, mustard, clover; the waste places give us elder and gorse.

Roses with fragrant foliage are not many, and none is so good and rich in quality as the Sweet Brier. R. *primula,* R. *setipoda,* the hybrid *wintoniensis,* R. *multibracteata,* and R. *glutinosa* are the main other sorts, apart from the fragrance of the flower stalks and 'moss' of the Old Roses; these all give off a little fragrance, but are especially delightful to handle and crush when the scent is more forthcoming, as with lavender and thyme, pelargoniums, and most herbs.

The main difference in these two types of fragrance is that in the petals the scent is formed and released by natural growth as the flowers expand, from minute cells on the surface. In leaves like those of mint and thyme the scent is formed and stored in cells and glands; it is therefore released only when the containers are bruised or broken. All the distillations of rose fragrance are made from the floral parts, not the leaves, and it has been an enormous industry in the Old World. It is recorded that rose-water was made as early as the year A.D. 810. Professor Flückiger, in 1862, published notices and extracts from the Imperial Library in Paris giving details from a Persian source. One of the provinces of Persia had to pay an annual tribute of thirty thousand bottles of rose-water to Baghdad, and the industry exported a large quantity

as far as Morocco and China. Certain districts gave especially fine
fragrance and high prices were paid for the finest products. Rose-
water was considered in ancient days to be the cure for almost
every ill. It is still used in cosmetics and as a popular cure.

It is said that the presence of an oily substance floating on the
surface of rose-water was first observed in Italy and Germany in
the sixteenth and seventeenth centuries, and when this was
separated from the water it commanded an infinitely higher price.
Slightly later this substance was separated and extracted in
Persia. This 'otto' or 'attar', as it is called, gave rise to a greatly
increased industry. Kaempfer mentioned that in 1684 the Persian
distilleries were in a very flourishing condition; the extract was
even more valuable than gold and was the scent most appreciated
and sought in various countries. I have not been able to trace what
species of rose was used; authors sometimes state it was R. *moschata*. As, however, R. *damascena* was subsequently used in India
and Bulgaria it would seem more probable that it was this rose.
The Bulgarian industry dates from the beginning of the eighteenth
century, and prior to the Second World War Miss Lindsay introduced from the Caspian Provinces of Persia a Damask Rose which
we now call 'Gloire de Guilan' and which she stated was used
for the extraction of attar. From some forgotten source I was
told also that another Damask, 'Ispahan', is similarly used in
Turkey.

The district of Kazanlik has given its name to R. *damascena*
'Trigintipetala', which we grow in Britain, and this is undoubtedly the rose growing in great quantity in Bulgaria. Mr V. M.
Staicov, of the Bulgarian State Agricultural Institute for Investi-
gation of Medical and Aromatic Plants, was kind enough to send
me pressed specimens and, later, propagating material of various
roses in his fields. In addition to this particular Damask Rose, a
form of R. *alba* almost identical to R. *alba* 'Semi-Plena' is also
grown. Both flower only once during the growing season.

A recent paper on the distribution of the oil in the flower parts
has been written [1] shewing that in the Bulgarian clone of Damask
Rose the oil is found in almost every part of the flower—petals,
stamens, calyx, etc.—but that most of it (92 per cent) resides in the
petals, which constitute 75 per cent of the weight of the flower.

[1] Staicov and Zolotovitch, 1957.

At daybreak the flowers start to open, developing a cup-formation; it is at this moment that they contain most oil, of which
nearly 30 per cent is lost by twelve o'clock and 70 to 80 per cent
by 4 p.m. Therefore, the harvesting has to be done from 5 a.m. to
9 to 10 a.m., and the gathered flowers complete with calyx are
processed the same day, since after twenty-four hours almost 30
per cent of the oil is lost, due mainly to evaporation. The oil is
today distilled by steam in large copper stills of about 250 to 500
gallons capacity.

The quantities are astronomical. About three tons of flowers
(approximately 1,200,000 blooms) are required to produce rather
less than 2¼ pounds of attar, and this amounts to the yield from
four to five acres of Damask Rose plants. Five to six tons of R.
alba are necessary to give the same quantity, but this rose is grown
on a very limited scale in Bulgaria. Mr Staicov tells me that the
cultivation of these roses in Bulgaria is concentrated in a pic-
turesque valley sheltered from the cold north winds by the
Balkan Mountains, while on the south the Sredna Gora is a check
to the dry, hot air penetrating from the Aegean Sea. The rivers
Toundja and Strema and their numerous tributaries bring
moisture and fertility. The climate is moderate and equable. The
Damask Rose grows best on well-drained, sunny mountain
slopes and hillsides, where the air is cool and damp, especially
during the flowering period.

The Kazanlik valley has become world famous as the 'Valley of
Roses', and it must be a great experience to be there in June, when
on crisp mornings the delicate fragrance is carried from the fields
and distilleries over the whole valley, in which 7,500 acres are
devoted to this crop. This area is steadily increasing. In the old
days the roses were grown in thick rows; now, Mr Staicov says,
the method is to cultivate them singly in the row, facilitating
mechanical tillage and control of pests and diseases, and thereby
greatly increasing the yield.

By the last week of May the harvest begins, continuing for about
three weeks; it is sometimes curtailed by a hot, dry spell, but is
prolonged in cool, damp weather, when the yield and quality of
the oil are higher. I had read elsewhere that R. *alba* flowers
slightly later and its flowers contain more stereoptene, which adds
increased 'oil of geranium', an adulteration frowned upon by

specialists but useful for lower-grade samples; a little book published in 1894, *Rhodologia*, by J. C. Sawyer, F.L.S., gave a fairly full account of the industry in those days. Now, Mr Staicov tells me, the Bulgarian State controls the whole of the production and guarantees absolute purity, and the attar is justly famous throughout the world not only on its own, but as an ingredient of high-grade perfumes and cosmetics. Many of us are familiar with the scent of attar through the flavour of the pink-coloured Turkish delight, and also I believe in marsh-mallow. But this gives only a tithe of the delight afforded by the pure liquid in a tiny phial which reached me from Kazanlik.

In Germany an industry was once concentrated near Leipzig, and the neighbourhood of Grasse in the south of France is still famous for its productions, but the attar, I understand, contains considerably more stereoptene.

It will be seen from the above that the rose through its scent has provided mankind not only with a priceless distillation but that the work necessary to extract tiny quantities of precious liquid has meant the employment of vast numbers of people, and the preservation for two hundred years, or more, of one vigorous type of Damask Rose, grown in the fields from division. This scent is, according to Dr Hurst, the product of the fusion of two roses, R. *gallica* and R. *phoenicea*. Through later hybridization with R. *moschata* and R. *chinensis*, the Bourbon and Hybrid Perpetual Roses were evolved, and not until towards the end of the nineteenth century was the 'dark red rose' beloved by our parents an established fact. Its scent was strong only occasionally, and bore a resemblance to R. *damascena*; thus the 'Damask scent' in dark red roses that one so often hears about is rather hypothetical.

I should find it difficult to say which rose scent I like best. To me, there are none that are objectionable. For pure sweetness and softness one cannot find anything to surpass the Old Roses, but the rich, fruity scents in the Hybrid Teas are also of special appeal, and their sharper, more exciting, scents fit their angular shapes and vivid colours, I think, very appropriately. Those who wish to delve into the fascinations of scent in flowers should read *The Scent of Flowers and Leaves*, by F. A. Hampton (Dulau), a little book of absorbing interest.

In addition to the prowess of R. *damascena* in the matter of distillations, R. *gallica officinalis* has equal claim to fame, for it was the particular rose that gave rise to another industry, that of the dried petals. From these conserves were made in great variety, and an enormous industry arose at Provins, near Paris, which still flourishes. There was a similar though smaller industry devoted to this rose for commercial purposes at Mitcham, Surrey. The Hungarian commercial variant, R. *gallica* ' Conditorum ', presumably was also used. R. *gallica* has the priceless character of retaining its scent particularly well after drying; possibly other roses may have this advantage but they have not been exploited commercially. The Provins industry exported products all over the northern hemisphere in vast quantities. Because R. *gallica officinalis* was often called the ' Red Damask ' in old books there is considerable confusion over these two. The petals were made into powder, syrup, jam, candy, cordial, wine, or just dried. Mrs Constance Spry used to make rose-petal jam from this species, as anyone who has sampled the resulting rose-petal cake will well remember.

The Hon. V. Sackville-West sent me this amusing extract:
[*From Louis XIII, aged four, to his father Henri IV, in 1605.*]

' Papa, all the apothecaries of Provins have come to me to beg me to ask you, very humbly, to give my company a different garrison-post, because my *gendarmes* like the *conserve de roses* and I am afraid they will eat it all and I shall have none left. I eat some every night when I go to bed. . . .'

Postscript, 1973 Edition

Further details regarding musk and musk roses occur in my book *Climbing Roses Old and New* (Dent, 1965, revised 1978).

17

Cultivation and Pruning

And when you plant your rose-trees, plant them deep,
Having regard to bushes all aflame,
And see the dusky promise of their bloom
In small red shoots, and let each redolent name—
Tuscany, Crested Cabbage, Cottage Maid—
Load with full June November's dank repose.

V. Sackville-West, The Land, 1927.

THERE HAS been so much written and spoken about cultivation during recent years that it would be superfluous for me to add a detailed chapter on this subject, and in any case I feel hardly competent. Gardening has become so scientific these days that the old rules are in danger of being forgotten. Even 'farmyard' is looked upon in doubt by the more scientifically minded; and the old potting shed is in danger of becoming a chemist's shop with the sterility of a clinic!

I am convinced that good cultivation calls for a few fundamentals, the first being *initial* deep digging, the second being the use of ground-cover either in the shape of carpeting plants or by a mulch of dead leaves or compost. That is nature's way. She does not grow her shrubs all alone on bare earth, but always with a complement of lowly foliage.

One of the least satisfactory ways of planting shrubs is to dig a small hole in an otherwise established border, and put the plant in. Seldom do they thrive with this minimum of attention. The ideal is to dig a large area, preferably the whole border; all plants benefit from this. There is no need to bury manure: it can be easily applied as a mulch a year later, when the shrubs have become well rooted and are ready for a little tonic. The important 'don'ts' are to avoid bringing to the surface the poor subsoil, and also to avoid planting in heavy soil when it is in a wet and sticky condition. It is impossible for nurserymen to deliver roses just when conditions are perfect, at the onset of the autumn rains; but shrubs can be 'heeled in' safely for weeks if necessary, awaiting suitable weather for planting.

If the ground is covered subsequently with a suitable mulch it will be found quite unnecessary to dig or hoe. I wrote fairly extensively about this in *Colour in the Winter Garden*,[1] and it works admirably on my light soil. In heavy damp soils the growing mulch is probably much safer than the mulch of dead leaves.

It is an extraordinary thing how rose-lovers are obsessed with the word 'pruning'. When one considers that a rose is, after all, only a shrub, more or less highly bred, it is the more remarkable that this idea of pruning should have been applied to them in such concentrated effect by the writers of rose books. The more highly bred the rose is, and by this I refer to the perpetual-flowering modern bedding roses, the more pruning is necessary to ensure the constant supply of bloom that is expected of them. And, of course, it is no good expecting to prune a shrub hard unless it is given plenty of nourishment in the ground to enable it to 'push' hard. The more you must prune to produce perfect blooms, the more you must feed; likewise the more you feed the more you must keep the plants within bounds. It is a vicious circle, but necessary with Hybrid Teas, Floribundas, and Poly-poms.

Most of the roses we have discussed in this book do not need this intense attention. In fact I would say that with very few exceptions all our shrub roses will give a better effect if not pruned at all than if they are constantly being snipped about. Let us leave out the Poly-poms and the Chinas and also the Hybrid Perpetuals for the moment and consider the species and larger hybrid shrub roses. Just as with any other normal flowering shrub, a healthy species rose will throw up great stems every now and again, and these gradually replace old stems. Therefore remove every year, if possible, and in February, one or two really old stems on which multitudes of small branches are growing. Usually they will be the darkest stems with the roughest bark and the most branching twigs. Their removal will allow the new stems more room, and it

[1]Phoenix House, 1957; revised edition, 1967.

should always be remembered that the best flowers are produced on side-shoots from the big branches of the previous year. The more constantly a shrub is encouraged to throw up new basal shoots, either by nourishing or pruning or both, the better the display will be.

The above remarks apply to all species and once-flowering hybrids; even colonizers like R. *spinosissima* need thinning out sometimes. If the rose is not perpetual flowering, or expected to give heps, the pruning need not wait until February but can be done *immediately* after flowering, which will save the plant from feeding the unwanted branches during the rest of the summer; thus it will probably throw up a new shoot at once. No pruning is necessary in the first spring after planting. Rugosa roses may be clipped over every February if a dense, bushy effect is required; their response in bloom will be surprising.

The roses in Part 2 of this book should be treated somewhat differently. Most are perpetual or recurrent-flowering and, as they owe affinity to the China Rose, they approach in style to the modern bedding roses. The Chinas themselves make much soft wood in late summer; every shoot bears a bloom, and the large basal shoots are crowned with a head of blooms. Obviously nourishment is necessary for so much effort to be satisfactory, but at the same time too much nitrogenous manure may cause the wood to be soft and to suffer in the frosty autumn or winter weather. They will need a careful inspection in February, and all small wood should be spurred back, as for Hybrid Teas. The occasional removal of an old branch is very helpful, but the bushes build themselves up gradually and need to have a number of stems retained more or less permanently.

Hybrid Perpetuals are mostly very vigorous. Shoots arising from the base during the summer may achieve 6 to 7 feet in height, and may often bear a cluster of blooms at the top. This is rather disconcerting for those who look upon their H.P.s as merely rather blowsy Hybrid Teas. They are much more vigorous and if they were not so erect could quite well be considered as normal shrubs. Unfortunately most of them are rather erect and lanky, and it is useless to reduce those long shoots to about 3 feet to try to keep the bushes to reasonable size. The way to achieve a glorious display is to bend the new shoots over and tie them to the bases of neighbouring plants; they will in this way bear flowers along their whole length. If grown on a fence, pillar or wall, these long shoots will flower only at the top in the following season if trained upright; by bending them or training them horizontally more flowers will be obtained, or they may be shortened if absolutely necessary. Small twiggy growth can be spur-pruned in the normal way in February.

Poly-poms need hard pruning, removing all weak twiggy shoots, and leaving the stronger wood slightly longer. Their main display is on the young wood of the current season and the more there is of this the better.

Hybrid Musks *can* be left unpruned, but pruning encourages the production of strong new shoots after midsummer with a corresponding increase of late bloom. Both these and the various shrub roses in Chapter 13 need, therefore, occasional removal of big old branches, and the shortening of shoots that have flowered; those that are not perpetual and do not produce heps can be pruned after flowering. Those which approach the species in their single flowers will need the same attention as species. It is best always to prune to an outward-facing bud.

In some districts it is very difficult to get farmyard or any other natural manure. The best substitute is a mixture of bone meal and hoof-and-horn meal, together with some kind of humus, garden compost, leaf mould, peat, etc. This can be applied, like manure, to the surface, or lightly forked in. The bruising of roots with tools is frequently the cause of suckers appearing, and this brings me to another subject.

One of the most controversial matters in horticulture is whether roses should be grown for sale on their own roots, or by budding them on an understock. R. *canina*, the Dog Brier, is generally acknowledged to be the best understock for Britain today and it provides some weak growers with vigour, and also is a very tough root which well withstands transplanting and handling. Unfortunately, while not nearly so prone to suckering as the common Rugosa-understock or R. *multiflora*, it is as yet raised from seed and occasional individuals arise that do produce suckers. This is one reason for the odd plant producing unwanted suckers; another, as I have said, is due to root-bruising; yet another is when the scion is inserted too high on the rootstock,

but this seldom occurs in up-to-date nurseries. The budding of
roses on to a rootstock has another advantage in small gardens; it
ensures that the colonizing roses do not run about and become a
nuisance. On the other hand if we want roses that have been
budded to run about we have only to plant them 3 inches too
deep and they will speedily root from the stem and start a colony
of their own.

Roses will root from cuttings, particularly those of Rugosa or
China derivation. Nowadays with the aid of science and mist-
propagation it may be that many more vigorous roses will be
produced on their own roots from cuttings. No doubt many of the
species are best grown like this but unfortunately own-root roses
do not make such a uniform crop as those which are on an understock, and that brings forth difficulties for the nurseryman. Roses
hybridize so readily that it is useless except in a few species to
raise them from seeds.

Fortunately shrub roses, old and new, are no more subject to
pests and diseases than modern bedding roses; in fact many suffer
not at all. Taking them as a whole I would say that one has less
trouble with shrub roses, and this is partly because, even though
some of them may get such diseases as 'black spot', they are
vigorous enough to survive and go on flowering year after year.
Diseased leaves are of course unsightly, but spraying is a tiresome
job and has to be done weekly to have any effect. I have known
gardens where 'black spot' has been successfully controlled by
attention to cultivation: avoidance of strong nitrogenous
manures, and the use of bone meal and compost. Aphides and
other pests can be controlled by using any of the reliable prepara-
tions on the market, for application systemically or directly.

As all of us like to grow roses in our gardens, all over the
country and in a surprising variety of local conditions, soils and
aspects, it stands to reason that only 'good-natured' plants like
roses could thrive as they do. It is also obvious that in some
gardens they will be more suited and healthier than in others;
'black spot' seldom occurs in towns, where the sulphur in the air
drives it away, but greenfly rather like towns, with their fences
and walls, and poor soils. But do not despair of growing healthy
bushes until you have tried bone meal, together with compost (or
other humus) in quantity, for a few years.

Envoy

THE WHOLE reason behind this book and *The Old Shrub Roses* has been to call attention to the roses that are not in the most popular groups. I was brought up to love Hybrid Teas and I still do, but besides these beauties, and the Floribundas, the genus Rosa has more to offer. In fact, at risk of repeating myself, I will go further and say that the H.T.s and Floribundas each represent but a tiny and stereotyped part of the bounty offered by the genus. Part of this overriding enthusiasm for these two groups can be put down to commercialism. They have been so pushed forward into favour that many rose-lovers have no idea of what other types of beauty are available. Over and over again people come to me at shows and elsewhere and say how much satisfaction they derive from getting to know the genus as a whole rather than suffering from a surfeit of one particular class. There is fortunately enough variety in the plants we can grow in Britain for every garden owner to produce, easily, a different effect from his neighbour if he so desires. If he decides to specialize in one particular flower or type of flower then only he is to blame if he has not first satisfied himself that the floral world has nothing more to offer him.

From my own point of view I find that the more roses I know the more I appreciate them, and I should like to make it clear that roses are only part of my love for flowers and plants. Knowing how many roses have been lost to cultivation already I send my book forth, in the hope that by helping to disseminate knowledge I shall help to awaken interest in the genus as a whole. Through being distributed roses will stand a better chance of surviving into the future, ready for the next change of fashion.

Having covered to the best of my ability the shrub roses both old and new I now feel I must not rest until I have dealt likewise with all the climbing and rambling species, and the Noisettes,

Banksians, and other old groups of climbers and ramblers. They merit re-appraisal as well.

Go, lovely Rose!
Tell her, that wastes her time and me,
That now she knows,
When I resemble her to thee,
How sweet and fair she seems to be.

Edmund Waller, 1606–87.

BIBLIOGRAPHY

Addisonia, New York Botanical Garden, 1916 et seq.
American Rose Annual, 1917 *et seq.*
ANDREWS, Henry C., *Roses,* 1805–28.
BEAN, W. J., *Trees and Shrubs,* 1949
Belgique Horticole, La, 1851–85
BOIS, Eric, and TRECHSLIN, Anne-Marie, *Roses,* 1962
Botanical Cabinet, Conrad Loddiges and Sons, Vols. 1–20, 1818–30
Botanical Magazine, The, 1786 et seq.
Botanical Register, The, 1815–47
BUNYARD, Edward A., *Old Garden Roses,* 1936; also in *The New Flora and Silva,* Vol. 2
CARRIÈRE, E. A., *Production et Fixation des variétés dans les végétaux*
Choix des Plus Belles Roses, Paris, 1845–54
CURTIS, Henry, *Beauties of the Rose,* 1850–3
DARLINGTON, Hayward Radcliffe, *Roses,* 1911
DRAPIEZ, P. A. J., *Herbier de l'amateur de Fleurs,* 1828–35
DUHAMEL DU MONCEAU, Henri Louis, *Traité des arbres et arbustes,* 1819
Floral Magazine, The, 1861–71 and 1872–81
Flore des Serres et des Jardins de l'Europe, 1845–67
Florist and Pomologist, The, 1862–84
Garden, The, founded by William Robinson, 1871 et seq.
Gardeners' Chronicle, 1841–
Gartenflora, 1852–1938
Garten-Zeitung, Berlin, 1882–5.
GAULT, S. Millar, and SYNGE, P. M., *The Dictionary of Roses in Colour,* 1971
GERARD, John, *The Herball,* 1597
GORE, Mrs, *The Rose Fancier's Manual,* 1838
HAMPTON, F. A., *The Scent of Flowers and Leaves,* 1925
HARIOT, Paul, *Le Livre d'Or des Roses,* 1904
HARVEY, N. P., *The Rose in Britain,* 1951
HILLIER AND SONS, Winchester, England, *Rose Catalogue*
HOFFMANN, Julius, *The Amateur Gardener's Rose Book,* 1905
HOLE, Dean S. Reynolds, *A Book about Roses,* 1870
Horticulteur Français, L', 1851–72
HURST, Dr C. C., in *The Old Shrub Roses* (G. S. Thomas), 1955 et seq.
Illustration Horticole, L', 1854–96
Illustrierte Rosengarten (M. Lebl, Editor), Stuttgart, 1875(?)–79
IWASAKI, Tsunemasa (edited by Ida Kuratavo), *Phonzo Soufo,* 1921
JACQUIN, N. J. von, *Florae Austriacae...icones,* 1773–8
——, *Plantarum rariorum horti Schoenbrunnensis...icones,* 1797–1804
JÄGER, August, *Rosenlexicon,* 1960

JAMAIN, Hippolyte, and FORNEY, Eugène, *Les Roses*, 1893
Jardin Fleuriste, Le, 1851–4
JEKYLL, Gertrude, and MAWLEY, Edward, *Roses for English Gardens*, 1902
JENNINGS, O. E., and AVINOFF, Audrey, *Wild Flowers of Western Pennsylvania*, 1953
Journal des Roses, 1877–1914
KINGSLEY, Rose, *Roses and Rose Growing*, 1908
KOMLOSY, *Rosenalbum*, 1868–75
LAWRANCE, Mary, *A Collection of Roses from Nature*, 1799
LEROY, André, *Histoire des Roses*, 1954
LINDLEY, John, *Rosarum monographia*, 1820
McFARLAND, J. Horace, *Modern Roses*, 1952
——, *Roses of the World in Colour*, 1937
MANSFIELD, T. C., *Roses in Colour and Cultivation*, 1948
Meehan's Monthly, 1891–1902
MEEHAN, Th., *Native Flowers and Ferns of the United States*, Vols. 1 and 2, 1897
MILLER, Philip, *The Gardener's Dictionary* (Figures), 1809
MOLLET, Claude, *Théâtre des plans et jardinages . . .*, 1663
MULLIGAN, B. O., in *R.H.S. Dictionary of Gardening*
Nestel's Rosengarten, E. Schweizerbartsche Verlagshandlung, 1866–9
NIETNER, Th., *Die Rose*, 1880
PARK, Bertram, *The World of Roses*, 1962
PARKINSON, John, *Paradisi in Sole Paradisus Terrestris*, 1629
PAUL, William, *The Rose Garden*, 1848, 1872 et seq.
Paxton's Magazine of Botany, 1834–49
Plus Belles Roses au début du vingtième siècle, Les, Société Nationale d'Horticulture de France, 1912
REDOUTÉ, P. J., *Les Roses*, 1817–24
Reeve's Drawings of Chinese Plants (R.H.S. Library), 1812–31, Vol. 2
REHDER, Alfred, *Manual of Cultivated Trees and Shrubs*, 1947
Revue de l'Horticulture, Belge et Etrangère, La, 1875–1915
Revue Horticole, La, 1846 et seq.
RIVERS, Thomas, *Rose Amateur's Guide*, 1837, 1877
ROESSIG, C. G., *Les Roses*, 1802–20
Rosenzeitung, Verein deutscher Rosenfreunde, 1886–1933
Rose Annual, The, National Rose Society
Roses et Rosiers, Paris, 187–?
ROWLEY, G. D., 'Some naming problems in *Rosa*', in *Bulletin van de Rijksplantentuin*, Brussel, 30 Septembre 1959
SABINE, Joseph, in *Transactions of the Horticultural Society*, 1822
SCHLECHTENDAL, D. F. L. von, and LANGETHAL, L. E., *Flora von Deutschland*, 1880–8, 5th ed.
SHEPHERD, Roy E., *History of the Rose*, 1954
SIBTHORP, Johannes, *Flora Graeca*, 1840
SIEBOLD, Phillip Franz von, and ZUCCARINI, Joseph Gerhard, *Flora Japonica*, 1835–70
SIMON, Léon, and COCHET, Pierre, *Nomenclature de tous les Roses*, 1906

SMITH, Tom, *Rose catalogues*, Daisy Hill Nurseries

STEP, Edward, *Favourite Flowers*, 1896–7

SWEET, Robert, *The British Flower Garden*, 1st and 2nd series, 7 vols, 1823–9 and 1831–8

THOMAS, G. C., *The Practical Book of Outdoor Rose Growing*, 1920

THOMAS, G. S., *The Manual of Shrub Roses*, 1957 et seq., Sunningdale Nurseries, Windlesham, Surrey

TRECHSLIN, Anne Marie and COGGIATTI, *Old Garden Roses*, 1974

WALLICH, Nathaniel, *Plantae Asiaticae Rariores*, 1831, Vol. II

WILLMOTT, Ellen, *The Genus Rosa*, 1910–14

WYLIE, A. P., in *Journal of the Royal Horticultural Society*, Vol. LXXIX, p. 555 et seq., December 1954

——, 'The History of Garden Roses', in *Endeavour*, Vol. XIV, No. 56, October 1955

Index

Main entries are denoted by heavy type. For notes on descriptions see p. 40.